PROTESTANTISM
IN AMERICA

PROTESTANTISM
IN AMERICA

(REVISED EDITION)

A Narrative History
by JERALD C. BRAUER

THE WESTMINSTER PRESS
PHILADELPHIA

Library of Congress Catalog Card No. 66–12686

Published by The Westminster Press®
Philadelphia, Pennsylvania

PRINTED IN THE UNITED STATES OF AMERICA

CONTENTS

Foreword

THERE IS, at present, no satisfactory history of Protestantism in America written for introductory seminary survey courses, for college students, or for adult laymen untrained in the technicalities of theology and history. This book is written for just such students and for adult laymen. It seeks to provide them with a concise yet comprehensive account of Protestant Christianity in America. The narrative style has been employed in an attempt to convey some of the excitement and drama which is its history.

That history is embodied in the past and present of many Churches. Because of this, some scholars insist that it is impossible to write the history of any movement called Protestantism in America. There are only the particular histories of many different Churches. This book rejects such a view and insists that it is possible to tell the story of Protestant Christianity in America. Nevertheless, the difficulty is real, and partially accounts for the fact that only ten such histories have been written in the past three hundred years, and of these, four have been written since the 1920's.

It is not easy to characterize Protestantism in America, but two characteristics seem to mark it. One is a constant free experimentation and search for a fuller manifestation of God's truth and will, and the other is a sustained effort to avoid going beyond the truth and light already known in the Bible and codified in certain basic beliefs and confessions. Thus Protestantism in America can be characterized in terms of a full, free experimentation and an enduring Biblicism.

In a statement which proved to be prophetic, Rev. John Robinson warned his Pilgrim congregation on the eve of their departure for the New World that "the Lord hath more truth and light yet to break forth out of his holy Word."

Here are the two basic elements: the necessity of searching for yet more truth and light, and the centrality of the Bible. Protestants in America faced both the opportunity and the necessity of relating the past histories of various Churches to new conditions in order to make the gospel relevant. Thus, as they helped to shape national life, they were shaped by it and as a result took on certain common characteristics. In their search for more truth and light they had to confront such common questions as religious liberty, democracy, large numbers of unchurched peoples, vast expanses of land, the constant influx of immigrant peoples, and even such a reality as the presence of a large number of Protestant Churches within any given local community. Their surroundings tended to enhance and drive them toward a positive similarity in spirit and in organization in spite of their diverse backgrounds and beliefs. All these Churches were stamped with an indelible mark; they were a part of a greater movement — Protestant Christianity in America.

The result was that all the Protestant Churches in America exhibited a certain spirit and embodied certain practices which made them closer to each other than to their European counterparts. All American Protestants have accepted religious freedom, and though none of the Churches have worked out the full implications of such a stand, it definitely sets them apart from European Churches in practice and in belief. Lutheran, Reformed, and Anglican exhibit an activism in organization and practice that is utterly foreign to their sister European Churches.

Thus, in spite of all the differences which exist between Protestant Churches in America — and these are profound — they are bound together in a single movement which gives them a certain character not to be found in their European brethren. In some cases they possess a Biblicism and orthodoxy that far outstrips anything to be found in their sister European Churches, either in intensity or extent. In other cases, they exhibit a certain willingness for free experimentation in belief and/or practice, which likewise is not present in their European counterparts. Protestantism in America is not, then, radically different from its European counterpart. Nevertheless, in America it is a much more cohesive movement which possesses a more definite set of common characteristics.

Nobody can write in this area without acknowledging a debt to the writings of Professor William Warren Sweet. In the author's case, the debt also extends to the classroom. The entire manuscript was read by my colleague, Professor James Hastings Nichols, whose many comments and insights proved extremely helpful. But above all, grateful acknowledgment is made to Professor Sidney E. Mead, teacher and colleague, who in classroom, in discussion, and in critical comment on the manuscript encouraged the author in his work, gave him invaluable help on questions of fact, and confronted him with a stimulating and challenging interpretation of Christianity in America.

Foreword to Revised Edition

THIS BOOK was originally written to fulfill a specific need in American Church history and in American cultural history. Its use has been so extensive among college students and in introductory courses at the seminary level that numerous reprintings were required. Since so many exciting and unusual things have happened to Protestantism in America during the 1950's and 1960's, moreover, it has appeared imperative that a revision of the text be undertaken. The Vatican Council alone would have been sufficient reason to revise and to note a new stage for the history of Protestantism in America. It is hoped that this revision, bringing the text up to date in the mid-1960's, will enable the book to retain its usefulness for students seeking to understand the nature and role of Protestantism in American life and in the history of the Christian Church. A new section of "Suggestions for Further Reading" has been provided as an aid to both students and their teachers.

Foreword to Revival Edition

1

The Churches Arrive

A FEW DAYS before Christmas, 1606, three small ships sailed from London. As they slowly passed down the Thames River toward the great open sea, excitement aboard ran high. These were Englishmen on their way to establish a plantation in America, the first in a long line of men and women who were to seek their fortune and freedom in the New World. Their religion was brought with them as naturally as their provisions of food and clothing. As good Englishmen planting a colony under the name of King James, they brought with them the official religion of England — that of the Anglican Church, or the Church of England.

What fate lay in store for these 105 men? They were adventuresome, seeking glory and fortune, certain in the conviction that they were acting in behalf of God and the king. Had not the Spanish and the French found fresh strength and resources in the New World? If England was to remain safe and secure, it too must venture forth into unknown rich lands. In 1570, Sir Walter Raleigh had failed to establish an English settlement in America, but this time a large company of men would succeed where a single man failed.

Aboard one ship was Rev. Robert Hunt, clergyman of the Established Church of England. Englishmen were out not only to make their fortune but also to win the savages to Christ. Was it not a shame that only French and Spanish followers of the pope sought to win Indians to Christianity? The precious souls of the natives must be saved from the Catholicism of the pope as well as from their own heathen practices.

So it was that the original instructions for the plantation demanded that the "religion now professed and established within our realm of England" should be regularly practiced by the colonists and spread "as much as they may amongst the savage people" around them. These were the instructions to be followed in the new colony of Jamestown soon to be founded.

One hot summer morning of the following year, the burning Virginia sun beat down on the Jamestown settlement. From under an old sail, stretched between several trees, a reverent voice was lifted in prayer. Jutting from the ground to form three sides were irregular rows of rough posts serving as the walls of the church. Uncut trees, lying where they were felled, provided the pews on which the worshipers sat with bowed heads. Standing behind a length of wood nailed to two trees was the minister, Robert Hunt. So the people gathered each morning and evening to worship according to the Anglican *Book of Common Prayer*. The Church of England had come to America.

Jamestown grew slowly and painfully. Within a year, fever, plagues, and Indian attacks had killed almost two thirds of the settlers, but under the leadership of Captain John Smith the little group that remained struggled courageously. Additional ships brought ever greater numbers of men. The charter of the colony was revised, and leadership changed hands as new governors were appointed. But death continued to make the greatest gains. Between the years 1607 and 1624, of the 14,000 who came, about 13,000 died.

The Church stayed with the struggling settlement. After the death of Mr. Hunt, the first pastor, a new chaplain was found. But the most impressive work was done by a later pastor, Alexander Whitaker, "the apostle to Virginia." By the time of his arrival, things had taken a turn for the better. Tobacco was introduced and proved to be the economic salvation of the colony. More settlers arrived, including a number of "marriageable" women who landed in 1619. The same year that beheld the joyous welcome of the women witnessed an event of profound importance — the first Negro workers were imported.

Whitaker began to extend the work of the Church. He contended that the preacher of the good news of redemption should be located in such a place that he could minister both to the natives and to the Englishmen. So he boldly sailed over fifty miles up the James

River and there established his parsonage and took over the farm land given to him by the colony. Nearby was the new settlement of Henrico. Work among the Indians made some progress under Rev. Alexander Whitaker, who was respected and trusted. Most famous of his converts was Pocahontas, daughter of the great chief, Powhatan. She married a planter, John Rolfe, and returned with him to England, where she was living proof of the effectiveness of Christian work among the Indians. Curious men and women crowded around to catch a glimpse of her. She was introduced to King James and his queen and made a fine impression. Unfortunately she died at Gravesend before returning to America. As one observer put it, " At Gravesend she met her end and grave."

In addition to the living example of Pocahontas, the written pleas of Whitaker appeared in England. He cried for more and better pastors for the New World to do the vast amount of work in the Lord's vineyard. Though his untimely death cut short his career, work among the Indians was not forgotten. It was very slow work and made few converts, but the intention of the ministers and people remained steadfast. In 1619 a college was proposed for the colony, one of the primary purposes being to teach the Indians; and a large grant of land at Henrico was given for its support.

On the surface everything appeared peaceable between the Indians and settlers, but early on Good Friday morning, March, 1622, the quietness of the scattered plantations was rent by bloodcurdling shrieks and savage attacks of the Indians. Within a few hours flames and smoke rolled into the sky as numerous homes and barns were put to the torch. Taken completely unprepared, the settlers were massacred before they knew what had happened. For a number of years they had lived peacefully among the Indians, hoping to convert them by a friendly attitude. Thus, some were killed at the breakfast table after they had finished sharing a meal with the Indians.

The attack was not unprovoked. A favorite of the chief had been slain a few days before. Probably his death was justified, but the Indians had no knowledge of that; so they planned revenge and hoped to drive the white men off their lands. They even borrowed the settlers' boats to attend a rendezvous at which plans were laid.

So sudden and unexpected was the onslaught that 347, almost one third, of the colonists were slain.

Thanks to the faithfulness of a Christian Indian, Jamestown and several of the outlying districts were warned. Men at these places were prepared for the attacks and easily defeated the Indians. But the damage was done. "Why did we not listen to the advice of Master Stockham?" Englishmen cried. "He told us that kindness would never make Christians of the Indians. Only when their priests and chiefs are killed will there be any hope to convert them."

So a new theory developed: "The only good Indian is a dead Indian." Plans for an Indian school were abandoned, and sincere efforts at Indian missions were to be a thing of the past for some time to come. The massacre of 1622 gave a legitimate excuse to carry out more fully what many men had long hoped to do — seize the Indians' land and handle them on the basis of force. Thus the early policy failed, not because too much kindness was used, but because it was used unwisely. Rather than correct the defects of a basically sound policy, the settlers in their sorrow, hate, and greed instituted a new approach of naked force.

Though work among the Indians came to a standstill, clergymen continued to work among the settlers. The bishop of London early accepted the responsibility of finding pastors who were willing to go to the Virginia settlements. The very charter governing Virginia stated that worship was to be according to the usage of the Church of England.

Also, at an early date the minister received his support from the state. Every settlement was required to provide land for the upkeep of the ministers; furthermore, every male over sixteen years of age was assessed in tobacco and corn to help to pay the pastor's salary. Thus the pastor's function appeared to be one related to the entire community.

The great difficulty was that the minister was not quite certain of his position. It was true that he had to be certified by a bishop before coming to America. In that way, the Church assured itself that the man was correctly ordained by a bishop, and that he supported the practice and the faith of the English Church. This also protected a new land from unscrupulous frauds.

A basic difficulty arose when clergymen arrived in America. Each local parish soon adopted the practice of electing a group of laymen as a "vestry" to govern the affairs of the congregation. It was their duty, when the church found a minister duly ordained and sent by bishops, to present him officially to the governor, who would then legally install the minister in the parish. Once he was so inducted into the parish, the pastor was secure for life unless he taught incorrect doctrine or became immoral.

The vestries, however, were usually unwilling to present a man to the governor, either because they were not certain of his merit or because they wanted to make certain that they retained a good share of control in local matters. So they simply hired the minister on a year-to-year basis and never presented him for induction.

Thus the ministers easily remained under the control of a small group in each parish — the vestry. How could the Church through its pastors and people present the full impact of its mission and message? The pastors were never certain of their status, and the vestry was jealous of its control of parish affairs. The governor carried on many functions that normally belonged to the bishops. The governor inducted ministers into office, deprived unworthy pastors of their parishes, suspended others, granted licenses to marry, and probated wills.

The result was that unworthy or lazy men often found their way into these insecure positions. There was a constant struggle for power between the clergy and vestry on one hand and between the vestry, clergy, and governor on the other hand. Many excellent pastors served in these early years, but they worked under great handicaps. In spite of the lack of bishops and Church courts, they did a magnificent job of ministering to the people and the society of the Southern colonies. Often at the mercy of the governor or of the vestries, they continued to preach, to baptize, and faithfully to guide their congregations.

Meanwhile, in England, another group of believers were driven to seek haven in the New World. In 1608, a group of Protestants called the Separatists fled from England and settled in Holland. There they hoped to find freedom to worship as they believed.

"Separatist" was the name given to those people, a type of Puritan, who were dissatisfied with the worship and practice of the Church of England; consequently, they withdrew from the Church and formed their own congregations. They argued that the Church was composed only of people who could be recognized publicly as Christians. There was no room for halfhearted believers. How could the Church of England be a true Church when it claimed that every citizen of the nation was also a member of the Church? Obviously, many of these so-called believers were not really committed to Jesus Christ.

They argued that God, in his goodness, had determined to save mankind, which had rebelled against him. Jesus the Christ was sent among men in order to make known God's saving will. So the Church was founded, the Bible was given, Baptism and the Lord's Supper — the sacraments — were offered, all that men might respond to God's call.

That was the way God had chosen to redeem rebellious and sinful mankind, if only they would avail themselves of God's way. This way was called a covenant or a compact. It was a type of agreement which was concluded not between two equal partners but between one who laid down all the conditions and one who was called upon to accept and fulfill those conditions. The reward was eternal life. Yet even the reward was a gift because God finally determined who would or would not respond to his covenant. They were the "elect" of God, known in the churches as the "saints."

Chances were that all people who found themselves living within God's covenant and sincerely striving daily after holiness in heart and life were among God's "elect." If they had responded to the love of God in Christ, had accepted his covenant, then they were driven to profess this faith and to join with others of the "elect" in order to found a congregation.

A local congregation was founded on yet another agreement or covenant. A group of believers confessed their respective experiences of faith to one another and determined to form a congregation as the Bible commanded. All who wished to join first had to give satisfactory proof in public of their living within God's covenant, and then they were allowed to sign the covenant which bound them together in a church. Thus the Church was composed only of the proved elect, gathered together in congregations that excluded the halfhearted and lukewarm.

This was a direct repudiation of the Church of England, which insisted that nobody could be absolutely certain of the elect or the damned. To be sure, replied the Separatists, one cannot be absolutely certain, but one can easily tell the really convinced Christians from the wicked. A whole nation cannot belong to the Church. One is not physically born into Christ's Church; one enters only through a spiritual rebirth; and until that happens one is not a full-fledged Christian and so not one of the saints.

Furthermore, these Separatists contended that the Bible provided a blueprint for the form of Church government and for worship, which the Anglicans ignored by continuing to use Romish practices in worship and to uphold bishops as the highest authority in the Church. Those things, the Separatists argued, were not Biblical.

There was no need for bishops who exercised vast powers, both spiritual and temporal, over the local congregations. Every group of converted believers was a complete church in itself. It could select its own pastors and set them aside through ordination for the task of preaching, counseling, and administering the two sacraments. No bishop's hand was needed here. Also, the Separatists refused to use the vestments of the Anglican clergy because they were continued from Roman Catholicism. *The Book of Common Prayer,* the Anglican book of worship, contained much that was taken bodily from the Catholic Mass. All this was to be swept away. Worship was to be simple and strictly Scriptural.

In vain did the Anglicans argue that those things not contrary to Scripture were permissible in worship. The Separatists replied that only things commanded in Scripture were allowable. Again, men might argue that of all systems of Church government that by bishops, called episcopal, was most successful, of widest use, and of greatest antiquity. "Non-Scriptural" was the retort.

In face of this, the Separatists refused to worship in the Established Church of England. They called upon true believers to separate themselves from the corrupt Church and to form independent local congregations. English authorities would not permit such deviation from the law of the land; therefore, they sought to force the Separatists into line. Because of such persecution they fled to Holland where they found freedom of worship.

After ten years of Dutch hospitality the small group began to worry about retaining their identity as Englishmen. They also felt that they did not have an opportunity to develop their type of Christianity to its fullest extent. So, when they read Captain John Smith's account of Virginia and heard from English merchants wondrous tales about America, they considered the possibility of moving.

But how to get to America? These were relatively poor men coming from the lower and lower-middle classes. Moreover, how would their religious beliefs be accepted? Negotiations with the Virginia Company, which owned the land around Jamestown, failed because the king refused to guarantee them liberty of conscience. After investigating several other possibilities, they finally accepted the offer of an English merchant, Thomas Weston, and associates. In order to get their fare paid and to preserve part ownership in the project they went into a voluntary joint stock company. The merchants provided all the equipment and passage and the Separatists provided their bodies and labor; thus, both owned stock jointly in the project. They were not servants or slaves, but partners!

A congregational meeting was held to determine the time and method of departure. It was impossible for the entire group to go at once, so a real problem arose concerning those who should go and those who should remain behind. It was generally agreed that the youngest and strongest members with the fewest personal ties should go ahead and prepare the way. Another problem was the location of their dear old pastor, John Robinson.

After discussion it was decided that if those volunteering should outnumber those remaining behind, then the pastor should accompany the volunteers. If a minority went over, then Mr. Robinson should remain behind and Mr. Brewster, the ruling elder and assistant to the pastor, should go. The majority decided to stay behind, so Mr. Robinson remained in Holland.

On July 21, 1620, the congregation met together for the last time. Their ship, *The Speedwell,* was ready in the port of Leyden. John Robinson preached a heart-warming farewell sermon and gave stirring advice to those departing. He reminded his congregation that they must follow him no farther than he followed Christ, and he urged them to be open to all truth from the ministry of others who live in Christ.

"Let us be certain, brethren, that the Lord hath more truth and light yet to break forth out of his holy Word. It cannot be possible that we have so recently come out of such great anti-Christian darkness and already stand in the full light of divine truth.

"Is it not a pity," he said, "that the Churches of the Reformation, starting so gloriously, have stopped short in their reforms? Lutherans stop with what Luther saw. Calvinists cannot be drawn beyond what was revealed and imparted to Calvin. God has not revealed his whole will to these men.

"If Luther and Calvin were living," he cried, "they would be as ready and willing to embrace further light, as that they had received. Search the Scriptures and learn the depth of the covenant God has worked out," he exhorted.

With the prophetic utterance ringing in their ears, "There shall yet be more light," the Pilgrims sailed for England, where, after abandoning the unseaworthy *Speedwell,* 101 of them crowded aboard the *Mayflower* and sailed for America.

As the ship approached America, it became evident that there was discontent among some who were not members of the Church. In order to assure a stable government, a majority of the men signed a civil compact, the Mayflower Compact, based on the Separatists' Church covenant. In it they covenanted and combined themselves into a civil political body with power to pass necessary and just laws. Thus their religious beliefs determined the basis of their political society.

The Pilgrims were landed farther north than they had planned and found themselves on the territory of the Council for New England. But they determined to remain, and they named their settlement "Plymouth," in honor of the last English city in which they had been. At last they were in a land where they could practice their faith to the fullest and live their lives as Englishmen. They were the first Puritans to come to the strange new world; truly they were as strangers and pilgrims, so they were named "the Pilgrims."

The first winter was dreadful. Nearly half the settlers died, and only because of help from the Indians did the others manage to pull through. At the time of the fall harvest in 1621, after a moderately successful summer, they had a grand banquet to praise God and celebrate their successful triumph over the wilderness. This was the origin of our American Thanksgiving Day.

Additional recruits joined them, but their beloved pastor, Mr. Robinson, was taken by death while still in Holland. Spiritual leadership fell on the shoulders of Elder Brewster. He proved an excellent leader, but the group were hampered by his inability to administer the sacraments and to perform marriages. He was not prepared for the ministry and was not called, so the Plymouth Colony got along without the sacraments for four years before an ordained clergyman arrived. He proved to be an Anglican and was rejected. Not until 1629 did they find a satisfactory pastor.

Under the leadership of Governor William Bradford the small group of Pilgrim church members retained control of the government. They argued that the purpose of the colony was to worship God according to his Word. All other things were secondary. The Church must be protected. Though the church members were in the minority, they allowed no religious alternative for the majority of the colonists. The Pilgrims stood secure in their understanding of God's Word, and it was offered to all on their terms. Any who did not like the Pilgrim practices were free to depart.

Plymouth Colony continued to grow, and soon became a settlement composed of a series of small towns. All were governed by the patents which the Pilgrims and their merchant partners had procured from the king. In 1626 they succeeded in buying out their partners in London, so they gained complete control over the enterprise. The purpose behind this move was to assure the continuation of their Church and faith. Nothing should be allowed to interfere with this.

As more settlers poured in, the Separatists held firm. Their Church stood open to all who could confess a satisfactory faith before the believers and would publicly own the covenant. But such people were few; thus, within a few years the Separatists were in a minority. They seemed satisfied with the light they had found years before.

Back in England a much larger and more powerful group were beginning to stir anxiously and to cast longing glances toward a new world of freedom. They too were Puritans, but, unlike the Pilgrims, they did not come from the poorer classes but were largely gentlemen holding estates of land and preachers who held university posts or great pulpits.

In most respects they believed exactly as did the Pilgrims. They were shocked at the vestments and worship service in the English Church. "Romish!" they cried. They deplored the inclusion of the whole nation in the Church regardless of the evil in many people's lives. Only membership in God's covenant and active participation in a local congregation marked one as a Christian.

But, in one important respect these upper-class Puritans differed from the Pilgrims. They did not want to separate from the Anglican Church, for in spite of all its corruption they thought it a true Christian Church. The Puritan aim was not to cut themselves off but to change the Church by remaining in it. This they tried to do by constant agitation in the English Government, by the appointment of so-called Puritan "lecturers" who would preach their views each Sunday afternoon, and by constantly protesting against the worship of the English Church.

Several times the powerful Puritan party was almost successful. When James I ascended the throne in 1603, he threatened to chase them out of England. It was an empty threat. But when his son, Charles I, became king, 1625, he selected as his right-hand man William Laud, bishop of London. It was Laud's intention to enforce the use of the English Prayer Book and to strengthen the rule of the bishops over the local clergy. This he hoped would produce one great, unified, well-ordered Church throughout England. In order to accomplish his goal, Laud used every measure of power available to him.

Under increasing pressure from Laud's new policy, the Puritans felt that they had little opportunity of changing the English Church, so they looked about for a chance to escape. They would find a way to purify God's Church; they would not be denied! Being men of some wealth, they bought enough stock in a company that possessed land in America to gain control of it. Within a short time they sent John Endicott with a group of Puritans to settle on some of this land. It was named " Salem," Massachusetts.

But the Puritans were not satisfied — they were only members in a commercial company which had a claim to land in America. How could they safely establish a purified Church on that insecure basis? Before they could take such a risk they had to be sure of two things. First, they had to be certain that they controlled the company so they would not be outvoted on any matter that pertained to their Church. Secondly, they had to have control of the new Government which they intended to establish in the New World.

A strange thing occurred in the spring of 1629. Somehow, the Puritans managed to get Charles I to grant them a charter for a new company, the Massachusetts Bay Company. This gave them the power of state to rule and govern all the king's subjects residing within the limits of the colony which they were to establish. On the basis of the charter they hoped to try a holy experiment — to found a Church and a State based on God's revealed Word.

Under the leadership of John Winthrop, the Puritans determined to make positive and unbreakable their control over the company and the charter. Unless they could protect themselves from all interferences from the crown and from their non-Church partners in the company, they could not freely go ahead with the holy experiment.

Late in the summer of 1629, Winthrop and his fellow Puritans persuaded all those not intending to sail for America to sell their stock in the Massachusetts Bay Company and to withdraw from it. Thus, there were to be no men left behind who might form an opposition group to the experiment in America.

When a great fleet of eleven vessels sailed, March, 1630, John Winthrop's boat, the *Arabella,* had a precious cargo aboard — the charter! This was the final step, and it was utterly new. Never before had a company set out for the New World carrying the king's charter with them. The Puritans felt that with the charter in their own hands it could not easily be seized by the Government, and revoked for some technical reason. Furthermore, there would be no opportunity for the company's English business representatives to surrender the charter at the first sign of trouble.

The charter was the symbol of the Puritans' new-found freedom. It was to be their constitution which prevented England from interfering with their Church and State. Based on it, the holy experiment was to go forward. Safe and secure in their rights, they poured vast numbers of talented and gifted people into the Massachusetts Bay area. In ten years over 20,000 men and women fled from England to their Puritan colony. Among them were 65 ministers of such high caliber and educational attainment as John Cotton, John Wilson, Roger Williams, Thomas Hooker, John Davenport, and Richard Mather.

They did not cut themselves off from English culture and the Anglican Church. Rather, they carried the best of English educational ideas and books with them. They hoped to transform and purify the English Church and State, to create a holy Church and nation dedicated to the will of God.

Before leaving for Salem, Pastor Francis Higginson had said: " We will not say, as the Separatists were wont to say at their leaving England, ' Farewell, Babylon! ' . . . but, . . . ' Farewell, the Church of God in England! ' . . . We do not go to New England as separatists from the Church of England; though we cannot but separate from the corruptions of it."

John Winthrop joined in a declaration which called the Established Church of England " our dear Mother " and referred to the Puritans as " members of the same Body." What the Puritans really wanted was a chance to establish a Church free from all corruptions. They never separated from it in England though they criticized it severely. In America they would rebuild it.

The churches they formed at Salem, Boston, Charlestown, Roxbury, and Watertown looked suspiciously like the Separatists' churches of Plymouth. It was to be expected, for the Puritans argued that that was what the true Church of England ought to be. Within definite limits, each local church was independent and suf·

ficient to itself. It was run on a democratic basis. That is, all who became members through a public profession of their faith and adopted the covenant were eligible to discuss and vote on all important problems of the church. From time to time councils of churches could be called for mutual advice and unified support, and their decisions were rigidly enforced by the civil magistrates as fathers in the Church.

Furthermore, the covenant of grace given to mankind through Christ Jesus held the same place in Puritan belief as in Pilgrim. It formed the basis of the believer's faith and also of that of the local congregation. All those who had an experience of God's saving grace and adopted his covenant made an agreement or a covenant with each other to form a local church based on God's will as revealed in the Bible. The purpose of the church made up only of God's chosen ones was to worship him, to spread his Word, and to strengthen each other's faith.

This local congregation elected and installed its own officers, often with the help of officers from neighboring churches. The officers were a pastor, a teacher, a ruling elder, and deacons. The pastor had oversight of the spiritual welfare of the people and also preached. The teacher preached and instructed children and adults in the fundamentals of the faith. The ruling elder performed many functions of an assistant pastor, though he could not administer the sacraments. Deacons took care of the finances and other material affairs of the congregation and saw to it that the widows, children, poor, and helpless were cared for.

The basic reason why the Puritans came to America was to reform completely the Church of England and to found a pure Church after God's design. To be sure, they wanted to improve their economic standards, but in these early years religion usually triumphed in a clash with profits. The way the Puritans used their charter was a good illustration of that. It was really a charter for a business enterprise, but to them was a charter giving freedom to establish a pure Church and a godly commonwealth.

So they started the holy experiment. God had shown man what he wanted in a Church and in a State. Did not God give man Scripture and reason as guides? What did God want? He demanded a Church of his chosen people faithfully converted to his true worship and carrying out his true will. And, God wanted a nation striving to live after holiness, righteousness, and justice. There could be a Christian nation as well as a Christian individual. God would settle for no less; his covenant demanded that much!

How was this ideal to be attained? The Puritan answer was at once simple and profound — the rule of the saints. The elect of God who formed the Church would also rule the nation; thus, the will of God would be done in private and in public Christian lives. Just as all problems in the Church were to be decided by all the believers searching and discussing Scripture, so in the State. The saints governed!

The only effective opposition to the holy experiment could come from two sources, the king or non-Church members. The Puritans rejected all attempts at English Governmental interference by appealing to their charter. The real danger lay in the requirement of their charter to elect freemen, who would have the right of participating in the election of the governor, deputy governor, and other magistrates. Thus, freemen had to be created, and the original requirements for freemen were only those of position and wealth.

In 1631 the Puritans took the only step possible to guarantee the success of their ideal. They worked out an oath that upheld the charter and religious view of the Puritans, and added a new requirement for freemen. Henceforth, only church members could become freemen or voting citizens. In this way the Puritans guaranteed that those men who held the real power of the State would be favorable to the religious experiment. As Governor John Winthrop put it, "we are bound to keep off whatsoever appears to tend to our ruin or damage."

The holy experiment progressed at a rapid rate. As a steady stream of people poured in, settlements sprang up in the Massachusetts Bay area, pushed inland and south to Connecticut. Ten or twelve growing communities were founded within a decade. In all these settlements the local church was the backbone of the community, and through its freemen the final authority in all matters civil.

The Puritans, unlike the Pilgrims, demanded a learned ministry and recognized all knowledge as a gift from God. Within six years after landing, the Puritans established a college, the first in America, in order "to advance learning and to perpetuate it to posterity; dreading to leave an illiterate ministry to the churches, when our present ministers shall lie in the dust." They named it after a patron, John Harvard, minister of the church in Charlestown.

The Puritans and Pilgrims did not forget their work with the Indians. The charters of both groups professed the desire to win the natives to knowledge and obedience of the only true God. The seal of the Massachusetts Bay colony pictured an Indian uttering the cry of the Macedonians to Paul, "Come over, and help us!" This work was carried on entirely by individuals on a personal basis. Though it never reached large proportions during the first ten years, it was, nevertheless, real. It was but one more example of the Church reaching out its arms with the good news of redemption.

So another great Church planted deep roots in America. It soon spread to absorb the Pilgrim group and with it laid the foundation of American Congregationalism. A great and powerful Church, rich in the fruits of the Spirit, dedicated to God's will in every aspect of life, it sought through its holy experiment to develop a nation and a Church that would guide people according to God's holy laws.

Early in 1634, a strange thing happened. A boat docked in what is now Maryland, bringing 2 Jesuit priests and 16 Catholic families, along with some 200 other people. Soon word spread through neighboring colonies: "Roman Catholics have arrived!"

All the Protestants in the colonies hated and feared the Roman Catholics. It was against Rome and its corruptions that Puritans and Anglicans had protested. Terrible wars had raged between Protestants and Roman Catholics during the previous century. Coupled with the deep religious difference was patriotic fervor. Spain and France, the two great Catholic powers, had explored America long before the English, Dutch, or Swedes. At the very time when Virginia was settled, Spanish Catholicism was reaching its golden era in Florida, and the French were pushing along the

St. Lawrence waterway and through the Great Lakes region. There was bound to be fear, hatred, and warfare between the two religious groups.

Thus, the coming of the Roman Catholics to Maryland placed the problem right in the midst of the Protestant colonies. Lord Baltimore, a Roman Catholic English nobleman, had been given a huge tract of land just north of Virginia, and the king had granted him absolute control over the area. Baltimore hoped to make it a place of refuge for Roman Catholics.

His son Cecil, anxious to make it a paying venture, laid plans to colonize the vast domain. He recognized that he could not find enough Catholics to settle the territory and make it a financial success. Furthermore, Cecil understood that it would be impossible to erect a Catholic colony between Anglican Virginia and the rapidly expanding Puritan New England. Thus, in order to entice Protestant laborers to the colony and in order to provide a safe haven for Catholics, he determined to pursue a policy of toleration toward all Christians who believed in God the Father, the Son, and the Holy Spirit. His plan was doomed to failure from two sides. The Jesuits were dissatisfied with their position and that of the Roman Church in the colony, and the Protestants were very uncomfortable with a neighboring colony which tolerated Roman Catholics.

Meanwhile, in the heart of the Atlantic seaboard another drama was unfolding. Between New England and the South the Middle colonies began to develop. These were to grow into such great colonies as New York, Pennsylvania, Delaware, and Jersey. They were to be the home of no one great Church, such as the Puritan, the Anglican, or the Roman, but they were to become the center of many Christian groups living together peacefully — the Dutch Reformed, the Lutheran, the Quaker, the Baptist, and the Presbyterian.

It was to be some time before all these Churches arrived on the scene, but in the earliest days, in the 1620's, the Dutch succeeded in establishing friendly relations with the Indians. Trading posts were developed on what is now Manhattan, and at several other places such as Albany, and near Philadelphia.

Trade brought settlers to the Dutch colony. In 1626, Peter Minuit was appointed governor by the Dutch trading company that held the land under a Dutch charter, and also through purchase from the Indians. He brought two deacons to visit the sick. But it was not until several years later that a Dutch Reformed pastor arrived. Dutch, German, and Scandinavian Lutherans were in the colony from the beginning, but they were allowed no freedom to worship in public. These Dutchmen were strict adherents of John Calvin, and they would brook no opposition.

Unlike the Puritans and even the Virginia Anglicans, these Dutch Reformed did not provide an adequate house of worship for over twenty years. Their first church was the upper floor of a horse barn. Niggardly in their own provision for worship, they would allow no others on Manhattan to provide for any other public worship services. Also, they made little provision for work among the Indians. The Church was there, but it was unable to perform its full function as long as it remained under the governor's control.

Lutherans first carried on independent worship in a settlement of the Swedes on the Delaware River. Three Swedish Lutheran pastors were busily at work when the Dutch captured these settlements in 1656. After the Dutch triumph, only one Lutheran pastor was allowed to remain.

Thus the early years witnessed the planting of the Christian Church in America. The Church came in many ways, using many languages. It came with the Anglicans, with the Puritans, with the Dutch Reformed, and with the Swedish Lutherans. To this day there is no one Christian group that embraces all the American people. It is strange, because each group thought that it was establishing its form of Christianity as the true and final form for the New World. This was not to be.

The great lesson these various groups had to learn in America was that the Christian Church brought its message of God's judgment and redemption in Christ through all Christian groups which faithfully attempted to carry that message and live under it. By 1646, 18 languages could be heard along the Hudson River alone. The gospel was preached in all tongues. The Christian Church was there preaching to the individuals, attempting to shape their lives and the life of their society. It was part and parcel of the life of each colony. It ministered to every side of life. It was seeking yet more light from God's Word for a new people and a new land.

2

Growing Pains

THERE WAS nothing spectacular or unusual in the arrival of Roger Williams and his wife at Boston in February, 1631. One more Puritan minister was warmly welcomed, and he was immediately offered the post of "teacher" in the Boston church. Within a short time Williams left Boston and in the span of a few years found himself in such complete disagreement with the Massachusetts colony that he was exiled. What happened that the colony founded as the holy experiment for the Puritan brethren soon became suspicious and intolerant of many of the brethren?

Roger Williams expressed his initial disagreement with the Massachusetts Bay Puritans over the point of recognizing the Anglican Church. He refused the position at Boston because that church recognized the Anglican as a true but corrupt Church and allowed its members while in England to commune in Anglican churches. Williams was a strict Separatist, desiring no relations whatsoever with what he considered the totally corrupt Church of England. An additional disagreement with the Massachusetts group was over the rights of the magistrates to punish those who broke the Sabbath. This was later to become the crucial point of debate between the leaders of the Bay system of Church-State relations and Williams, the forerunner of the American system of separation of Church and State.

Neither Williams nor Massachusetts was happy in the other's company, so he proceeded to the Separatist Puritans in Plymouth, the Pilgrims, where he became assistant to the minister. There he argued the Separatist position with such zeal that even the Pilgrims were somewhat uneasy, since they wished to retain peaceful rela-

tions with their strong Massachusetts neighbors and with the
homeland. Only a handful of followers and a number of Indians,
whose languages and customs he learned, were appreciative of
his work.

Within two years Williams returned to the Bay colony in an
unofficial capacity in the Salem church. There he found a minister
and congregation sympathetic to his views and determined to retain their independence over against the Massachusetts authorities
and the other congregations. He also encountered the old suspicion of the officials and the ministers. Massachusetts was in no
mood to tolerate critics of the holy experiment. They were in danger of losing their charter to the crown, and pressure was constant
from opponents in England. In order to defend themselves against
the impending threats, they armed their colonists and required a
special oath of promised support from all residents. The holy experiment had to be protected at all costs.

Once more Williams protested against the acts of the magistrates
and refused the oath on the grounds that it was sacrilegious, a taking of God's name in vain by Christians and nonbelievers alike in
order to keep the magistrates in power. This the officials could not
tolerate. In 1635, Williams was summoned before the highest tri-
bunal of the colony — the General Court — composed of the governor, the deputy governor, the assistants, the representative deputies
of the freemen, and the Bay ministers who were invited to attend.

In addition to the above views, which supposedly attacked the
authority of the magistrate, Williams, while at Plymouth, had also
criticized the very charter itself. He maintained that the Indians
alone owned the land and that the king had no right to grant it
through a charter. If this were true, it was an attack on both the
powers of the king and the rights of the colony, and it was criticism repeated at the very time when the colonists were trying to
hold their charter.

Roger Williams was not silenced at this trial. He continued his
attack on the colony until he was once again ordered before the
magistrates in October of that year and sentenced to be banished
from the colony. But the execution of the sentence was delayed
because of his ill-health, until the authorities heard of his continued

preaching. Then they determined to ship him back to England, and, learning about this, Williams fled from Salem in a violent snowstorm in January, 1636.

Not knowing where to go, he stumbled through the wilderness until he was saved by a band of Indians whose friendship he had won while in Plymouth. He had always been kind to the natives, and in this his greatest time of need they did not fail him. In the spring he settled in what is now Rhode Island and named his settlement "Providence." There he put into practice those beliefs he had taught in Salem.

Soon he came to doubt the validity of infant baptism on the ground that it was unscriptural, and that a child could not consciously accept in faith the baptismal covenant. Though he later repudiated this Baptist position, he became known as the founder of the first Baptist church in Rhode Island. Soon other Baptist churches developed in that state.

Roger Williams represented the first real break in the New England holy experiment. At a later date he engaged in a spirited controversy with John Cotton on the right of the magistrate to coerce a man into the truth. The Puritans argued that the object of their experiment was to establish a Scriptural form of government, both civil and churchly. This included the right of the magistrates to make and enforce such laws as would develop and uphold a Christian community.

The magistrates were called "nursing fathers" of the churches. They investigated the fitness of the clergy, gave advice on disputes between churches, determined where new ministers should be located, and upheld the moral law of the community. The ministers, on the other hand, preached election sermons each time new magistrates were to be selected. In the sermon they attempted to bring to bear the Word of God as it applied to current problems. Many times they gave advice to the magistrates. Thus, minister and magistrate served to check each other, both were responsible to the church members, and ultimately all were under God's will as revealed in Scripture. God's will was to be made to prevail in the public life of the nation as well as in the personal lives of the citizens.

Roger Williams had no argument with making God's will supreme in public as well as in private life. He disputed the method used by the Puritans. You cannot force the conscience of any man. You cannot make laws of faith. John Cotton contended that they were not forcing any man's conscience. But when a man sees the truth, his conscience tells him to follow it, and if he refuses, then the State has the right to compel that man to listen to his conscience. The laws of Massachusetts were not intended to suppress the conscience but to aid it by making hardheaded men obey it.

All this was rejected by Williams. He argued that there are two areas in life, both ruled by God but in different ways. In one, the area of natural life, of society, and of government, man lives according to the laws and customs of that life. In the other, the area of grace, man lives only by the direct call from God. You cannot force the second area by laws in the first. But, also, you cannot leave God out of the first. The insights of the gospel are carried into all of life voluntarily, indirectly, never perfectly, but always under the judgment of God. The State cannot interfere with the Church, and the Church cannot make laws for the State.

Little wonder that Roger Williams was rejected by the Bay Puritans! He undercut their whole program. If his criticisms were true, then the colony didn't even own its own land, and the crown of England was without power in America. What would the English critics say when they heard this? Furthermore, if the magistrates had no power to enforce forms of worship and to prevent insidious beliefs from arising, how then could a holy commonwealth, pleasing to God, be established? Roger Williams' beliefs were felt to be dangerous to the welfare of the State both from the spiritual and from the temporal point of view. His view of the relations between the powers of the State and the religious beliefs of the citizens was the forerunner of the American ideal of the separation of Church and State; hence his great importance.

The exile of Roger Williams did not mark the end but the beginning of troubles in the holy commonwealth. Further unrest and dissatisfaction were seen in the reaction to Mistress Anne Hutchinson, one of the outstanding women in Boston. A gifted woman with powers of persuasion, she was convinced that all the ministers of the Bay, except her pastor, John Cotton, preached more on good works than on grace.

This the ministers and magistrates could not tolerate, and it became a point of contention when an entire group adopted that point of view. In November, 1637, after her friends had been defeated, several exiled, Mistress Hutchinson was brought to trial for disparaging the ministers and for holding meetings in her home in order to criticize the clergy. The court found it exceedingly difficult to trap her, and it was only in reply to the question of her theological certainty that she gave her opponents an opportunity.

She replied that she was certain in the same way that Abraham was positive he should not sacrifice his own son — by an immediate revelation. To this the deputy governor replied, " How! an immediate revelation."

Governor Winthrop summed up the feelings of the court when he said, " Now the mercy of God by a providence hath answered our desires and made her to lay open herself and the ground of all these disturbances to be by revelations, for we receive no such."

Anne Hutchinson was banished and fled to Rhode Island. The magistrates had to dispose of her because, from their point of view, she had denied the whole basis of Church and commonwealth. She had attacked the theology of the ministers, and by emphasizing the personal operation of the Holy Spirit in revealing the truth of Scripture, or truth apart from Scripture, she was denying the very foundation of the holy experiment — that of Scripture as interpreted by the ministers in the midst of the congregations. This would destroy all obedience to law, both private and public, and replace it with individual fancy. So they argued.

Meanwhile the colony was giving other indications of growing pains. Some of the members were dissatisfied with the strict control of the magistrates, and they wished better land. So a large number of them moved to Connecticut with their minister, Thomas Hooker. Though they were willing for all good citizens to have a hand in electing those who were responsible for government, they too insisted that only church members could be in actual positions of authority. So, in spite of their dissatisfaction with the Massachusetts arrangements, their system of government was not radically different.

In the 1640's internal difficulties of Massachusetts were further complicated by events in England. Parliament and King Charles I were at war. The Anglican Church was pulled down, and a coalition of Presbyterians and Congregationalists, the latter called Independents, ruled supreme. Both groups looked suspiciously at Massachusetts.

The English Independents practiced toleration of all Christian groups except the Anglicans and Roman Catholics; thus, they were astonished at the intolerance of Massachusetts. The Presbyterians could not understand why the American Puritans would not admit good Presbyterians to full communion and to the privilege of voting. It is true that Presbyterians held a different idea concerning the right of synods or Church assemblies to legislate for local churches and to ordain or examine ministerial candidates. But the theology of the two groups was essentially the same.

In 1646 a remonstrance was presented to the magistrates at Boston by a group of dissatisfied men. Among them was Dr. Robert Child, a Presbyterian. It asked that all Englishmen be given their essential rights and freedom apart from any religious requirement. Furthermore, it asked that all members of the Church of England be allowed to commune in the Massachusetts churches. This was a bombshell exploded among the magistrates.

As Dr. Child prepared to sail for England, the authorities burst into his cabin and declared him under arrest. A careful search of his belongings revealed a petition addressed to the House of Commons. It asked for an investigation of the Massachusetts Government, the appointment of a royal governor to guarantee the freedom of Englishmen, and the legal recognition of Presbyterianism. Dr. Child was rushed from shipboard to jail and later, with his fellow petitioners, was heavily fined. He subsequently returned to England.

As a result of the repeated attacks on the holy experiment, an attempt was made to strengthen the government and to pacify the unrest of the dissatisfied. In 1648, *Laws and Liberties,* embodying the laws of the colony, was published. Now every man knew exactly his responsibilities and his rights. Some of the discontent was pacified by the extension of certain local privileges to non-Church members, but the central control of the colony remained unchanged.

Criticisms from England had to be met. In face of Presbyterian opposition, the magistrates invited the Puritans' churches to a meeting where theological issues were to be discussed. The final formulation of the consensus was known as the Cambridge Platform, 1648. This was American Puritanism's first confession of faith concerning doctrine and Church government.

They silenced English Presbyterian and Independent criticism by the adoption of the Westminster Confession of Faith, which was the product of a group of English Puritan divines called together by the House of Commons, 1643–1649. By its adoption, the American Puritans upheld the same beliefs as did their English brethren.

Both held that God, not man, decides who will be saved. He picks his elect. In his time before Christ, God gave man a set of Commandments to obey, and he gave certain men the grace to live in his laws. This was the old covenant, or the covenant of works.

But God did not forget his people. He sent his only Son, Jesus the Christ, who perfectly fulfilled and revealed God's will and exhibited how he felt toward man. He created the Church, the sacraments, and preaching. Whoever received grace to repent his sins and to trust unreservedly in God as seen in Christ was saved. Through preaching, baptism, and the Lord's Supper, and through membership in the Church, he came under the new dispensation of God — the new covenant or the covenant of grace.

Thus the Puritan believed that God was holy, mighty, fearful in wrath, but also loving and forgiving. He had graciously bound himself in his covenant. Men could depend upon this. Hence the importance of men's coming to church, hearing his Word, and reverently partaking of the sacraments.

There was one point which appeared on the surface as a basic difference between the English Presbyterians and the New England Puritans. The Cambridge Platform insisted that the Church existed in its fullness in each local congregation which selected its own ministers and officers for the church. In the hands of the congregation were the keys of discipline. In theory, no presbytery composed of

elders and ministers from all the churches of a particular locality
could exercise power over any local congregation as to the selection
of a pastor, the formulation of doctrine, or the exercise of discipline.

Supposedly, then, no body such as a synod or presbytery had any
power over congregations. Such meetings as the synod at Cambridge
were only gatherings of congregational representatives to combine
their wisdom on particular problems and to offer advice. Though
no congregation had to accept this advice, they were to receive the
synodical declarations with " reverence and submission."

The fact was that the synod did not produce merely advice; it
produced a confession of faith which included even the form of
Church government. The synod did not have to insist on the congregations' accepting the declarations and confessions of the synod.
Steps were sure to be taken by the civil magistrates against any
individual, church, or minister that deviated from the synod's declarations or advocated something contrary to the generally accepted
beliefs or practices.

The magistrates, after all, were the "nursing fathers" of the
Church, and in the face of heresy or anything disruptive of the peace
in Church or State, they punished and executed discipline. In practice the Government played the role of a presbytery or a synod in
administering rebukes and discipline, which the clergy decided was
necessary against such people as Roger Williams, Anne Hutchinson, or Robert Child.

Strongly fortified by the declaration of the Cambridge Platform,
the Puritans turned to a strict control of all opposition within the
holy commonwealth. In 1656 a "plague" descended on New England. At least, that was the way the Puritans received the Quakers.
Mary Fisher and Ann Austin arrived to spread the teachings of
George Fox. They were opposed to all externals in worship, to all
sacraments, to all ministerial offices. The important thing was the
divine light present in the breast of every human being. When,
through the Spirit, one turned to the light within and followed it,
he became a child of light, living in peace, fellowship, and unity.
True worship then became silence, broken only by the inner witness
of the Spirit who compelled the believer to testify to his presence.

Mary Fisher and Ann Austin were promptly put in jail and

deported, but soon more Quakers poured in from the safe base of Rhode Island. A series of strict laws were passed by the magistrates. Finally, in 1658, the death penalty was decreed for all Quakers who returned after banishment. Some were beaten unmercifully with whips, others were branded, and three had the right ear cropped.

This was typical treatment for that day. Though the magistrates had no final excuse for such actions, they greatly feared the Quakers. One Sabbath service as the congregation in Newbury listened to the sermon of their pastor, the door burst open and in walked a young woman stark naked. She cried out: "Woe to those who hide from their sins. All are known unto God. All shall be thus revealed openly in the last days."

Other Quakers interrupted meetings and shocked the congregations which could see no symbol of the openness of sin in the lack of clothing. Some Quakers stood up during or after the service, and with their hats still on contradicted the preacher. Little wonder that the authorities feared and detested the Quakers.

In 1659 two men were hanged according to the new laws against the Quakers. The following year Mary Dyer, who had twice returned seeking martyrdom, was hanged until dead. In 1661 the last Puritan execution of a Quaker took place.

Though the Puritans tried to defend themselves by the plea that they were defending the public peace, they were roundly condemned in England and by the Rhode Island Baptists. By the mid-1670's, Quakers were protected by the English law and could conduct non-religious business in New England.

Not only did the Quakers attack the colony and its holy experiment, but the Baptists did as well. Roger Williams marked only the beginning of Puritan troubles. By the year 1651 a sufficient number of Baptists were located in Massachusetts to merit a visit of fellow Rhode Island Baptists. Three were seized on such a visit to Lynn. Two were heavily fined, and one, refusing either to pay the fine or to let the others pay for him, was given the usual treatment of being whipped.

In 1654 the congregation of Cambridge Church was shocked by a statement from Henry Dunster, the highly respected president of Harvard College. While a baptismal service was in progress, he arose to dispute the practice of infant baptism as un-Biblical and proceeded to take each point from the pastor's sermon and to answer it with Baptist views. He was silenced, stripped of his Harvard presidency, and publicly rebuked.

Thus the Quakers and Baptists joined the ranks of those dissatisfied with the Puritan holy experiment. Both stressed the conscience of the individual believer and the consequent inability of the magistrate to control the soul of man. The Puritan argued that if one wished a godly nation as well as godly individuals, one must be willing to keep men in line by laws. The Commonwealth was dedicated to God, and the aim was to make certain that it remained so committed.

While the Puritans were busily engaged in fighting off all open attacks on the holy experiment — by England, by Roger Williams, by Anne Hutchinson, by dissatisfied planters, by Presbyterians, and by Quakers and Baptists — a more subtle enemy was striking telling blows against it. Success brought prosperity, and prosperity brought indifference.

The second generation was gradually taking over the leadership of the colony. A new type of growing pain was revealed, and it had permanent destructive consequences. Would these children, who reaped the fruits of their parents' labors, prove faithful to their parents' beliefs? The settlements were showing definite signs of economic prosperity. Soon many became more interested in their financial advance than in their spiritual condition. They continued to be good, moral men and women, but somehow the old zeal was cooling; growing pains had dire effects on the heart.

One of the first signs was the small number of people presenting themselves for membership in the churches. Many had been baptized and taken into the Church as children of the saints. Did not God make his covenant between his elect and their children? They, in turn, were expected to make a public profession of their faith and to " own the covenant " when they grew up. But they did not!

This created a difficult problem. As children of the founders, they were in a position of responsibility and authority. But until they were full church members they could not have full rights of citizenship. In a sense, the holy experiment had broken down. There was no real principle of continuity from father to son which had within it both a religious and a political center. Who was to rule the colony if the saints' children would not own the covenant?

After a good deal of discussion and argument a compromise was reached. It was known as the "Halfway Covenant." Those who were baptized into the Church as children of the saints could retain a halfway connection with the Church simply by promising to live a Christian life and to raise their children in the fear of the Lord and to bring them to baptism.

These halfway members could not have the Lord's Supper, but they were still under the control of the Church; so they could vote on some of its nonspiritual problems and could keep all their privileges as citizens. Many were not satisfied with this and rigorously opposed it, but the Halfway Covenant triumphed.

In a sense, it was the deathblow to the holy experiment. The early Puritans demanded public proof of deep faith in the Lord Jesus Christ before one could become a church member. Only on this basis could one select those who would be responsible for the government. Henceforth, the only requirement for a minimum connection with the Church and thus for the right of citizenship was a promise to live a moral life. Trust and faith in God were replaced by an effort to live a good life as the test of church membership and political responsibility.

Two questions were never seriously asked. Where does one find the source of strength to live the good life? What happens to a holy commonwealth that is no longer ruled by professing saints? It seems that these deeply religious questions had passed into the background. Membership in the Church appeared to be a political and social necessity. It no longer reached the center of man's life.

Then a long series of troubles hit New England, and men began to question the source of their difficulties. In 1673 the Pequot Indians went on a rampage. A three-year bloody war followed. Homes were burned, people were slaughtered, towns were destroyed, and hatred against the Indians was fanned anew. Even nature conspired against the Puritans. Terrible fires broke out in Boston and the plague was the worst in years.

In face of such events, the New England Puritans called a special synod in 1679. There, two questions were asked:

" What are the evils which have called the judgment of God upon us? "

" What is to be done to reform these evils? "

The synod agreed that the evils responsible for the recent catastrophes were such things as pride in heart and body, a spiritual falling away, excessive profanity, breakdown of family life, and failure to observe the Sabbath. They insisted that God would be pleased only when the people repented of these sins and turned to him. To aid in this, the synod suggested that congregations exercise closer discipline and that the magistrates also enforce public discipline.

But the synod did not halt the woes of New England, nor did it rejuvenate zeal. A terrible blow was struck in 1684, when Massachusetts lost its charter and was given a royal governor. This man was an Anglican! To make matters worse, he compelled the Puritans to allow him and his followers part-time use of one of their churches. Several times the Puritan service was prolonged while the governor was forced to wait outside before the church was ready for his use. But the Anglicans had gained an entrance into the very heart of Massachusetts. That from which the Puritans had fled was now introduced in Boston by the governor.

To check the loss of zeal in the churches and to assure a common point of view over against growing opposition, an attempt was made to furnish a careful check on the pastors and congregations. According to the Cambridge Platform, synods had no real jurisdiction or authority over local congregations or pastors, but now even the Government was no longer interested in enforcing discipline. Soon ministerial associations sprang up to fill in the gap. Increase Mather, greatest of the second-generation Puritan divines, took part in an English scheme of co-operation between Presbyterians and Congregationalists. This system he proposed on his return to America.

The Massachusetts Proposals, 1705, advocated by Increase Mather and his son Cotton, represented an attempt to exercise discipline on all pastors and churches at some point beyond the local congregation. In order to do this, ministerial associations were to be given power over pastors' profession of beliefs and life, and a group from each association was to continue between association meetings with power to supervise certain questions within congregations.

John Wise fought these proposals as contrary to New England beliefs and advocated the rights of the local congregations. Though he verbally defended the old New England idea, it is interesting that he defended it more on the basis of reason and human rights than on the basis of Scripture, and this defense of congregational independence later provided arguments for advocates of the revolution against England. However, this theory appeared to overlook the actual power of discipline which was carried on by the civil magistrates in the earlier Congregational system.

Massachusetts churches refused to accept discipline and control over the local congregations. In 1708, however, the Connecticut churches adopted the Saybrook Platform, embodying the check on ministers and the association control over congregations. The churches in every county were formed in consociations. This marked a step closer to the Presbyterians, many of whom were among the New England Puritans. The children of the holy experiment found it impossible to maintain the faith without the recognition of a power beyond the local congregation.

Meanwhile, the Anglican churches in the South were having growing pains of their own. The vestries had grown in importance to such a degree that they were able to select their own successors and so become self-perpetuating. The clergymen were at the mercy either of the vestries or of the governor. There were no bishops and no ecclesiastical courts to regulate discipline. In one way this system left vastly more power in the hands of the local unit than did the New England Puritan congregational system. Parishes were usually of a huge size, often too large to handle, and there was a lack of ministers. How could the Church perform its task?

In 1689 steps were taken to improve the situation. The bishop of London was responsible for the clergy in the colonies. Since he could not be there to function, he determined to delegate his authority to commissaries. These were clergymen residing in the colony who would be commissioned to exercise certain functions of the bishop. The greatest of these commissaries were James Blair of Virginia and Thomas Bray of Maryland. Though both of them did a tremendous job, they could not ordain, confirm, or make final ecclesiastical decisions.

The best answer to the Anglican difficulties was found in the formation of two societies at the turn of the century, the Society for Promoting Christian Knowledge founded in 1688 (S.P.C.K.), and the Society for the Propagation of the Gospel (S.P.G.) in 1701. Thomas Bray was instrumental in the founding of both. The former undertook to supply books and printed matter for the churches in the colonies, while the latter sent out missionaries to work with the king's subjects and with the natives. All such ministers were directly under the supervision of the secretary who exercised a strict discipline over each of them. Even their salaries came from the S.P.G., and they were a closely knit, faithful, hard-working group of men.

Their greatest work was done in New England and in New York. They entered the Puritan stronghold and founded churches in Connecticut and Massachusetts. In 1722, all New England was shocked when six outstanding Puritans, including the president of Yale College, left the faith of their fathers to enter the Anglican Church. The S.P.G. was doubly feared and hated in New England because it continued to agitate for a bishop in America. The Puritans felt this would only reintroduce the prelacy from which they had fled.

The Anglican Church continued to spread. It naturally moved into the other Southern colonies as they were settled. As South and North Carolina drew more people, the Church of England moved in and became the official religion of these colonies, supported by public taxes. This was in spite of the fact that in neither colony were the Anglicans in the majority.

New Amsterdam fell to the English in 1684 and was renamed "New York." Though the English allowed the Dutch Reformed Church to receive public support by taxation, they sought the official establishment of Anglicanism as the religion of the colony. This was accomplished in the late seventeenth century.

Roman Catholicism was having trouble in Maryland. Settlers poured in from Virginia and from New England. An Act of Toleration was passed in 1649, the first in America, guaranteeing freedom of worship for all Christians who professed faith in the triune God. This was based not on principle but on necessity, but even it could not hold off the storm. Repeated attempts by Protestants to take over control of the colony finally succeeded in 1689.

Little wonder the Protestants would not rest. They feared Roman Catholics in their midst and were especially aroused at the presence of Jesuit priests. By 1702 the Anglican Church became the official religion of the colony, although its members were not in the majority.

Thus appeared the strange spectacle of the Anglican Church setting itself up, under the protection of the governors, as the official religion of five colonies. Was this the way to guarantee the Church's success in carrying out its mission and message? Apparently not. Establishment did not bring the Church success in America. It did not produce a godly, disciplined, hard-working ministry. In fact, it discouraged better men from coming to America. It did not produce a consecrated, disciplined laity. It bred indifference, discontent, and even contempt. The Anglican Church did not do its best work because of its establishment in America but in spite of it!

Meanwhile another type of " holy experiment " was taking place in Roger Williams' Rhode Island and in the Quaker William Penn's Pennsylvania. Both welcomed all Christians to their colonies and offered to all colonists complete toleration. Williams violently disagreed with the Quakers, charging them with replacing God's revelation in Scripture with their own fancy spun out of the " light within." But he would not use the " sword of steel " against the Quakers or other religious groups. As a result, Rhode Island became first their refuge and then their stronghold.

After a visit from George Fox, 1672, the Quakers in America began to expand their work already under way in New England, in New York, and in the South. Their real opportunity came with the establishment of Pennsylvania by William Penn in 1682. Earlier, Penn and fellow Quakers had promoted a colony in what is now New Jersey, but that was only a prelude of what was to come.

Penn believed that the colony could be ruled by himself in conjunction with a free assembly. He deplored force, war, or any type of coercion. His colony was to be built on toleration, persuasion, and moral integrity. When Roman Catholics were persecuted in Maryland, they fled to Pennsylvania and made it their headquarters. The Indians found in Penn one of their most faithful white friends.

Come to Pennsylvania where you can have land, a home, a wife, a family! Come to where you can worship God freely according to your own conscience. There you will serve in no army. You have no money? Your way can be paid. In a short time you will be free to work for yourself!

These were thrilling words to thousands of war-weary Germans and dissatisfied Scotch-Irish. Soon immigrants were flowing into Pennsylvania in a mighty stream. Philadelphia rapidly became the largest city in the colonies. Englishmen, Quakers, Baptists, and Anglicans settled in and around Philadelphia. German Lutherans, Mennonites, and Reformed moved into the heart of the colony and settled on rich farm land. Large numbers of sturdy Scotch-Irish Presbyterians, weary of the contradictory policies of the crown, left Ulster, Ireland, for the frontier of Pennsylvania.

Thus the Protestant Church came with the Churches of all these peoples. The German and Scotch-Irish were barely beginning to arrive. They did not come in large numbers until after 1710. But at that time the Scotch-Irish came in large waves.

Francis Makemie, one of the great early leaders of Presbyterians, traveled widely in Maryland, Delaware, Virginia, and Pennsylvania. He was in close contact with the New England Puritans and found fellowship with many Presbyterians who had come out of New England. In 1706 he and six other clergymen founded the Philadelphia Presbytery. The Scotch-Irish furnished ever-increasing numbers for the Presbyterian Church, but New England still furnished the leadership and the inspiration. The Presbyterians were to develop in strength until at the time of the Revolution they and the Congregationalists formed the two most important Church bodies in the colonies.

Philadelphia soon became a center for Baptists as well as for Quakers, Anglicans, and Presbyterians. A number of these Baptists came from Wales. They were strict followers of John Calvin's doctrine of God's determining grace. About the same time that the Presbyterians were founding their first presbytery in Philadelphia the Baptists founded the Philadelphia Association, 1707.

Growing pains were evident in many ways. Instead of one great Church in America, every fresh wave of immigrants brought other Churches, each feeling that it had more light yet to exhibit. By 1700 almost all the major Churches found today in America had representatives in the colonies. In spite of the division into many Churches, the Church was truly at work in America. All groups professed allegiance to the God revealed by their Lord Jesus Christ and sought to express their faith in worship and daily activity. Naturally, that worship and activity varied from group to group, and from year to year.

One of the ways that faith expressed itself was in the continuation of Indian missions. The " heathen " were not to be forgotten. Great difficulties were encountered. Numbers died from white man's plagues. It was difficult to stay with any group as they wandered about. But most damaging of all was the poor example set by the colonists.

Perhaps the greatest of the Protestant missionaries to the Indians was Rev. John Eliot. Possessing great skill in languages, he mastered an Indian dialect and preached to the natives. In 1661, after fifteen years' work among them, he published a New Testament in their language. He also translated a number of Puritan tracts for them and gathered them into typical New England communities. In 1660 they formed their first covenanted church and became known as the " Praying Indians."

About the same time the Mayhew family started mission work on the famous island, Martha's Vineyard. They too gathered Indians into typical Puritan communities, and devoted three generations of work to them.

In 1673 the terrible Indian war, King Philip's War, broke out and raged for three years. One tenth of the male population of the New England colonies was slain. In their hatred against all Indians, the colonists attacked the " Praying Indians " and others who had been converted. This war practically ended all work among the

Indians. Once more the old theory prevailed—"the only good Indian is a dead Indian."

The outgoing life of the Church was expressed in another important area of life—education. The Puritans, in particular, were determined that their people should be able to read and write so as to understand the meaning of God's Word. The Massachusetts Bay colony organized in individual towns grammar schools that were supported by subscription, though the town was to pay for the poor. The congregation within the town usually provided the officers for the school.

Puritans wanted a godly and learned ministry. A large number of the 65 pastors who came during the first decade were educated at Cambridge University. To insure the continuation of such a ministry, a college was opened in 1636. The following year it secured a legacy from John Harvard and so took his name. The college prospered and more than satisfied the desires of its founders. However, it became a bit too liberal for the Mather family and other leading Puritan clergymen. So, in 1701, another college was started in Connecticut. After a donation of books from a merchant, Mr. Elihu Yale, this became known as Yale College.

The Anglicans were not idle. They had wanted a school for the colony and the natives as early as 1620. Their plans never materialized. Under the leadership of James Blair, commissary for Virginia, funds were raised in England. A substantial gift from the sovereigns William and Mary resulted in the charter for the school, and it opened its doors in 1693. Needless to say, it took the names of its greatest benefactors.

Growing pains may have plagued the Church, but it did not forget its responsibility to the total life of its members. It attempted to discipline those who continued to ignore their obligation. It reached out in the field of education as it recognized that knowledge and Christianity are not to be separated but go hand in hand. It attempted to win the natives to Christ. All this was in the face of a lagging zeal and a growing interest in things of the world for their own sake.

3

The Great Awakening

OCTOBER 29, 1727, was a quiet, crisp New England night. The bright moonlight shimmered on the trees and grass, casting eerie shadows and lighting dark recesses. Suddenly the stillness was broken by a faint rumbling which grew in intensity. The earth began to shake and tremble. Women screamed, babies were awakened, men fell on their knees and prayed.

Had God come to destroy faithless New England? Just six years ago he had visited them with a terrible plague of smallpox, in which several hundred people died. Men wondered if this was not the divine wrath poured out against New England's sins.

The earthquake spread more terror than damage. For a short time people repented of their coldness of heart, but this did not last. People no longer had the commitment of the founding fathers. They could become halfhearted church members through the Halfway Covenant. It was not unusual to find a whole New England community baptized and holding some relation to the Church. Many were invited to the Lord's Supper in the hope that they would be converted to the Lord.

The early Puritans were familiar with the spiritual temperament which fluctuated like a barometer with each change in the weather. Their answer had always been strict discipline of those in the congregation and a renewed appeal to the covenant and to conversion. Discipline, covenant, and conversion — these formed the arsenal with which John Cotton, and later Increase Mather, fought deadness of heart.

Like all good Puritans they stressed God's initiative and man's heartfelt response. God had taken the initial step in providing through his covenants an offer of salvation to man. His Word, his sacraments, and his Holy Spirit brought men to realize their election. Men had to feel their sin, their worthlessness, and God's forgiveness.

This experience, which might be sudden or gradual, took place within the means ordained by God. So men were urged to hear God's Word, to obey his commands, and to avail themselves of his grace. If they were of the elect, those chosen by God, they would respond in utter trust. This was conversion. The result was a new life lived in the fellowship of the saints under the strict control of the Church.

Successful periods of conversion grew infrequent. It was difficult to reach these self-satisfied New Englanders. They would respond when disease struck or when the Indians became restless, but no great outpouring of the Spirit was noticed during the first thirty years of the eighteenth century. Large numbers of unconverted men, those who had never experienced the depth of their dependence on God, were communicants in the churches. Morality was at a low stage.

In December, 1734, Jonathan Edwards preached a series of sermons that struck home in a marvelous way. His first sermon was on "Justification by Faith." In it he denied every attempt of man to base his security on his own power or choice. Either salvation was from God or it was not possible.

As his series of sermons progressed, men and women began to groan and cry out during the service. Their consciences were stricken with their unworthiness. Edwards did not leave a single loophole. God's way with man was grounded in the very nature of things, for he was the creator and sustainer of all things. Reason and conscience both pointed to the justice of his treatment of men.

Little wonder people cried out in fear. Either they were damned eternally or they were saved. They could be saved only by God and in his way. But they had not followed his way or heeded his will as revealed in Christ Jesus! Were they all, then, damned? Apparently so — unless they repented from their sins and turned from their evil ways. Only God could lead them to this point. They had best listen closely to God's demands and offer.

People crowded to Edwards for advice. Hundreds were converted. A little child of four years experienced the forgiving grace of God. Jonathan Edwards was no fool, but one of the greatest intellects America has produced. He carefully guided those souls seeking comfort. He rooted out all false conversions based simply on imagination and emotions.

Soon the news of the Great Awakening spread from Northampton, Massachusetts, to other communities. Revivals spread throughout New England, sporadic and unconnected.

There had been an earlier renewal in New Jersey, but it was unconnected with that of Edwards. A German preacher, Theodore J. Frelinghuysen, had ministered among the Dutch Reformed in the 1720's. Unlike Edwards, who always delivered a restrained, carefully reasoned sermon, Frelinghuysen was eloquent and passionate. He condemned the external, formal piety of his listeners and demanded an inward conversion of the heart which would produce the good life. So a revival spread among the Dutch Reformed and produced a cleavage in their ranks.

The Great Awakening took hold among the Presbyterians as well. Rev. William Tennent, Sr., developed a school for pastors in a log cabin at Neshaminy, Pennsylvania. Out of this " Log College " came a series of young men who preached conversion sermons in a winning way. One of the leaders in promoting the revival was Tennent's son, Gilbert. Under the direction of the Log College men, numerous sinners were brought to a renewed commitment to God. New Jersey, New York, and Pennsylvania were the early centers of this Presbyterian awakening.

The man who bound the separate revival movements into a great unified effort was a young Anglican preacher, George Whitefield, who arrived in 1739. He toured the colonies, drawing vast throngs as he spoke in all the Protestant denominations or in great public gatherings. A close friend of John Wesley, the founder of Methodism, he remained within the Anglican Church and promoted its evangelical wing.

One day in Philadelphia, 1739, thousands of people crowded around the courthouse steps to hear the great evangelist from England. A portly young man in his early twenties strode up the steps, turned, faced the crowd with upraised arms, and launched into his sermon. With great effectiveness he portrayed the fallen, helpless condition of man, the unspeakable love of God, the judgment of man's reason and conscience convicting him of his failure, and God's gracious redemption in Christ. Hundreds were in tears. Others groaned as their hearts were moved. But George Whitefield kept them well in hand.

So persuasive was George Whitefield that even Benjamin Franklin emptied his pockets in answer to an appeal for money to establish an orphanage in Georgia. He urged his friends never to go to hear Whitefield with money in their pockets. This was a high tribute from penny-wise Franklin. All Whitefield's energies were thrown into the orphanage appeal and the Great Awakening. Everywhere he went crowds gathered from near and far. Farmers left their work and hurried to the cities. Merchants closed their shops. Once a court was postponed.

Whitefield traveled through the colonies from one end to the other. He bound together the many local revivals and made of them one great movement which swept the country. Jonathan Edwards welcomed him. The Tennents opened their churches and hearts to him. His fervent sermons, preached without manuscript, dramatically painted the picture of man's damnation and God's redemption. This was not essentially new to New England Puritans. There was newness, however, in the freshness and vividness with which it was said, and also in the lack of the old Puritan doctrinal exposition.

Whitefield returned to England in 1740, but he was to make five additional evangelistic tours in America. He died while on a preaching tour in 1770, and was buried under the pulpit of the Presbyterian church in Newburyport, Massachusetts. Under his inspiration the first colony-wide movement took place. The Great Awakening united the colonies in one great movement.

The extension of the movement was not all for the best. It did help to unify the various Protestant groups, and to produce a common point of view. Whitefield preached in pulpits of all the major denominations. But discord as well as unity was a product of the Great Awakening. Even the common theological point of view, which cut across denominational lines, was opposed by some.

One of the first indications of disharmony was in the Presbyterian Church. For quite some time the Scotch-Irish ministers, called the "Old Side" group, had been opposed to the New England trained and Log College "New Side" Presbyterians. The Old Side said that the New Side men were not true Presbyterians, since their beliefs were not correct, and the revivals were proof of their incorrectness. The emphasis on the converted man and the method of conversion distorted good Presbyterian doctrine.

In 1740, Gilbert Tennent preached a sermon on "The Danger of an Unconverted Ministry." In it he attacked those who did not emphasize the necessity of a regenerated or holy life for the ministry. "Our Lord will not make men ministers till they follow him."

But this was contrary to the Old Side orthodox view, which stressed the strict adherence to a confession of faith and argued that the presbytery, and ultimately a synod, determines the fitness of a man for the ministry on the basis of his education and doctrinal beliefs, and an external call from a congregation. But the ministry is not just another profession, argued the revivalist; it is the result of the call of God. No institution can make a man a true minister of the gospel if that man is not converted by God.

A bitter battle followed, in which the Old Side accused the revivalistic New Side of invading parishes by traveling around to preach. The revivalists retorted that the Old Side would not allow the people to hear converted pastors. So fierce was the battle that the pro-revival New Brunswick Presbytery was put out of the synod in 1741. The split remained in the Presbyterian Church until 1758. Thus disunity and dissension were also products of the Great Awakening. The Presbyterians were left with an Old Side party, opposed to revivals, and a New Side party, in favor of revivals.

In March, 1743, men were busy rushing around New London, Connecticut, knocking on doors to invite people to a special meeting. Rev. James Davenport, famous Congregational revivalist, was in town. The previous year he had traveled through New England imitating the procedures of Whitefield, but his spirit was utterly different from that of Whitefield. He would gain the right to use a pastor's pulpit and then denounce that pastor before his congregation as an unconverted man. As he preached, his voice would grow in shrillness until it reached a vibrating singsong. Often he would close his eyes and rock back and forth as if in a trance. This was the worst side of the revival.

"Come to the wharf this afternoon and see the Lord's will done," was the word spread through New London, Connecticut, on March 6. Mr. Davenport was holding a special service, and people were urged to bring all worldly possessions that they idolized. A great fire was to be lighted.

As a woman threw rings and a silver necklace to the flames, she cried out that they were the devil's toys. Another flung a beautiful gown and a rich cloak onto the smoldering pile. All around men and women were chanting, singing, and praying. Mr. Davenport was pacing about, exhorting his followers to sacrifice their idolatrous love for worldly things. Suits, velvet breeches, wigs, hoods, and books — from the pens of " unconverted " pastors — were added to the bonfire. And into that fire went the last shreds of the spirit of unity that still bound together those opposing and those upholding revivals.

The hitherto restrained opposition now broke forth. One group of Congregational pastors produced a *Testimony* opposing the revivals and deploring their results. A far larger group responded by publishing a *Testimony* of their own, which deplored irregular practices of men such as Davenport, admitted some excesses, but upheld revivals and the Great Awakening as a gift from God.

The seat of opposition was in and around Boston under the able direction of Rev. Charles Chauncy. In 1743 he published *Seasonable Thoughts on the State of Religion in New England*. It contained a collection of all the extravagances of the revival. Though Chauncy admitted that some good came from the Awakening, he argued, on the basis of the extreme cases, that the evil far outweighed the good.

Chauncy upheld respectability, sobriety, and reason in the Christian life. These were sufficient, for they were the best evidence that one was in a state of salvation or on the road to being saved. He was strongly suspicious of any display of the emotions in religion. After all, religion was a sensible thing and the last thing it should produce was emotional disturbance.

Chauncy was speaking for one side of Puritanism. He was the spokesman for the shrewd Yankee businessman. Puritanism had always held to the moral uprightness and reasonableness of the Christian, and by 1740 this had produced the hardheaded, respectable, rather cold and calculating merchant. His religion was a reflection of his state, and Chauncy was, in reality, defending this position.

There was another side of Puritanism which the successful Yankee businessmen and their pastors had outgrown — the deeply stirring piety that trembled before a holy God and drove men to acts of love and mercy. Jonathan Edwards replied to Chauncy in a series of writings and reminded him that religion involved the whole man, emotions and reason.

The man in Christ, moved by the Spirit of God, has a profoundly emotional experience. Why not? Is not religion related to the very heart of man — his will? What he wills, that he will do. But what determines what he wills? Custom? Reason? Yes, all these things. But above all, it is his whole past life, all his desires, that which he wants most of all! Only when God's Spirit shows man the true aim of his desires and grants him a new heart and will, only then can man turn to God.

So, argued Edwards, we must expect the Spirit of God to work through such channels as the revivals. Granted the excesses, they must be overcome and guarded against, but the work must go on. The Great Awakening was a good thing misused by a few men. It should not be thrown out because of that misuse!

Jonathan Edwards not only defended the place of emotion in religion, but went far beyond and questioned what Chauncy meant by reason and a good moral life. He was convinced that Chauncy held a very shallow view of reason and morality. So he plunged deeply into a discussion of the meaning of all reality — of the whole universe. He was one of the greatest thinkers America has ever produced. His defense of the revivals and of emotion in religion rested on a broad argument which included God and the nature of reality itself.

Chauncy never answered him. The revivalists, safe behind the defense of Edwards, went on their way, forgetting that Edwards said that religion deals with both the heart and the mind of man — with the total man. The rejection of Edwards and the resulting divorce between reason and religion was a rejection of the spirit of earlier Puritanism. This had dire consequences for the future of American Christianity. On the other hand, Chauncy and his followers went their separate way, stressing cold, hard morality, apart from a warm piety. This was to culminate in Unitarianism.

Agitation over the revivals spread among the Baptists as well. The older Rhode Island Baptists, stressing the free will of man and standing for an educated ministry, were to be found mostly in Rhode Island, Massachusetts, and Connecticut. They were comparatively few in number. Generally speaking, they were suspicious of the excesses of the Great Awakening.

As a result of the revivals a large number of churches were founded outside the officially recognized State-established congregations. This was particularly true in New England. These Separatists would allow preaching only by a converted ministry, and demanded that a congregation be composed only of known saints.

This was where the Baptists won new followers. What was more sensible than to limit membership only to those who as adults consciously professed their faith and were baptized? Thus a large number of Separatist congregations cut themselves off from the State-supported Congregational churches and became Baptists.

All these were revivalistic Baptist churches. They were strongly resented and opposed by the older or regular Baptists, but the future was in the hands of the Separatist group. They had to fight vigorously in New England in behalf of Roger Williams' famous principle of separation of Church and State. Their greatest leader and organizer in the campaign was Rev. Isaac Backus, a former New England Separatist turned Baptist.

But the very opposition and dissension produced by the Great Awakening became responsible for a new life in the churches. It led to a rapid growth of the Presbyterians and the Baptists, and it led to the introduction of a new religious group, the Methodists. All was not loss!

The New England Separatist Baptists turned to the South and found a fruitful field of activity. A number of these men had come under Whitefield's influence. Converted, they moved away from infant baptism to the necessity for adult baptism as a mark of professing faith. These men were drawn mostly from the lower classes, and they disdained education as a hindrance to the Spirit. They upheld the absolute independence of the local congregation, and they took pride in their preachers who were common laborers like the rest of the folks.

In the South, as in New England, the Baptists were persecuted by the State authorities. They were accused of disturbing the peace and of keeping people from working by turning their attention to revivals. In a way they did disturb the peace by their highly emotional and dramatic preaching, but really not enough to merit persecution on the part of the State. The real rub was that they were Baptists who held incorrect beliefs and refused to support the established Church, be it Anglican or Congregational.

Persecution and suppression only produced more Baptists and gave them the mantle of martyrs. They had a phenomenal growth in the Carolinas and in Virginia. This was the first step in the direction of Baptist predominance in the South which exists even today. It also marked them as one of the great religious groups in America.

Meanwhile the Presbyterians were having some success in the South, though largely in Virginia. Log College men visited that state and soon had large numbers attending the services. In 1748, Rev. Samuel Davies settled in Virginia and became the center of the movement. The Old Side Presbyterians sided with the established Anglican Church and attacked the New Side Presbyterians. But the revivalists won both the respect of the magistrates and the hearts of the people. They increased while their opponents decreased. It was not until 1758 that the two groups reunited.

Another fruit of the Great Awakening was the beginning of Methodism in the South, especially in Virginia. John Wesley, a close friend of Whitefield, was probably the greatest single figure in the revival of religion which swept England starting in 1740. He organized his followers into closely knit, well-disciplined groups which existed as special societies within the Church of England. Pressure was always present to break with the Anglican Church and to form a separate Methodist Church. Wesley would not hear of it.

In the 1760's Methodist missionaries and laymen were active in New York; however, their work was marked by only average success. The real heart of American Methodism, small though it was, was to be found in the South, and it benefited from the Great Awakening.

A young Anglican pastor, Devereux Jarratt, was converted in the Presbyterian revivals, and he continued to preach revival sermons. His work, in turn, converted a number of men who later became active, often leaders, in the Methodist movement. Jarratt was strenuously opposed by many of his fellow Anglican pastors and was accused of being "a fanatic Presbyterian."

During the 1770's he came in contact with Wesley's men and immediately recognized them as brethren in Christ. Here were men in the Anglican Church who felt as he did. Praise God, they would perform a mighty work! Under the joint efforts of Jarratt and traveling Methodist lay preachers much of southern Virginia, and some of North Carolina, was covered by Methodist circuits. Although Jarratt refused to join them when they broke from the Anglican Church, his work was responsible for the sound and extensive activities of the Methodists in the South. But even with this activity the Methodists remained as a group within the Anglican Church, and far smaller in numbers than the three great Churches — the Congregationalists, the Anglicans, and the Presbyterians. Even the Baptists were much larger.

In 1742, Henry Melchior Mühlenberg, a Lutheran pastor, arrived in Pennsylvania. He was trained in the famous Pietist university, Halle. The German Pietists also stressed the necessity of a conversion experience and, consequently, a strict moral life. By this time there were a number of Lutheran congregations in Pennsylvania, New York, Virginia, the Carolinas, and Georgia. Most of the Swedish Lutherans on the Delaware had been absorbed into the

Anglican Church. But the others held firm, hoping for pastors. They would not use untrained men and were suspicious of the revivals.

One year previous to Mühlenberg's arrival, Count von Zinzendorf came to America. He was the great leader of the Moravians, who were German Lutherans and Bohemian Pietists. Zinzendorf hoped to form a great united Protestant Church in which each Church would retain its individuality but unite on common essentials. He was working with a number of Lutheran churches in Pennsylvania when Mühlenberg arrived.

Mühlenberg decided at once that the greatest need of the Lutheran congregations was not for some vague union of all Protestants but for adequate pastoral care by devoted ministers. Fakes and quacks had succeeded in gaining control of the churches on the frontier because nobody was there to check their credentials.

In a heroic manner Mühlenberg set out to bind together the scattered Lutheran congregations, to give them adequate pastoral care, to preach, administer the sacraments, and to work out a common worship service. Under his leadership the first Lutheran synod, called the Ministerium of Pennsylvania, was founded in 1748.

Though Mühlenberg himself was not a revivalist, he was sympathetic to the piety of the revivalists and opened his pulpit to Whitefield. In turn he preached in German and Dutch Reformed churches and in Anglican churches. He represented the warm, personal religion of German Pietism, coupled with a strong orthodox Lutheranism which insisted on adherence to the historically formulated Lutheran doctrines. Theology was not to be ignored in favor of the emotions. This was to become a distinctive mark of Lutheranism in American Protestantism. The major problems of the Lutheran Church were those of an educated ministry and the use of a strange language, and they were to plague Lutherans for some time.

The German Reformed, like the Lutherans, had difficulty in obtaining an educated ministry. For practical reasons they co-operated with and received support from the Dutch Reformed Church of Holland. In 1746, Rev. Michael Schlatter arrived. He played the role of a Mühlenberg for the German Reformed. As did his friend in the Lutheran Church, he took a mediating position between two extreme parties — the Pietists and the strict Confessional orthodox.

Not only did the Great Awakening account for the new status of the Presbyterians and Baptists and the arrival of the Methodists; it also resulted in a new way to reach the many unchurched. How were the thousands of indifferent people outside the Church to be brought within? At this time America had fewer church members than did any other so-called Christian nation. Revival preaching, use of the Word, sacraments, and pastoral ministry, and strict congregational discipline was the answer.

The people were ripe for a revival. Living on the frontier, their lives always in danger from Indian attacks, struggling against nature for a living, accustomed to the raw, untamed life, these people were prepared for revivalistic religion which touched the emotions. Those in the cities were just as prepared for a resurgence of the emotional side in religion.

A great ingathering of souls resulted. It is estimated that between 40,000 and 50,000 people joined the Church in New England alone. This was the pattern in the other sections. Through the revivals the Churches reached out and touched more people than at any previous time in America. Here was a method of bringing the people to God. It took for granted that men were separated from God and that they had to be born anew.

The results were astounding. A new life pulsated through the Churches. Grasped by the love of God in Christ, men poured out this love to their fellow men. As members in the great Kingdom of God, they sought to express its meaning in life around them.

Indian missions took on a new appearance. Once more young men volunteered their life's work with the natives. Young David Brainerd poured out his zeal and energy in their behalf until he died a burned-out man in the home of Jonathan Edwards.

Eleazar Wheelock had such success that he hoped to open a college for Indians. One of the converts, Samson Occom, made a great impression in England and helped to raise funds for the institution. In 1769, Dartmouth College, named in honor of Lord Dartmouth, who helped to raise funds in England, was founded by Wheelock for the specific purpose of training Indians. Even Jonathan Edwards spent a long period of his life laboring among the Indians at the Stockbridge mission in western Massachusetts while he was producing some of his greatest theological treatises.

This new life in the Churches resulted in the establishment of a number of colleges and other institutions. Whitefield's famous orphanage in Georgia became an inspiration for a number of similar homes for children. Out of a charitable school and academy in Pennsylvania, 1755, there emerged the University of Pennsylvania. Likewise schools such as the Anglicans' King's College (Columbia), 1754, and the Baptists' College of Rhode Island (Brown), 1769, gained support from the fresh energy of the Churches.

One of America's great universities came directly out of the Great Awakening. It was the continuation of William Tennent's Log College as the College of New Jersey, 1746. This Presbyterian college later became Princeton University. A whole series of " Log Colleges " sprang up, and some proved to be permanent colleges. Thus the revivals produced a new spirit manifesting itself in missions and education.

One of the finest fruits of the Great Awakening was the increased opposition to slavery. Ever since the introduction of Negro slaves into Virginia in 1619, many Christians had been uneasy about the buying and selling of their fellow human beings. Others had defended it.

To the Biblical statement that in Christ " there is neither Greek nor Jew, . . . bond nor free " the reply was made that this pertains only to man's soul, not to his external bodily condition. Slavery exists because of sin.

Students of Jonathan Edwards believed that Christian love must be shown to mankind in general. It cannot be stopped by a small limited application. Negroes and Indians were part of the great human race and should, therefore, be objects of love as much as any other being. In the 1770's, Samuel Hopkins, one of these students, took a stand against slavery.

The real opposition to slavery, however, was carried on independently of the revivals but benefited from the atmosphere of the revivals. Anthony Benezet and John Woolman, both Quakers, devoted their lives and talents to opposing traffic in human bodies

Woolman, in particular, gave all his time and devotion to the concern of traveling around to various Quaker meetings and speaking his mind against slavery. He had a sensitive, highly spiritual personality, which on one occasion led Indians to grasp what he was saying though they could not comprehend the language he used.

The Great Awakening had changed the American religious scene. New groups forged to the front in importance. All groups had to decide for or against revivals. A new kind of leadership replaced the older leaders, and the fresh vital life pouring through the Churches expressed itself in colleges, orphanages, Indian missions, and antislavery feeling.

But most important of all was a subtle shift in emphasis. Formerly the Puritans had emphasized God's covenant — what he had done. This was found in Scripture and in doctrine, and a correct understanding of both was essential. This was taught and made real in the Church. But revivalism tended to stress, not so much what God had done, but how man had responded. Earlier revivalists such as Edwards and Whitefield did not make this error, but later men did.

This led to several new developments in American Christianity. So much stress was laid on the response of the believer to the love of God in Christ that there was a danger of overemphasizing man's emotional states. The real concern was with how he felt. Did he feel guilty? Did he show this guilt so that all could see it? Was his conversion experience convincing? Did it have the proper marks? How man felt and reacted became more important than what God in Christ had done for man.

Again, the converted man came under the rule of God, the reign of Christ in God's Kingdom. This brought him a new will, a new heart, a new knowledge of God's will. Each man had to experience this individually and personally. Having experienced conversion, he would show it in his actions, so his actions became all-important. How was he living? Did he show God's will in action? The really important thing was not what man believed but what he did. So the emphasis was placed on man's activity, with less and less regard for doctrine, theology, or the Church as the chosen instrument of God.

Finally, a new shift was evident in the different way men recognized religious activities. Formerly all the Churches granted that the Church was responsible for all life — personal and social. But now, the later revivalists saw God at work primarily in the conversion experience and in the resulting life of Christian good works. The conversion experience and its fruits were from God. But what of the rest of life? What of knowledge, of government, of economics? Did not the Church have some responsibility for these? Yes, but only through converted men can God's will be shown in those areas. God is related only to the saved individuals. The world is essentially in sin and so is evil. Therefore only converted men really know and do what is right. Both the place of the Church and the importance of worldly activity suffered at the hands of revivalism.

What, then, happens to the Church's mission and message to the whole of life? The Puritans knew that God's will could never be done perfectly, but they also knew that some actions are closer to his will than others, regardless of a man's being converted or unconverted. One could find God's will and action in many places besides the conversion experience. One of the fruits of the Great Awakening was a surrender of the Church's mission and message as related to the intellectual, political, and economic life of man. No longer was the old Puritan ideal of a holy commonwealth completely dedicated to God the primary goal of New England. Interest was now shifted to God's reign in man's heart. Meanwhile, while many remained unconverted, one could not hope for a holy commonwealth.

4

Religion and Revolution

THE YEAR 1740 found the colonies in a state of fear and yet confidence. Life was still not easy. Indian attacks were a constant menace, and the Roman Catholic French and Spanish forged an iron ring to the north, south, and west. How could the ever-increasing numbers of people move beyond the eastern seaboard if enemies held the territory all around them?

Canada was in the hands of the French. Their fur traders and trappers traveled down the Ohio and Mississippi rivers, pushed into western Pennsylvania, northern Ohio, and northern New York. They were small in numbers but strong in heart. With the French trappers went French Jesuit priests. These men were out to win the savages for Christ. Sacrificing European comforts and customs, the Jesuits went among Indian tribes and shared their way of life in an attempt to improve that life.

Within a half century the Jesuits had lost many martyred priests but had succeeded in winning a number of converts, and, more important for France, they also had won the friendship of a large number of the Indians. Not interested in forming permanent settlements, they did not appear to be such a threat to the Indian way of life. The French planned to use Indians in driving the English off the frontier and in confining the colonists to the seaboard.

Another threat to the English was the Spanish settlement to the south. Spain was a strong Roman Catholic power, eager to expand from Florida northward and westward to Georgia and the Carolinas. Constant raids and warfare marked the relations of the southern English colonies and their hostile neighbors. Little wonder that the English hated and feared these other groups in Amer-

ica. Not only were they French and Spanish; they were also Roman Catholics. For over one hundred years after the Reformation,
the Catholics and Protestants had fought bloody battles in an attempt to crush each other. The hatred and suspicion born of the
warfare was still very much alive.

From time to time the rivalry and hatred of the enemies broke
loose into all-out war. Longest and most bitter of these struggles
was the famous French and Indian War throughout the 1750's.
During the early years of fighting the French and their Indian allies
had the best of the struggle.

English frontier settlements were wiped out. Fire, torture, and
tomahawks drove them back. The Indian allies of the French were
encouraged to undertake raids against the helpless, scattered families in the backwoods. No mercy was shown, for it was a fight to
the death. For the Indians it meant preserving their land under
French protection. For the English colonists it meant the right to
move west to new land, the conquest of the French threat, and the
defeat of a Roman Catholic power.

The English were not without their Indian allies, because the
strongest of all the eastern tribes, the Iroquois, fought on their side.
However, the English could not use the Indians to full advantage
because white leadership meant little to them. Jesuit priests accompanied the Indian tribes from French territory on their raids and
in their battles. This was done in order to control the savages. Protestant colonists claimed it was done to incite them to greater cruelty and atrocities. Whether the priests were responsible or not,
they were present at several of the bloodiest massacres of the war.

The clergy of the colony rallied the people to the side of freedom
and justice. They abhorred the Roman Catholic French as infidels
who would bring slavery to the people of America just as they had
enslaved the French Protestants on galley ships. Where was freedom in France or in New France?

Jonathan Mayhew exhorted his Boston parishioners: "Do I behold these territories of freedom, become the prey of arbitrary
power? . . . Do I see the slaves of King Louis with their Indian
allies, dispossessing the freeborn subjects of King George, of the inheritance received from their forefathers, and purchased by them

at the expense of their ease, their treasure, their blood! . . . Do I
see a Protestant, there, stealing a look at his Bible, and being taken
in the fact, punished like a felon! . . . Do I see all liberty, property, religion, happiness, changed into slavery, poverty, superstition,
wretchedness! "

"And are we willing to give up our civil Rights and Privileges,
and become subjected to Tyranny and arbitrary Government? And
are we willing to give up our Religion? O! for God's sake, let us
think of our Danger, and labor to prevent our Ruin. Your All lays
at Stake " — so cried another preacher to a group of soldiers.

Thus the clergy preached about the privileges and freedom of the
English colonists as contrasted with the government of the French
king. They raised troops, fought in battles, and served as chaplains. Above all, they kept alive a certain tradition in the people, a
heritage which stressed freedom to worship God and good government under decent laws.

After a long struggle, in 1763 the English emerged triumphant.
They stripped the French of Canada, took over all the land to the
Mississippi River, and drove the Spanish out of Florida. The New
World was open to English expansion, and the threat of Roman
Catholicism was removed. All the colonies rejoiced, for it was now
possible to settle down and reap the sweet fruits of victory.

But there was a price to pay for the victory, and when the time
of reckoning came it produced even greater dissension between the
motherland and the colonies. The British had won the victory and
had gained a world-wide empire; but now the question emerged
as to who should pay the bills for the protection and security of the
empire.

For years there had been tensions between the colonists and the
motherland. England determined to use its colonies to build up its
own wealth and security; consequently, it passed a number of laws
carefully regulating colonial economic life so that England stood
to benefit. Over the years England had passed laws regulating the
commerce and taxes of its colonies. At times no objection was raised,
but at other times protests were loud and vigorous.

Now, faced by a huge debt from the recent French and Indian
War, the British determined simultaneously to make a peaceful set-

tlement with the Indians, to keep a large army intact in order to preserve peace, to pay off past debts, and to handle future expenses by a series of colonial taxes. So they put into effect a tax on molasses, a basic colonial commodity, and passed the infamous Stamp Act, which placed a tax on all newspapers and legal documents. These taxes were to furnish the money to pay off the war debts.

Once again the New England Puritan preachers awakened to this new threat to their liberties. This was not the first time clergy and colonists had challenged the actions of the British parliament. Was not the very founding of Massachusetts based on a charter that granted certain privileges and liberties to the people? Friction was long-standing and grievances had come down through the years. No sooner were the French defeated than the English turned their backs on the charters and proceeded to rule as they wished. So argued some of the colonists.

The English argued that the king in parliament has every right to tax English subjects in order to pay the cost of maintaining peace and prosperity. Taxes were to be relatively small in that they were to be levied on only a few basic items.

Against this the colonists asserted that Englishmen could not be taxed without having the opportunity of consenting to that tax. Their colonial charters guaranteed that right. But the British and their sympathizers replied that the charters gave no such independence from parliamentary control, and to flout legal parliamentary actions was to go against the powers that were ordained by God to rule England under law and custom. So the arguments raged throughout the colonies. Particularly in New England voices were raised on both sides. And what were the ministers doing? Did they apply the same arguments against the British king and parliament that they used against the French? They did, but with greater effectiveness because they were arguing as Englishmen with Englishmen.

They contended that their commonwealth was founded on a compact that was drawn up between their fathers and the king. This sacred contract formed the fundamental law of the land whereby their relations with England were to be determined. It embodied the rights of all freeborn Englishmen to liberty and property. So long as both parties observed the rights and duties of this compact there would be peace, harmony, justice, and security. But when one party to a compact or covenant breaks the fundamental agreements of the compact, he not only violates the terms of contract, but he also violates the laws of God which are embodied in that compact. That is what parliament did! Under the guidance of the clergy and a group of radical agitators, bands of men were established, and they adopted the name "Sons of Liberty." They wrote and spoke against the Stamp Act. People were enrolled in a great protest boycott against all British imports. Home spinning and weaving was encouraged. Meanwhile British merchants suffered such a severe loss of trade that they forced parliament to abolish the Stamp Act.

At this news the pulpits resounded with glad tidings. Tyranny had been defeated! The founding fathers had been vindicated. Sermons were preached recounting the dreams and actions of the first Puritan settlers so as to teach the people the heritage which they possessed. The repeal of the evil act became an act of deliverance from slavery.

Meanwhile another danger had been growing in the New England and Middle colonies. For several years a group of New England Anglicans were busily engaged in an attempt to bring bishops to America. Such a move required an act of parliament, so it raised anew the question of parliament's rights over the colonies. Furthermore, it re-created the specter of lord bishops as the right arm of the crown ready to undercut the people's liberties. The descendants of the Puritans could not forget their fathers' persecution at the hands of bishops such as Laud.

The Church of England had no intention of introducing bishops as a means of political control. It was purely a religious matter intended to deal with specific shortcomings in Church organization. Only bishops could ordain, confirm, and exercise discipline through ecclesiastical courts; therefore they were desperately needed in America. The past history of Puritan colonists prevented them from understanding the Anglicans' need.

The S.P.G. was active in New England, winning converts, establishing churches, and pleading for bishops. During the Stamp Act agitation these men proved loyal to England and opposed all actions intended to overthrow the tax. Therefore, the New England Congregational clergy felt that asking for bishops was all part of a great plot to deliver the Puritan colonies back into the hands of king and bishops.

The same pastors who fought the Stamp Act battled against the introduction of bishops. Again, the center of opposition was New England Congregationalism and Middle colony Presbyterianism, two of the largest Churches. These two groups held a series of joint meetings to develop a strategy. Articles were written in newspapers, pamphlets were turned out by hundreds, and eloquent sermons were delivered from pulpits. All the arguments boiled down to two major points. Bishops were but another form of tyranny — spiritual tyranny — and, as such, they perverted the gospel by their hunger for power and pomp. Furthermore, spiritual tyranny was but another step in the direction of political tyranny. Loss of religious liberties meant a loss of political liberties.

So important was the agitation over bishops that it turned the attention of the entire population to the questions of parliamentary rights and fundamental liberties. Even the great patriot John Adams admitted that it caught the attention of the common people and made them aware of the basic questions.

Event piled upon event, building up to a grand climax. Undaunted by the rejection of the Stamp Act, the British parliament instituted a new series of economic restrictions. The colonists could not determine where the pinch was greatest, on their pocketbooks or on their political liberties. To aid in the enforcement of these laws, British troops were housed in Boston homes. This was the end!

In March, 1770, a thrill of horror passed through the colonies when British regulars fired on a crowd gathered in Boston commons, killing five and wounding others. Excitement from that had hardly died down when, in 1773, there occurred an act that led to the revolution. In order to save the East India Company from bankruptcy and in order to reassert its authority to tax, parliament dispatched a vast quantity of tea to the colonies. It was to be sold cheaply but with the abhorred tax included. Merchants and laborers were aroused.

Late one night a mob of Bostonians disguised as Indians converged on the piers, boarded the boats loaded with tea, and dumped the cargo into the sea. This was the famous Boston Tea Party of 1773. Other ports followed with even greater violence, and in one case ship and cargo were burned.

The governor was furious, and the English people and parliament did not take lightly the insult of the " Boston Tea Party." A series of strict regulations were passed which placed Boston and Massachusetts directly under royal control. The commander in chief of British troops in Boston, General Gage, was appointed governor.

As regulations grew in severity, the Puritan clergy rallied the people, and revolutionary agitators such as Samuel Adams cried for action. In 1774 another blunder of the British strengthened Puritan suspicions that a concerted effort was under way to repeal the religious and political liberties of the colonies. The so-called Quebec Act again raised the heated issue of Roman Catholicism. The territory of Quebec was extended southward to the Ohio River and westward to the Mississippi River. In this vast Quebec territory, not English common law, but French civil law was to prevail. Also, the British pledged themselves to support Roman Catholicism in that territory in the same way that the French had done.

Suddenly all these actions appeared as part of one great plot that would culminate in the triumph of Roman Catholicism. Did not the support of the Catholics and the agitation for bishops prove it? So the clergy attacked the Quebec Act as a danger to religious and civil liberty, the frontiersmen attacked it as a sellout of their territory, and the merchants and land speculators agreed. The entire nation was aroused.

In April, 1775, hostilities broke out with the battles of Lexington and Concord. The die was cast! The colonies were in open rebellion against the constituted authorities. What would the Churches and the clergy do? Which side would they back, or could they remain neutral? Did they have the right to take any side?

It was clear from the past actions of the Puritan clergy in times of crisis that they would have a good deal to say. For years they had preached about the fundamental rights of men, that governments were the result of a compact, that disloyalty to the compact or its laws called for adjustment, and that all people were responsible to the laws of God.

One pastor wrote his reaction to Lexington and Concord in a newspaper article, saying: "King George the Third, adieu! No man shall cry unto you for protection. . . . Your breach of covenant; your violation of faith; . . . have dissolved our allegiance to your crown and government. . . .

" O my dear New England, hear thou the alarm of war! The call of heaven is to arms! to arms! Behold what all New England must expect to feel, if we don't cut off and make a final end of those British sons of violence, and of every base Tory among us. . . .

" We are, my brethren, in a good cause; and if God be for us, we need not fear what man can do. . . .

" O Thou righteous Judge of all the earth, awake for our help. Amen and Amen."

To the south, Virginia girded itself for battle under the guidance of Thomas Jefferson, George Washington, and the stinging words of Patrick Henry: " If we wish to be free; if we mean to preserve inviolate those inestimable privileges for which we have been so long contending; if we mean not basely to abandon the noble struggle in which we have been so long engaged . . . we must fight! I repeat it, sire, we must fight! An appeal to arms, and to the God of hosts, is all that is left us.

" . . . The gentlemen may cry, ' Peace, peace! ' but there is no peace. The war has actually begun! The next gale that sweeps from the north will bring to our ears the clash of resounding arms! Our brethren are already in the field! Why stand we here idle? What is it that the gentlemen wish?. . . Is life so dear or peace so sweet as to be purchased at the price of chains and slavery? Forbid it, Almighty God! I know not what course others may take, but as for me, give me liberty, or give me death! "

The appeals to God were not mere camouflage, nor were they simply a justification for the immediate action to be taken. For many years ministers in America had preached on the grounds of obedience and rebellion. They were not satisfied that subjects should obey any and all orders from a Government. On the contrary, they insisted that government was based on law superior to itself and that it had its origin in the consent of the people. When that law was disobeyed or when the people's consent was ignored, then the Government committed treason and was to be punished by the people.

One minister clearly expressed these views to a local company of artillerymen when he said: "Whoever makes an alteration in the established constitution, whether he be a subject or a ruler, is guilty of treason. Treason of the worst kind: treason against the State. . . . That we may, and ought, to resist, and even make war against those rulers who leap the bounds prescribed them by the constitution, and attempt to oppress and enslave the subjects, is a principle on which alone the great revolutions which have taken place in our nation can be justified."

He went on to argue that all great Protestant divines stood for this principle and he quoted Luther, Calvin, Melanchthon, and Zwingli. Thus it was that long periods of preparation paid off. The New England ministers were among the first to enunciate the doctrines that became the basis of the American Revolution and the Declaration of Independence.

Not all ministers agreed in this. A vast majority of the Congregationalists and almost all the Presbyterians, under the leadership of John Witherspoon, president of the College of New Jersey and a signer of the Declaration of Independence, were in favor of the colonial cause. A small number of these clergymen, however, remained Tories, faithful to the king. As always, there was a vast body, probably the majority, of clergy who were conservative moderates. Only slowly were they won to the Revolution.

It was among the Anglicans that the largest numbers of loyalists were found. Especially the S.P.G. men in New England were king's men. Many of them fled with the British armies and served as chaplains. Others showed their courage by facing rifle fire as they preached from their pulpits.

In the South, the Anglican churchmen were almost entirely for the Revolutionary cause. These were the men who opposed the introduction of bishops as an encroachment on the rights of the local vestries. They agreed with the New England Puritans in upholding the liberties and property of the colonists. Almost two thirds of the signers of the Declaration of Independence were from the Anglican

Church; hence, there was a great cleavage in their ranks.

The Lutherans, Baptists, Reformed, and other groups proved faithful to the cause of independence. All gave unsparingly of their time and men, and chaplains were furnished from all groups. The handful of Roman Catholics of Maryland and Pennsylvania also proved faithful to the Revolutionary cause. No one group can be singled out for special acclaim. Perhaps, of all groups, the New England Congregationalists did most, because of their years of preaching about the covenant and about a government responsible to the people.

One group that temporarily suffered as much as the Anglicans were the Methodists. John Wesley, their great English leader, wrote a series of pamphlets in which he pleaded for nonresistance on the part of the Methodists and condemned the Revolution. As a result Methodists were in bad repute, and a number of their leaders had to go into hiding. Fortunately, Francis Asbury, greatest of the preachers sent over by Wesley, remained in America and favored the colonial cause. All the American-born ministers were for the Revolution. But the stand of Wesley and his preachers tended to identify the movement with the British cause.

Some Christians refused to fight on either side as they believed that all war was wrong. As a consequence they were misused by both sides. The Quakers and the Moravians especially suffered greatly on this account during the Revolution. One of the most regrettable incidents of the entire war was the unprovoked slaughter of a large number of pacifistic Moravian Indians in Ohio. This dark blot rests on the American armies, though the British also misused Christian Indians.

So the Church working through the churches faced the question of revolution and came to the conclusion that there was a point where people might and should rebel against their Government. Governments were ordained of God, but they were ordained in such a way that they were responsible to God and to the people over whom they ruled. Government did not exist for itself and did not determine its own ends. It existed to fulfill certain laws of God, and when it failed to do this faithfully, it could be called to task by the people.

It was not easy for the Church to reach such a decision. Some of its members disagreed. But all agreed that in time of distress, war, and destruction, the Church had to offer succor and redemption; so it performed its acts of mercy and love in ministering to the sick and dying. The Church was carrying on a full ministry to man, both in his personal relation to God and in his relationship to his fellow men in society.

5

Turning Point

NEW YORK streets were crowded with joyous throngs of cheering people pushing and shoving, trying to get a glimpse of the hero of the hour — General George Washington. On that December day, 1783, long lines of soldiers stood at rigid attention, the winter sunlight glittering on polished buttons and cold steel. Strong winds sweeping up the Hudson whipped the flags and put the sting of freshness and vigor into the gathered crowd.

A great roar arose from the throng as Washington appeared on the steps, saluted his men, and briskly strode to the landing where a boat waited for him. Then as cannons blazed, guns boomed, and church bells resounded, the victorious leader took his departure. The revolution was an accomplished fact. Peace and victory went hand in hand — a new nation was born, independent of the British Empire.

Effects of independence were evident in all the states. Men walked with heads held high — they were now truly free men! But free men faced a mighty task of replacing English control with a government that would express the principles for which they had fought. They could no longer depend on Europe for guidance and strength. Gone were the ties with the Old World. How were they to bring order and peace among the thirteen independent and self-ruling states? What was to happen to the many Churches?

Nobody had a simple answer, but all men realized that something new had to be created. The various colonies had learned to work and to fight together against the English. They then banded together in a confederation of states, each retaining its independence but all co-operating on a few matters of general interest.

Just as the states had to find a new way of working together so all the Churches, no longer dependent on their European mother Churches, had to discover new methods of living and working in America. One year after the end of the war, over fifty Methodist ministers, the followers of John Wesley, met in Baltimore, December, 1784, to take action.

Still dependent upon the Anglican Church for sacraments, they felt that the time had come to go beyond the status of a mere society or club within the Church of England. The preachers were determined to form an organization independent of the Anglican Church. With no disrespect to their founder, they saw the necessity of developing a new Church in a new nation so that the gospel might be brought to all. One question uppermost in the minds of all was their relation to John Wesley. This was one of the chief topics of conversation among the preachers.

John Wesley had asserted his rights as a presbyter to ordain men for a ministry in America, thereby denying the necessity of ordination by bishops alone. As a result he was denounced by the Church of England as an unfaithful priest. He sent Thomas Coke to America as a superintendent, or "bishop," with instructions on founding a new Church and with directions as to worship and general practice. Wesley was willing to launch a new American Church, but it was to be under his spiritual control.

While American Methodists held Wesley in great esteem and respect, they did not feel it necessary to follow all his instructions. Some they ignored, others they modified, and a few they followed. Wesley had appointed Francis Asbury cosuperintendent with Coke, but Asbury felt that the American Methodists should elect their new leaders. The American brethren agreed with him, so he and Coke were elected to their office of superintendent. After election to office Asbury allowed himself to be set apart for the office of "bishop." He saw that if the Methodist Church was to grow in a new nation, it must control itself and not be subservient to its founder, John Wesley.

So a new Church was born at the same time as a new nation — the Methodist Episcopal Church and the Confederation of American states, both independent of English domination. This new Church had bishops acting as superintendents, so it was called the Methodist Episcopal Church. It met in a series of local annual conferences and in a great triennial general conference. It worked out a series of strict rules on discipline, adopted a confession of faith, and provided for preachers who traveled from point to point serving many congregations — the famous circuit riders. The Methodist Episcopal Church was organized and ready to move with the people as they went west. At this time it was one of the smallest Churches in America, but within a few decades it was to be one of the largest.

The Congregational Church was the largest and most influential Church at this point in American history. It had no institutional ties with England and possessed no central agency to give itself national representation. In face of the threat of Anglican bishops, the Congregationalists drew closer to the Presbyterians, with whom they felt a theological affinity. Out of this was to come a mutual plan of mission activity to cover the nation. The Baptists, of the same size as the Presbyterians, were in much the same position as the Congregationalists. They had no important institutional ties with England, and they vigorously opposed any national or central organization.

Meanwhile things were happening in other American Churches. Six months before Washington's departure from New York and before the Methodists' Baltimore Christmas conference, an Anglican priest from Connecticut quietly sailed for England. The New England Anglicans were determined to have a bishop at any cost because they felt the Church could not do its work without bishops. In the winter of 1784, Samuel Seabury was consecrated bishop by three Scottish Anglican bishops because the English bishops refused to ordain him on the grounds that he could not take the necessary oath of loyalty to the crown.

But what of the rest of the Anglican Church in America? Its great strength was to be found in Pennsylvania, New York, and in the South, and these men distrusted their New England brethren because of their English sympathies during the war.

In 1782 the entire American Episcopal Church was stirred by an article from the pen of Dr. William White, of Philadelphia. He offered a plan to form a national Episcopal Church that did not necessarily require bishops. His drive for a nation-wide Church was ably backed by another famous patriot and Anglican priest, Dr. William Smith, friend of Benjamin Franklin and former head of the College of Philadelphia.

In accordance with White's plan, a general convention was held in Philadelphia in 1785. There a constitution and name were settled upon — the Protestant Episcopal Church of America. Out of this meeting came the selection of candidates for bishops, and by 1787 White and another man had been consecrated in England as bishops.

Two years later at Philadelphia, a great convention was held which healed the breach between the New England clergy and the other Episcopal clergymen. Again, the impact of the Revolution was noticeable. Laymen were active as voting delegates in all conventions. The second largest colonial Church was ready to act with the new nation.

The fresh vigor pulsating through the nation could not be channeled by a loose confederation of states; something stronger was needed to guide the energy in a creative direction. The Churches were no exception to this rule. The Methodist and Episcopal Churches quickly founded organizations capable of national extension. No longer would they be dependent upon the mother Churches of Europe. Advice they would take and influence they would accept, but direct interference was no longer to be tolerated. This was the general pattern among the Churches — a turning point had been reached in American Protestantism.

The Presbyterians were no exception in this movement. One of the outstanding pro-Revolution Churches, they stood high in prestige and were rapidly growing in numbers. By 1780 it was evident that their organization, centering in a Joint Synod and ten presbyteries, was not sufficient.

Unlike their Scottish brethren, who developed an organization from the top down, the American Presbyterians', like the American government, was built from the bottom up. By 1788 they had approved the formation of a General Assembly to be composed of ministerial and ruling elders elected annually by the presbyteries. First had come the presbyteries, then the synods, and finally had come the national General Assembly. Simultaneously, the Presbyterians gave their followers a worship service, a catechism, and a confession of faith. They too stood ready to move with the American people, possessing a strong organization implemented by worship and doctrine.

What happened among two of the largest American Churches was closely paralleled by the smaller foreign-language American Churches. For some time the Lutherans under the leadership of the Mühlenberg family retained a fraternal and spiritual relationship to German Lutheranism. Cut off from Europe and dependent on themselves, they gradually adopted the English language and strengthened their own synodical organization. Each new wave of German immigrants increased both their problems and opportunities. They were, however, a Church independent of Europe. The Dutch Reformed and German Reformed, both dependent on the Church in Holland for funds and leadership, broke away from such ties and formed independent Churches. Everywhere the new spirit of freedom asserted itself.

The organization and independence of the Churches in the new confederation, though of great importance, was of far less consequence than another development in American Christianity. Slowly but steadily the Churches had been moving in a direction which some disliked, which others preferred, but which none could prevent — the establishment of religious liberty.

In Puritan New England the Congregational churches were convinced that the Church played such an important part in the life of the community that the State should uphold and support it by law and with money. Six other states felt that way about the Church of England.

How could the Church make its full impact upon all of society unless it was part of that society by law? Men argued bitterly over the vexing question. The Puritans said that the holy commonwealth could truly be holy only if the State were based on God's will as revealed in the Bible. It was the Church that provided the moral power to make the commonwealth holy. It conveyed God's love and judgment to men and so made them instruments of his will.

So it was that all but four of the thirteen colonies had some one

Church, such as the Puritan or Anglican, which was the only official Church. Such an "established" Church was supported by taxes levied by the State on everybody who lived in the community. Baptists living in Massachusetts paid taxes to keep up the Congregational churches.

Meanwhile a series of forces converged to bring about the greatest turning point in the history of American Christianity. No nation in the history of the world had ever established complete religious liberty, in which no one religion was publicly supported by taxes and where all religions were fully equal before the law of the land.

Pennsylvania stood as a beacon, a symbol of a group of colonies in America. This group was known as the Middle colonies. Situated between New England and the South, they became the seedbed of the American ideal of religious liberty.

From the very beginning William Penn had determined to establish " a free colony for all mankind that will come hither."

He forthrightly stated: " I abhor two principles in religion and pity them that own them. . . . The first is obedience to authority without conviction; and the other is destroying them that differ from me for God's sake."

Penn was determined that nobody should be forced to pay taxes to support a Church in which he did not believe, and he saw to it that the " Great Law " of Pennsylvania, adopted in 1682, guarded against such an unfair practice.

The law stated that no man or woman shall " at any time be compelled to frequent or maintain any religious worship, place, or ministry whatever, contrary to his, or to her, mind, but shall freely and fully enjoy his, or her, Christian liberty, in that respect, without any interruption or reflection."

Penn advocated this position on principle. He believed, as did all good Quakers, that true belief could not be enforced by law or constraint but could come only through God's gracious spirit. The consequence of his stand was that all religious groups found freedom in Pennsylvania.

Philadelphia became a center, not only of the Quakers, who founded the city, but also of the Presbyterians, Episcopalians, and

Baptists. Out on the frontier, in the mountains and wilderness, hardy German Lutherans and Reformed as well as the militant Scotch-Irish Presbyterians were to be found. When the Roman Catholics were driven out of Maryland by the Protestants, the priests and some of the laity fled to Pennsylvania, where they found shelter.

Almost every Church of consequence found room to settle in the Quaker state. Relatively unknown and somewhat unusual groups such as the peaceful Mennonites, the hard-working Moravians, the very peculiar semimonastic Ephrata community, and the German Baptists, called Dunkers, all established settlements in Pennsylvania. All were non-English-speaking; most used German.

Under such conditions the principle for which Penn stood was strengthened and deepened. He too hoped to build a community dedicated to the will of God, but he was sure it could be done in a way different from the establishment and support of only one Church. He was convinced that all Christian groups living and working together in harmony, though disagreeing at many points, could actually erect a state dedicated to God's will.

Pennsylvania flourished. Some of Penn's ideals were not realized, particularly the belief that no force should be used against one's enemies. The Scotch-Irish and the Germans on the frontier had to face the threat of the Indians and the encroachment of the French; hence, they used arms not only in defending themselves but in enlarging their holdings.

Though Penn's ideal of a peaceful commonwealth renouncing all war was not possible, his ideal of many types of Christians living and working together within one state was a pronounced success. Pennsylvania's green valleys bloomed; the rich, fertile soil produced abundant crops. Its great metropolis, Philadelphia, became the largest city in the colonies and was soon the economic center of the British American colonies.

Thus, Pennsylvania demonstrated what Rhode Island had earlier proved, that a sound, peaceful, and prosperous, as well as God-fearing, colony could be built on the basis of religious liberty.

What happened in Pennsylvania was paralleled in the other Middle-colony states. New Jersey and Delaware also contributed to the ideal of religious liberty. Both were somewhat under the control of their larger neighbors, New York and Pennsylvania, but they finally established themselves as independent colonies. Just as in Pennsylvania, many types of Christians flocked to Delaware and New Jersey. Swedish, Dutch, German, and English people brought with them the Anglican, Presbyterian, Lutheran, Quaker, and Roman Catholic faiths. Even some Puritans settled in those states. Together, all proved the principle so important in the development first of toleration and then of religious liberty — where no single Church has a fairly substantial majority of the people it cannot hope to have a Church supported by law. This the Middle colonies learned by experience.

In New York the situation was at first different, but finally here also was established the principle of religious toleration. Settled first by the Dutch and then captured by the English, the Churches of these two people, the Dutch Reformed and the Anglican, held a privileged position in the colony. They were supported by public funds, and the Anglican Church was the State Church in six counties.

The large influx of people not interested either in Christianity or in the established Anglican Church made necessary a system of toleration. That is, though the Anglican Church was supported by the New York colonial government, it could not control the wishes of a great majority of people who were either indifferent to or openly hostile to the Anglican religion. Some toleration was absolutely necessary. But this did not come automatically.

In the fall of 1706 a Virginia Presbyterian, Francis Makemie, had stood before Governor Cornbury of New York. He had been invited to preach by New York Presbyterians as he traveled through the city on his way home. Could a minister of the gospel deny the request of fellow Christians? Certainly not! He had preached; so he stood accused of preaching to Presbyterians in a city where the Church of England was the official religion.

The governor demanded that he post money to assure his intent never to repeat his offense. This Makemie refused to do. Off to jail he went for six weeks until he was finally released on bail. At his trial, his lawyers argued that he had every right to preach in New York without first gaining the permission of the governor.

The Anglican Church was not the official Church of the whole province.

His case ended with the plea that the State of New York was composed mostly of "foreigners and dissenters; and persecution would not only tend to the disuniting us all in interest and affec tion, but depopulate and weaken our strength." Why frighten away all such possible colonists by the threat of persecution? Let the gospel be preached by and to all these groups so long as it was done in good order. Francis Makemie was acquitted.

The Church of England remained the official religion in several counties, but it could not control the religious life of New York. Like all the other Middle colonies, New York found that no one religious group could control the religious life of the province.

The example and experience of the Middle colonies was not the only positive factor driving American Christians to seek yet more light on the perplexing problem of the relation between Christianity and the State.

Revivalism, coming out of the Great Awakening, tended to by-pass the usual way of relating Church to State. It was not interested primarily in the State support of the Churches, it was interested only in the soul's relation to God. Was a man saved? Had he been deeply moved by his sin? Had he undergone the experience of the forgiveness of sins in Jesus Christ? As a result, was he living a pious or godly personal life?

All this was in a different direction from the sedate Church-State establishments. Revivalists also forsook the genuine theological interests of Jonathan Edwards. They were not concerned primarily with doctrines but with experience and proper living. Not interested in speculation or in institutions, they were suspicious of the clergy, who were constantly talking about true doctrine or about the Church as a visible institution to be supported by the State.

Thus the revivalists were usually opposed by some Presbyterians, the Anglicans, and most Congregationalists. The latter two groups felt it was necessary to expound true doctrine and to be of influ-ence on society through the State support of the Church. Only in this way, they argued, would the full impact of the Church be possible. So they insisted on the State's suppressing all false forms of the Christian religion and on the recognition and support of their own beliefs.

Naturally the revivalists opposed this point of view. They contended only for the godly life which was born of the conversion experience. True life, not true doctrine, was basic. Thus they stood against any attempted control of religious life and experience by a minority of Christian believers.

Meanwhile, another movement developed in America which also worked against the favoring of any one Church. This movement was strong among a group of leading Americans which included Benjamin Franklin and Thomas Jefferson. They were not opposed to Christianity, but they felt that there were only a few truths in it that were essential for men.

Franklin said: "I never doubted . . . the existence of the Deity; that he made the world, and govern'd it by his providence; that the most acceptable service of God was the doing good to man; that our souls are immortal; and that all crime will be punished, and virtue rewarded, either here or hereafter. These I esteem'd the essentials of every religion; and, being to be found in all the religions we had in our country, I respected them all, tho' with different degrees of respect, as I found them more or less mix'd with other articles, without any tendency to inspire, promote, or conform morality, serv'd principally to divide us, and make us unfriendly to one another."

This type of belief was called deism. It was not interested in specific Christian beliefs or in speculation about Christian truth. It was interested in the moral principles of the Churches. Deists felt that Jesus was the greatest teacher who had ever lived, and that he taught in a clear fashion the moral laws on which the universe operated. There was no possibility of his being the Christ, or the Son of God, or of being a savior or redeemer of man. His function was to proclaim and make clear the laws which governed life.

Thomas Jefferson felt the same as Franklin and a number of others. To the extent that various Churches helped people to discover and follow the moral law, the deists respected them. To the extent that they insisted on the discussion of Christian beliefs about God, Christ, the Holy Spirit, the sacraments, or the Church, these various Churches disagreed with each other and so produced disunity. This the deists rejected.

Jefferson attempted to find the heart of the Bible in the teachings of Jesus and compiled a book on the subject entitled *The Life and Morals of Jesus of Nazareth*. If only all the Churches would stress the simple basic principles to be found in Jesus' teachings, which are also found in all great religions, then all dissensions would disappear.

The deists were opposed to the clergy of a State Church which tried to enforce its belief on all people. All religions held the central few truths, but these were not what the law enforced. Rather, a State Church demanded obedience to an entire body of doctrines which were not essential for religion; thus, the deists opposed that position and advocated freedom of the conscience. They were friendly toward all Churches that emphasized the teachings of Jesus but suspicious of all that spoke of the divinity of Jesus the Christ, the redeemer of mankind.

The mild deists such as Franklin and Jefferson were in agreement with the Christian revivalists on many things. Both wanted to destroy State-established Church relations as contrary to true religion. Both were suspicious of clergymen who controlled politics. Both emphasized that religion was not concerned with doctrine but with right living as outlined in Jesus' teachings. For the deist this was a very personal thing based on the reason of each man and the law of the universe. For the revivalist also religion was a very personal thing arising only out of a personal conversion from sin to righteousness through the Lord Jesus Christ.

Thus the first victories for religious liberty were won in those states where revival Christians combined with mild deists to overthrow the entrenched clergy. Pennsylvania and Rhode Island no longer stood alone.

At the time of the Revolution, Virginia was undergoing "an intense internal struggle for religious liberty." Almost since the beginnings of Virginia the Church of England was supported by land given by the State and by taxes collected from all the people. The Baptists and Presbyterians, as well as other Church groups, objected to the State support of the Anglicans.

Of all Churches, the Baptists were most faithful in their protest. They wanted no State support for any Church. During the war they sent a petition to the Virginia Government stating that "at a time when this colony, with others, is contending for the civil rights of mankind, against the enslaving schemes of a powerful enemy . . . the strictest unanimity is necessary among ourselves."

They asked that they "be allowed to worship God in their own way, without interruption, that they be permitted to maintain their own ministers, and name others, that they be married, buried, and the like, without paying the clergy of other denominations."

Up and down Virginia went the Baptist ministers gathering names in petitions pleading for religious liberty, for exemption from laws favoring the Anglican Church or any Church. They had to be reckoned with as they were a growing Church employing revival methods, and common people heard them gladly.

Meanwhile the Virginia Presbyterians were not inactive. In the years immediately before the war, their great leader, Samuel Davies, had led the fight to gain at least toleration for all Churches dissenting from the State establishment. Now, some Presbyterians favored support by taxation for all the religious groups in Virginia. But the Hanover Presbytery was opposed to such a plan and argued for complete religious liberty.

The Virginia debate raged with heat and intensity. Patrick Henry favored some kind of support by taxation for all religious groups. Washington was uncertain. Jefferson and James Madison joined with the dissenting forces to lead the fight against establishment.

In 1784, when it appeared that toleration for all groups but not genuine religious liberty would triumph, James Madison wrote the famous *Memorial and Remonstrance on the Religious Rights of Man*. In it he said:

"Religion, or the duty which we owe to our Creator, and the manner of discharging it, can be directed only by reason and conviction, not by force or violence. The religion, then, of every man, must be left to the conviction and conscience of every man, and it is the right of every man to exercise it as these may dictate. The right is in its nature an unalienable right."

As a result of the combined efforts of the dissenting Churches and the mild deists such as Jefferson and Madison, full religious liberty was established by law in Virginia in 1785.

The very words of the act were taken from an earlier proposal of Thomas Jefferson. It stated:

"To compel a man to furnish contributions of money for the propagation of opinion, which he disbelieves, is sinful and tyrannical; . . . even the forcing him to support this or that teacher of his own religious persuasion, is depriving him of the comfortable liberty of giving his contributions to the particular pastor whose morals he would make his pattern. . . .

"*Be it therefore enacted by the General Assembly,* that no man shall be compelled to frequent or support any religious worship place or ministry whatsoever, nor shall be enforced, restrained, molested, or burthened in his body or goods, nor shall otherwise suffer on account of his religious opinions or belief; but that all men shall be free to profess, and by argument to maintain, their opinions in matters of religion, and the same shall in nowise diminish, enlarge, or afflict these civil capacities."

The precedent was set! A State had thrown off public taxes and support for a Church. Henceforth all Churches were equal before Virginia law. The State had no right to interfere with religious practices so long as they did not advocate immorality or treason. The Churches could expect no financial support from the State. What started as a principle in Rhode Island and Pennsylvania developed into a necessity in Virginia, and rapidly in the other states as well. Nevertheless, these states demonstrated their friendliness for the Christian religion through the payment of chaplains' salaries and through the granting of tax exemption to religious institutions.

In the spring of 1787 an important convention met in Philadelphia. People gathered outside the doors of the convention hall as the delegates assembled. The crowd broke and made way for George Washington and James Madison from Virginia. A short time later Benjamin Franklin made his appearance.

The crowd buzzed in an excited manner. Nobody except the delegates was allowed inside. What was going to happen? Since

1781 the states had worked together under the Articles of Confederation. So many problems arose that the states were in a dangerous crisis. How could the government be improved so as to overcome their major problems? For this reason the Philadelphia convention was called.

In September, when the convention finished its work, the states were confronted, not with a few changes in the Articles, but with an entirely new Constitution for a Federal republic, a truly national government. Early in 1789 the required nine states had ratified the new Constitution, and George Washington was elected first President. The United States of America had been born.

Among the articles of the new Constitution and the very first amendment in the Bill of Rights were the following statements on religion:

"No religious test shall ever be required as a qualification to any office or public trust under the United States."

"Congress shall make no law respecting an establishment of religion, or prohibiting the free exercise thereof."

Thus religious liberty was established for the national government by law. Many were dissatisfied with such an arrangement. Some states felt the necessity for a religious test for national public office. Again, the dissenting Churches led by the Baptists co-operated with the politicians to overcome the opposition.

In 1788, Massachusetts called a convention to debate the acceptance of the new Constitution. The Congregational Church was established by law in that state and was convinced that only the combined efforts of Government and Church, both supported by public laws, could produce a peaceful and godly commonwealth.

In answer to the objection against the lack of religious test for an officeholder under the new Constitution, Isaac Backus, outstanding Baptist minister, gave a stirring speech. In it he said:

"And I shall begin with the exclusion of any religious test. Many appear to be much concerned about it, but nothing is more evident, both in reason, and in the holy Scripture, than that religion is ever a matter between God and individuals; and therefore no man or men can impose any religious test without invading the essential prerogatives of our Lord Jesus Christ. . . . And let the history of all nations be searched, from that day until this, and it will appear that the imposing of religious tests hath been the greatest engine of tyranny in the world."

Mr. Backus won his point. For years he had fought against unfair taxes levied by the State on all people to pay for Congregational churches and ministers. He could not defeat the system in Massachusetts, but he could see it prevented under the national Government. The state voted to accept the new Constitution, with its provision of religious liberty. It took almost another fifty years for Massachusetts to declare religious liberty within its boundaries, but the first irrevocable step was taken in 1788 at the urging of Isaac Backus, the Baptist minister.

So the great turning point both for the nation and the Church had been reached. Driven by necessity and by the truth derived from the Baptist and Quaker interpretation of God's Word, the nation and Churches had decided for religious liberty.

This was utterly new in the history of Christianity. It raised a host of questions. How would the Churches survive? Where would money come from? Would not Christianity be greatly weakened, if not wiped out? How could the Churches relate their message of judgment and redemption to the State and society? What of the problem of religious instruction in the face of State indifference or perhaps hostility?

Indeed the Churches had searched God's Word and will in history and had found a blazing new light. Henceforth they had to depend only on the sword of the spirit. If the nation was to be made holy, it could be done only by persuasion. Thus the Church faced at once its greatest threat and its greatest opportunity. Religious liberty brought many problems as well as many blessings.

6

New Frontiers

It was late Christmas night, 1793, in Paris. A little man sat hunched over a table in a garret room. As he wrote feverishly, the flickering candle cast strange shadows on the dark walls and low ceilings. Thomas Paine was in haste to finish a manuscript before the gendarmes would come to arrest him.

A few years before, he had been an international leader, the author of *Common Sense,* a 1776 tract that inflamed the determination of the colonists in their revolution against England. A friend and collaborator of Franklin and Jefferson, he had hastened to France to take part in the new revolution. When the extreme radicals gained control and the guillotine became master of France, Paine knew that in spite of his love for liberty, he was a marked man.

That Christmas night, 1793, he was taken prisoner and was led away to a long confinement. Before leaving, he was allowed to turn over his manuscript to a friend. It was entitled *The Age of Reason.* The second part was not completed for another two years, and the entire work appeared in 1795. Though Paine was to survive its publication by almost fifteen years, he considered it his last testament to mankind.

The purpose of the book was to combat atheism by defending what he believed to be the "true religion." He called for a rejection of the creeds and beliefs of the Churches of his day "too absurd for belief, too impossible to convince, and too inconsistent for practice." They would, he thought, render the heart torpid or produce atheists or fanatics.

"My own mind is my own church!" This was the battle cry of Tom Paine. Men were now living in a new, vital age — the age of reason. The superstition of Protestantism was almost as bad as that of Catholicism. But what then was the belief of Paine? Who was God and how was he known? Was God only the image of man's mind, as was the Church? No, there is a God, and he can be known. But God cannot be known in the life, death, sufferings, and resurrection of Jesus as the Christ.

Man learns to know God through His operations in nature — in the steady movement of the seasons, spring, summer, autumn, and winter; as one gazes at the starry heaven above, as one notes the vast multitude of living forms, one recognizes that God has made them. Said Paine, "The only idea man can affix to the name of God is that of a first cause, the cause of all things."

Christianity teaches nonsense when it speaks of the holiness of God, of his absolute sovereignty, or of God as suffering love. On the contrary, says Paine, God is "the almighty lecturer" who teaches man by placing his rules and laws in the universe. Man does not learn of God through the Bible, which contains numerous errors and many vulgar passages. "*The Word of God is the creation we behold,* and it is in this Word, which no human invention can counterfeit or alter, that God speaketh universally to man."

Here is a new theology. "That which is now called natural philosophy . . . is the true theology." From this study one learns that there is a God who is to be thought of as a professor or a lawgiver. From his laws which govern the universe one learns of his nature and will. Man learns to be kind as God through nature is kind to him. Man learns that if he breaks the laws of life he will be punished.

Here was a direct attack on the Christian Church! Paine clearly declared that his own mind was his church, that science was his theology, and that the world was his Bible. The cross was utter foolishness. Christian worship was a deliberate misleading into the paths of ignorance. The Bible was a collection of fables, false stories, and some moral truths.

The impact of *The Age of Reason* was tremendous. Christian ministers attacked it as a book from the devil. The mild deists such as Jefferson were also shocked. While they agreed with many of Paine's ideas, they were not prepared to go so far as he on many points; and they were forthrightly opposed to spreading such ideas among the great masses of people. Nevertheless, Paine found a ready audience. In a vigorous new nation where men felt the full sweep of independence in their own freedom of thought and action, such a point of view held great appeal. As new land was opened on the frontier, so here was a new frontier opened in thought. Both beckoned to the sturdy son of the New World.

The fact that Paine wrote his treatise in France gave it twice its usual appeal. Not only was he one of the great leaders of the American Revolution, he was also one who spoke from within the glorious French Revolution. The newly created United States of America watched with not a little interest the struggle of the nation that had helped it to win freedom from England. So, many of the anti-Christian writings of the French, leveled primarily against Roman Catholic tyranny, but also in passing against all Christianity, found their way into eager American hands.

Soon little groups were organized around the principles set forth in *The Age of Reason*. Deistic literature was printed and spread up and down the coast, while men and women united in a common faith in reason or common sense. Every person was created equal and so everyone was entitled to use reason in order to understand religious truth. Clergymen were responsible for perverting the true religion of humanity.

In New York, in 1794, a former Baptist preacher gathered a group of like-minded people and formed the first official Deistic Society. Elihu Palmer, though blinded by a plague, was a gifted, capable leader. He was bitterly opposed to all organized Churches and said that "Moses, Mohamet, and Jesus can lay as little claim to moral merit, or to the character of the benefactors of mankind, as any three men that ever lived upon the face of the earth. . . . Their existence united perhaps cost the human race more blood, and produced more substantial misery, than all the other fanatics of the world."

Against the superstitious beliefs of the Churches, Palmer cried that he upheld the pure, undefiled principles of nature. He announced that the new age of reason and philosophy had dawned. His mission in life was to see that the true religion was spread. So the Society became the center from which to work.

Soon other societies were developing, none very large and none having sufficient money; nevertheless, they survived. In addition to preaching and lecturing, they spread deism through newspapers and pamphlets. Several newspapers and magazines were started, but none proved too successful. Meanwhile, the organized movement spread to Baltimore, Philadelphia, and Newburgh, New York.

Tom Paine's writings proved to be one of the major factors accounting for the spread of deism. Skepticism and unbelief were rampant. So serious did matters become that the General Assembly of the Presbyterian Church issued a public warning in 1798 that unless America turned from deistic infidelity, God would assuredly visit his wrath upon it.

Though such radical views were widespread all along the Atlantic coast, they were perhaps even more prevalent on the frontier. Many of the people who moved westward were largely indifferent to Christianity to begin with. Deism appealed to these men and women who in their rough freedom fought out their own battles. It was good to have one's own mind as one's own church.

It was not surprising that large numbers of people in America were not interested in Christianity. Many had come only to seek economic security. Furthermore, the war did its usual job of lowering morals and turning the people's attention to other matters. Less than ten per cent belonged to the Churches. When religious liberty was established by the Federal Constitution it meant that in many states people had no formal ties with the Churches unless they joined by choice. Thus, the Churches received no support from the Federal Government and had to find their own solution to the problem of winning people to Christ.

Tom Paine was eagerly read on the frontier. Subscriptions to the deist papers were gathered from Kentucky. Deism had spread out over the mountains into the Ohio Valley, into Tennessee, and into Kentucky. The capital, Lexington, became the center of deistic freethinking. By 1793 the Kentucky legislature no longer wished to have a chaplain present. The Presbyterians feared that most of the people in the state were infidels.

So the Church faced a genuine threat. This was no genteel deism satisfied that the churches were a great force for moral good in society. This was a movement that attacked the Christian conception of God, scoffed at the Bible and sacraments, detested the ministry, and denied the necessity of the Church. It was not satisfied to confine these beliefs to a small circle of learned people; rather, it wished to preach from the housetops, win the rugged common man, appeal through lectures, newspapers, tracts, and magazines. The Churches were in a desperate battle.

Westward ho! New frontiers were calling. A promised land lay beyond the eastern seaboard mountains. Before the war men began to find their way through the barrier to the wilderness region. Tall tales were brought back concerning the fabulous wealth of the new section. But these were not simply fables; the stories were based on fact. West of the mountains lay a vast region threaded by rivers that emptied into the mighty Father of Waters, the Mississippi. Bounded on the north by the Great Lakes, on the south by the Gulf of Mexico, and on the west by the Mississippi, it contained a territory so large that France, Germany, Great Britain, Italy, the Netherlands, and Belgium could be fitted in, with room to spare.

This was a beautiful region rich in virgin timber, resplendent with rolling hills and gentle valleys, full of vegetation and wild game — a prize waiting to be captured. There was a variety of climate to fit the widest range of temperaments. Cold, freezing winters in the north; long balmy springs in the central part; hot, humid summers in the south. The earth offered an overwhelming harvest of all types of crops and an unbelievable quantity of minerals and metals. Here a new empire could be built.

People to conquer the frontier were plentiful. Within the new nation itself there were large numbers of those who were dissatisfied with their lot on the Atlantic coast. Some had come over as bonded servants, had served out their time to pay for their passages, and were eager to move on and find a place for themselves. Others had failed in the east and wanted a fresh start.

The War of Independence prepared the nation for the westward movement. Soldiers, having fought the British and won the victory, looked about them for the spoils of that victory. What could be a better prize than unlimited land? George Rogers Clark had gone out to the frontier capturing British forts and laying claim to the Mississippi and Ohio valleys for the colonies. The British gave in.

As soon as the war was over, the streams of European people began again to flow into America. They settled first on the coast and then pushed back over the mountains and westward. Here was a chance for the common man! What if the speculators did control the land? A good man could wrest out his living and become his own master. Fortune and adventure, hard but promising work, beckoned the unfortunate, the dispossessed, and the wealthy.

Four routes were open to those pressing westward. The earliest, most popular, and easiest route was through the famous Cumberland Gap into the bluegrass region of Kentucky. Shortly before the Revolution, Daniel Boone had pioneered this route. A more difficult passage could be made from Alexandria, Virginia, over the mountains and into Kentucky. The gateway to the southern part of the Ohio Valley was provided by the Ohio River, on which the pioneer could embark at Pittsburgh. To the north, eager settlers could leave from Albany, New York, travel to Buffalo, and follow the shores of the Great Lakes.

The first push was in the south from Virginia and the Carolinas into Kentucky and Tennessee. Starting slowly before the Revolution, slackening during the fighting, the migration burst as a flood after the peace. By 1790 two districts boasted populations larger than Rhode Island and Delaware, two of the original colonies. By foot, wagon, horse, and boat people moved into the new territory.

This became the age of road building, for without adequate roads contact could not be maintained with the settlers. To the north and to the south turnpikes were constructed so people could move into the wilderness. Rivers were dredged and canals were built. And the people poured through by the thousands. By 1790 slightly over 100,000 people had settled in the Mississippi Valley, but within ten years, by 1800, over 375,000 were to be found there.

Where did all these people come from? Many came directly from the states. The Ohio River Valley was settled in the north by New Englanders and in the south by Virginians and folks from the Carolinas and later from Kentucky. The British Isles supplied most of the immigrants who moved out on the frontier, but Germany sent its share as well.

There was a rhythm to the settlement. Sometimes a whole community or a large section of a New England town would move west to the frontier. When this happened all the institutions of society and civilization were transplanted, the schools, churches, and political organization being carried with the people. But such a plan was followed only by certain New England communities.

Mostly frontier settlements were made by individuals. The genuine frontiersman was the hunter who broke the paths into the wilderness and lived by his wits, his rifle, and his brawn. His was a rough, crude life full of danger. A family was not unusual for this pioneer, but families also shared the dangers and hardships of the woodsman.

Their homes were crude shelters made of unhewn logs and roughly tanned skins. Food was provided by the slain wild game, the fruits of the forest, and a few crops cultivated in the most primitive fashion. Clothes, candles, and other household necessities were made by the mother and children. Few were the things provided by civilization — the rifle, the ax, gunpowder, pots and pans, and occasional trinkets.

Isolation and constant danger were the lot of the woodsman's family. Cut off from neighbors by miles of forests and hills, utterly self-reliant, they faced the challenge of the primeval land alone. Only the barking of the family dog, the neighing of the horse, or the cries of the children broke the silence of the woods, and a few hundred yards beyond the cabin clearing these faint sounds of civilization could no longer be heard. Silence and isolation breeds strength but also a vague uneasiness.

To make the silence more ominous there was the constant threat of death. Prowling through the forests were bands of Indians. In the midst of the silence one had to keep alert for the telltale sounds and signs of the dreaded savages. Often they would strike without any warning, killing the entire family and leaving the cabin and clearing in flaming ruins.

One frontier farmer of the 1780's expressed the constant fear and the effect upon the human spirit in the following way: "We never sit down either to dinner or supper, but the least noise immediately spreads a general alarm and prevents us from enjoying the comfort of our meals. The very appetite proceeding from labor and peace of mind is gone: we eat just enough to keep us alive: our sleep is disturbed by the most frightful dreams; sometimes I start awake, as if the great hour of danger was come; at other times the howling of our dogs seems to announce the arrival of the enemy: we leap out of bed and run to arms; my poor wife with panting bosom and silent tears takes leave of me, as if we were to see each other no more; she snatches the youngest children from their beds, who, suddenly awakened, increase with their innocent questions the horror of the dreadful moment. She tries to hide them in the cellar. . . . Fear industriously increases every sound; we all listen. . . . We remain thus, sometimes for whole hours, our hearts and our minds racked by the most anxious suspense: what a dreadful situation, a thousand times worse than that of a soldier engaged in the midst of severe conflict. . . . At last finding that it was a false alarm, we return once more to our beds; but what good can the kind sleep of nature do to us, when interrupted by such dreams. . . . I am not a superstitious man, but since our misfortunes, I am grown most timid, and am less disposed to treat the doctrine of omens with contempt."

In addition to the Indians, death threatened through the forces of nature. Long, hard, freezing winters took their toll. Dreaded diseases would strike and, with no help present, the family fought alone either to triumph or to death. Wild animals also were a menace. Many were the ways nature could curse as well as bless the man of the frontier.

After the hardy woodsman and his family came the settled farmers who made their livelihood not directly from the forest but from the soil. And after the farmer there came small villages, the need for churches and schools. But even then the frontier placed its stamp on the lives of these people.

In the earlier stages of the westward movement there was little evidence of civilized manners. Life was crude, tough, and hard. Because of the isolation of families there was a real self-sufficiency, a rugged individualism, and an independence. People were not interested in social niceties but in survival. They worked hard, they swore hard, they drank heavily, and when they played, they played with abandon.

Underneath the rough exterior of the frontier there was a genuine social concern. Once the farmer class began to take over, a social co-operation was evident. Men and women got together to build homes and barns for each other. On such gala occasions there was heavy drinking, singing, and great funmaking. The frontier relaxed just as thoroughly and completely as it worked. There was also hospitality on the frontier for all who traveled the lonely trails. Having left behind the securities and niceties of civilization, they had not totally forgotten a concern for their fellow men in the wilderness.

When Peter Cartwright, famous Methodist frontier preacher, was on a five-hundred-mile trip home to Kentucky, he found himself utterly destitute. An example of frontier hospitality is found in his treatment both by private frontiersmen and frontier taverns. As he said: " When I came to the first tavern . . . my money was out. What to do I did not know, but I rode up and asked for quarters. I told the landlord I had no money, had been three years from home, and was trying to get back to my father's. I also told him I had a little old watch, and a few good books in my saddlebags, and I would compensate him in some way. He bade me alight and be easy."

Needless to say, Cartwright was charged no money for his stay.

Just as the deism of Tom Paine posed a problem for the Churches as a new frontier in thought, so did the physical frontier present the Churches with a challenge.

As the people moved out to the frontier, how were the Churches to keep up with them? How could they meet their needs? Was there any chance of the Churches ministering in such a wilderness? With no support by taxation where would the Churches get funds to work on the frontier? Such were the questions faced by the Churches.

Several of the Churches responded nobly to the new challenge. All were concerned to work with people on the frontier. At the close of the war the largest and best equipped Churches in the new nation were the Congregationalists, the Episcopalians, and the Presbyterians. They were all concerned with the people in the West.

The Congregationalists could not escape the question of ministering to frontier folks because many of their own people had early left the settled communities of New England and had pushed north and west into the great space of New York State. In order to send ministers to and to provide Churches for such people they began to found state missionary societies in the late 1790's. Congregationalists conceived of their task as bringing the gospel and education to the masses; so they insisted on sending only fully educated pastors who represented not only the gospel but also the best in Christian civilization.

The Presbyterians held similar views. As they had a large number of Scotch-Irish members living in western Pennsylvania, they were among the first to see the problems of the frontiersmen. They too insisted on a thorough education for the minister, whose task it was to function in a community as a teacher as well as a pastor.

For some time the two groups worked together. Though they held different views of Church government, they were quite close on their view of what was Christian truth and how it was to be preached and taught. In the early 1790's the General Association of Connecticut exchanged delegates with the Synod of the Presbyterian Church.

As the two Churches faced the tremendous need of the frontier they saw that they could best meet the challenge by co-operation and not by competition. In 1801 they drew up what was called the Plan of Union. When Congregational and Presbyterian people were found together on the sparsely settled frontier they were to combine to form a single congregation and were to call a pastor from either denomination, depending on which they could get. The congregation would then relate itself to the denomination of the majority of the members and would so conduct its discipline. Presbyterian or Congregational churches were each to remain affiliated with their own group, but they were to call either a Presbyterian or a Congregational minister. He might retain affiliation with his own denomination. Rather complicated provisions were suggested for the settlement of disputes.

So the Presbyterians and Congregationalists were prepared to work together on the frontier in order to win the people for God's Kingdom. They followed the people out to the frontier and formed united congregations. One thing was lacking, however; they did not have enough trained men. Since they refused to use untrained men it meant that some people would be without a ministry. How could a single pastor residing in a frontier village minister to the lonely settlers out on the fringes of the frontier? At best he could contact only those within the immediate vicinity.

The Episcopalians at the time of the War of Independence were a large and wealthy Church, but they suffered greatly from the war. They were suspected of being pro-English. The New England Episcopalians were, but most of the Southerners were not. Still the stigma remained, and their work was hampered. Furthermore, until they obtained bishops they were at a disadvantage. It is interesting that it was not until the second decade of the nineteenth century that they moved out to the frontier. Perhaps this is partially due to the fact that the masses of men and the common people who first settled the frontier were never much attracted by the Anglican Church. The fact was that as the Church moved westward with the people, the Episcopalians soon lost their position of leadership in the New World.

The Baptists and Methodists were more successful in meeting the needs of the frontier peoples than were any other denominations. In face of the new challenge to the Churches their view of the ministry and the Christian faith was most successful in finding and holding the people of the west. Furthermore, they were from their inception Churches of the common people, the underprivileged.

After the War of Independence and the founding of the new nation, the Baptists found themselves in an enviable position. They had fought for freedom both political and religious. Among the Protestant Churches they above all others had always appealed to the common people, to the uneducated and the dispossessed. They could claim a share in the victory.

Baptists were foremost in the first movements from the south onto the frontier. This was to be expected because of their vast supply of ministers. The Baptist preacher was often a layman who possessed a "fuller measure of the Spirit" and so could preach effectively. He was untrained and unsalaried; he worked his land as did any farmer. After he had proved his "calling" by acceptable preaching, he was licensed and later ordained to the ministry. The local congregation exercised judgment in such matters.

For the Baptists there was no waiting for a trained and educated ministry; thus there was no shortage of ministers and no impediment to the Church's reaching the people. The frontiersman preferred one of his own kind chosen by his own approval as a member in the church. Sometimes several Baptist ministers were present in a vicinity, though one was usually official minister of the congregation. They could afford several in one community because of each supporting himself by his farming.

The Methodists suffered during the War of Independence because of their membership in the Anglican Church and because their leader, John Wesley, after first defending the Americans, later turned against the colonial cause. But the Methodists persevered in their work; and as soon as they formed a national organization in 1784, they were ready to move with the people. In their first bishop, Francis Asbury, they had a leader who was both astute and brave.

The great advantage of the Methodists was their organization worked out in England by Wesley and adapted to the needs of America by Asbury and the early preachers. The Methodist minister was not "settled," but traveled on a circuit, preaching at as many as twenty or thirty "appointments" along the way. Wherever possible these horsemen of the Lord formed "classes" of Methodists, each under the care of a lay class leader during the minister's absence. Often those classes grew into churches. Furthermore, gifted laymen were urged to preach after first being licensed as lay exhorters. Thus there was a constant supply of men to handle preaching and discipline in the absence of the minister.

Methodist circuit riders were the shock troops of the Lord on the frontier. Unmarried, completely devoted to their work, they spent themselves freely. Often traveling with nothing in their saddlebags but the Bible, hymnbook, book of discipline, and sleeping equipment, they risked all for the Lord Jesus Christ. Quick to preach, ready to help, they worked day and night. A barn, a rude cabin, a schoolhouse, a clearing in the forest — all places were fit to be used to preach the gospel.

If the people moved out to the frontier, the Church went with them. All groups attempted to follow their people. The foreign-language groups such as the Lutherans went with their people out on the Pennsylvania and Ohio frontier. But the work of reaching the great mass of common men who spoke English fell to the Baptists, Methodists, Congregationalists, and Presbyterians.

The Methodists had always made their appeal to the poorer, uneducated, and dispossessed peoples. The frontier was no exception. With their lay preachers and circuit riders they could the more easily meet the challenge of people spread in isolated regions. Perhaps they could not bring a minister who was both teacher and expounder of the gospel, perhaps they could not supply schools in the earliest days; nevertheless they did not fail to supply large numbers of fervent exhorters for the Lord.

The Church faced not only this threat but also the greater threat of indifference and vast numbers of unchurched peoples. Circuit riders and lay preachers marshaled Christian forces for the grand onslaught. But even with the Church's victory there went a danger. Where would Christianity find the resources to judge and criticize as well as to answer the needs and prejudices of the frontier and its gospel?

7

Revivalism to the Rescue

EXCITED STUDENTS at Yale College gathered in a dormitory room to plan their strategy for victory. It was the opening fall term of the year 1795. A new president of Yale, Rev. Timothy Dwight, had recently been installed. Given their annual opportunity to select a subject for public debate, the students picked a topic which they were certain would be rejected. It was, "Are the Scriptures of the Old and New Testament the Word of God?"

The students were astonished and full of glee when the new president accepted the proposed subject for debate. Never before had they been allowed to pick so radical a subject. The "poor new president" simply did not understand what he had done! He was giving the young deist students an opportunity to prove the foolishness of the Bible and so of Christianity.

Calling to each other in names adopted from deist writers, they gathered their forces for one great onslaught on revealed religion. They would show what would happen if a deist were given a free chance to state his views publicly and fully! This had to be an airtight case, so they worked feverishly and hard. Students ran in and out of the room with the writings of Tom Paine, Voltaire, Rousseau, and D'Alembert. They carefully perused the Scriptures, noting instances of supposed contradiction. They scrutinized the doctrines of the Christian religion, attempting to show their absurdity.

Finally they were prepared. The big day arrived. All the students and faculty were present for the annual debates. Mr. Dwight reminded the students that they were encouraged to take whichever side they wished; nobody would be held responsible for upholding the negative side. In fact they were encouraged to do so for the sake of debate. The students smiled and winked at each other. If only this naïve new president knew what was in store for him!

So the debate commenced. Student after student presented and upheld the view that the Old and New Testaments could not be called the Word of God. They pointed to the language difficulty. Why would God choose to speak in any one specific language which might easily be misunderstood? Even translation was not always satisfactory as it did not always convey the original sense of a passage. Would an almighty God who wished to make known his will choose such an uncertain method? Furthermore, they cried, just look at all the strange fables, impossible miracles, terrible murders, and atrocities on the pages of the Scriptures. How could this be the Word of God?

Mr. Dwight stood up. A large, distinguished gentleman, he carried his weight with dignity. As he glanced about the room straining to catch the expressions on his students' faces, they recognized a scholar who was almost blind from long hours of study. Starting with a sincere compliment to the students for their attempt to explore the question, he proceeded to a thorough discussion of the issue. He had little difficulty in demolishing every argument of the students. He demonstrated how God had revealed his will in Scripture for the edification of the Church; he pointed to millions of people who had found God there, in their changed lives, and in the supremacy of Christian truth over all other forms of truth.

The students were astonished! Never had they heard such a full, frank, and reasonable discussion of the problem. Deism was defeated. Lyman Beecher, great Congregational preacher, wrote later of Dwight's impact on the student body:

" Before he came college was in a most ungodly state. The college church was almost extinct. Most of the students were skeptical, and rowdies were plenty. Wine and liquors were kept in many rooms; intemperance, profanity, gambling, and licentiousness were common. . . .

" That was the day of infidelity of the Tom Paine school. Boys that dressed flax in the barn, as I used to, read Tom Paine and believed him; I read and fought him all the way. Never had any propensity to infidelity. But most of the class before me were infidels and called each other Voltaire, Rousseau, D'Alembert, etc."

Six months of steady preaching against deism helped to strengthen the cause of Christianity at Yale. But many boys still were not positively converted to the Christian religion. In 1798 some of the students took the Bible from the Yale chapel and never returned it.

Meanwhile revivals began to sweep New England and spread to include both churches and schools. These new revivals also included a political interest. Dwight and other preachers combated French infidelity, imported through Tom Paine, and its supposed results in Jefferson's political party. Revivalists argued that good morality, good government, and a proper understanding of Christianity went together. Any who supported Jefferson supported deism and thus supported an irreligious movement.

Thus they tried to rally the people around revival Christianity and the Federalist political party which opposed Jefferson. The revivals were successful in gaining converts but unsuccessful in politics. Jefferson won and the nation was not destroyed morally. As a matter of fact, it grew and expanded.

Within Massachusetts and Connecticut, the stronghold of the old-type Puritans, the Congregational Church was still established by law and supported by public taxation. With the victory of the Jeffersonian party, first in the nation and then in the states, the Congregationalists were in danger of being cut off from State support. Dwight and Beecher argued that infidelity and Jeffersonianism would destroy Christianity in the State and open the door to immorality. So the revivals once more became a means of winning Christians to fight the disestablishment of the Church.

Lyman Beecher painted a terrible picture of what would happen if infidels won the election:

"Thus would political atheism suspend the kind attraction of heaven upon us, and let out the storm of guilty passion and, by one disastrous move from stem to stern, make a clear breach over us, sweeping away what patriots and Christians and heaven have done to render us happy."

He argued that the Jeffersonian plea for the equality of men was a false plea. The poor could be protected only on the basis of revealed religion.

"My beloved countrymen: If there is an eye in the universe that pities you, or a heart that feels for you, or a hand stretched out for your protection especially, it is the eye and the heart and the hand of heaven — it is your cause that the Christian revelation espouses. . . . It is the Bible, and the Sabbath, and the preaching of the gospel, and the schools, and the virtue, and the enterprise, and the equality which Christianity creates which dispel the darkness and open the prison door, and knock off the chains, and break off the yoke, and take off the burdens, which have in all nations and ages been the lot of persons in your condition."

Up and down Connecticut and Massachusetts rode the best revivalists. A systematic plan was worked out whereby both states were to be covered by revivals. They were conducted with zeal and sobriety. Their aim was to produce stable, moral, and enlightened Christians. But their plan failed. In 1819, Connecticut cut off the tax support for the Congregational Church, and in 1833, Massachusetts did likewise. Religious liberty and separation of Church and State had finally won!

Meanwhile the eastern revivalists found another battle on their hands. From within the bosom of the Congregational Church, a group of men around Boston gradually worked out a position that was contrary to the general Christian belief concerning God, Jesus Christ, and the Holy Spirit. These new men were later named Unitarians because they believed that God was one and that therefore Jesus as the Christ was not both full God and full man. They argued that they were more concerned with the reasonableness of Christian beliefs and with a decent moral life.

The Congregationalists replied that such a misinterpretation of Jesus as the Christ would eventually destroy true Christian religion and true morality. Again revivals were called to the rescue! In order to win back people in and around Boston, Lyman Beecher invaded Boston and preached a series of impressive revival sermons in which he upheld the usual understanding of the Christian faith.

The success of the eastern revival was considerable. Unitarianism was confined largely to the Boston area. Deism was stopped. Students at the colleges and universities were converted and great numbers again presented themselves for the ministry. Within six months, 75 out of 235 students at Yale were converted.

While the eastern revivals were slowly getting under way in the 1790's, religion out on the frontier was facing dark days. Not only was deism posing a threat, but also the problem of distance was proving difficult.

Before the Churches could make an impact on the frontier they had to contact the people. But before people could really be touched by the gospel, they had to be brought into groups. The small towns dotting the frontier were not favorable to religion. They were hide-outs for men fleeing from justice.

Peter Cartwright, famous Methodist circuit rider, tells of his boyhood days in Kentucky:

"Logan County, when my father moved to it, was called 'Rogues' Harbor.' Here many refugees, from almost all parts of the Union, fled to escape justice or punishment; for although there was law, yet it could not be executed, and it was a desperate state of society. Murderers, horse thieves, highway robbers, and counterfeiters fled here until they combined and actually formed a majority. The honest and civil part of the citizens would prosecute these wretched bandits, but they would swear each other clear; and they really put all law at defiance and carried on such desperate violence and outrage that the honest part of the citizens seemed to be driven to the necessity of uniting and combining together, and taking the law into their own hands under the name of Regulators. This was a very desperate state of things."

How could the Church prosper under such conditions? People were spread out over great spaces, miles apart. Indians, though defeated in great battles, still lurked in small, marauding bands. Criminals collected in frontier towns threatened the security of the farmers and other honest citizens. So distance and solitude were not the only hazards faced by the Churches.

Such people and such conditions could be met only with a gospel that hit head on. The revival preacher was the answer. But revivals were nothing new in the Churches. For many years ministers had preached with the primary object of convicting people of their sin and of showing the forgiving love of God in Jesus Christ.

These sermons were direct and to the point. They painted a picture of sin, death, damnation, and salvation in bold strokes and with lurid colors. The results were astounding. People would be stricken with remorse and cry out for mercy. Often their lives would be completely changed as a result of the experience. This was the form of gospel that appealed to the frontiersman.

One of the men who helped to bring revivalism to the frontier was James McGready, a Scotch-Irish Presbyterian. A powerful preacher who was famous for his eloquence and zeal, he traveled in the Carolinas converting sinners to the new life. Though not an impressive-looking man, his voice had an unearthly, somewhat ghostly tremor and his piercing eyes would not let one sinner rest.

Hear him as he exhorts his listeners:

" The fool hath said in his heart, ' There is no God.'

" He died accursed of God when his soul was separated from his body and the black flaming vultures of hell began to encircle him on many sides. Then all the horrid crimes of his past life stared him in his face in all their glowing colors. . . . The remembrance of misimproved sermons and sacramental occasion flashed like streams of forked lightning through his tortured soul; then the reflection that he had slighted the mercy and blood of the Son of God . . . was a poisoned arrow piercing his heart. When the fiends of hell dragged him into the eternal gulf, he roared and screamed and yelled like a devil. Then while Indians, pagans, and Mohammedans stood amazed and upbraided him, falling like Lucifer . . . sinking into the liquid, boiling waves of hell, and accursed sinners of Tyre and Sidon and Sodom and Gomorrah sprang to the right and left and made way for him to pass them and fall lower down even to the deepest cavern in the flaming abyss. Here his consciousness like a never-dying worm stings him and forever gnaws his soul; and the slighted blood of the Son of God communicates ten thousand hells in one. Now through the blazing flames of hell he sees that heaven he has lost. . . . In those pure regions he sees his father, or mother, his sisters, or brothers, or those persons who sat under the same means of grace with him, and whom he derided as fools, fanatics, and hypocrites. . . . They shine brighter than the

sun when he shineth in his strength and walk the golden streets
of the New Jerusalem; but he is lost and damned forever."

Sinners cried out for help — some wept, others moaned, many
were stricken in conscience and determined to follow the Lord. So
the revivalist preacher made his impact. Many centuries previous
a great scholar, Anselm of Canterbury, had used the identical text
as a basis for an elaborate and very intelligent discourse to prove the
existence of God. Now, on the frontier, the same text became the
basis of a highly charged emotional appeal to leave off cursing, swearing, and sinning, and to accept the Lord Jesus Christ.

Up and down the frontier valleys, over the mountains, into the
woods, traveled the preachers. Always their approach was the same
— appeal to the raw feelings of the frontiersmen, move them to
repentance, and offer the redeeming love of God in Christ. Their
message was heard.

Soon large numbers of people were converted. Little congregations and churches were gathered. What did it matter that often
the believers had to walk ten miles each Sabbath? They had been
called by the Lord! Indifference, deism, and hostility were attacked.
The Church would not surrender or forget the masses on the
frontier.

Just as the Great Revival was getting under way in the west,
around 1800, the frontier developed a new form for the revivals.
Because people sometimes had to travel several miles to reach the
place where the preaching took place, they could not leave early
enough to return home the same night. Therefore they began to
bring equipment for camping on the spot. Also, the Presbyterians
encouraged such activity by their great outdoor " sacramental meetings," which lasted several days. Soon there developed what were
called "camp meetings." People would come from miles around
and bring provisions for several days.

One of the first such meetings occurred in July, 1800, at Gasper
River in Kentucky. The meeting started on Friday, continued during Saturday, and that evening nobody went to bed. Instead, the
whole camp was swept by an outbreak of repentance and confession.

First, people discussed quietly among themselves. Soon the earnest conversation spread like a flame from group to group. The

excitement and tension mounted. People began to cry out. Old men and women, little children, young folks, parents — all began to cry for mercy. Turning and twisting, wringing their hands, beating their breasts, they struggled to be released from sin and to experience the new birth in Christ.

All night the ministers and converted Christians rushed about the camp praying and exhorting. In the darkness of the night, broken by the flaming campfires and the smoking torches, strange shadows reached out from the surrounding forest — the probing fingers of the evil one trying desperately to clutch the sinners striving for release. Here and there a cry of victory broke through the moaning as a saint was born.

Nobody slept. On Sunday several ministers again mounted the rough platform and led the singing with great booming voices. Again the people fell to praying and preaching. Nobody wanted to cease praying, singing, exhorting, and listening. Even food was forgotten for the time.

Finally, all participated in the Lord's Supper — the great culmination of the meeting. Large numbers had been won for the Lord. The violence and indifference of the frontier had met its match. The camp meeting was a new way to preach the gospel. Henceforth the church building was to play a different role on the frontier. No longer was it to be so much the place where sinners were convicted. Rather, it became the place to which converted saints returned in order to show the effect of their religious experience.

The camp meeting, born of the necessities of the frontier, soon grew to be a regular part of the frontier life. In place of the earlier haphazard, unplanned meetings, the camp meeting arose controlled by the ministry and used as an instrument to further the Lord's work. It was employed by all the large frontier Churches — the Methodists, the Baptists, and the Presbyterians. It spread from Kentucky to the Carolinas, Tennessee, Virginia, Pennsylvania, and to Ohio. From there it went to the entire midwest.

The largest of these early camp meetings was held in August, 1801, at Cane Ridge, Kentucky. It was jointly sponsored by the Methodists and Presbyterians. For several months before this great meeting other meetings had been held in the area; thus, many were looking forward to Cane Ridge. The meeting was to begin on Friday and end on Wednesday.

On Thursday the roads leading to Cane Ridge were crowded with horses, wagons, and people. From miles away one could see clouds of dust arising as the long, slow columns wound through the passes and over the bumpy roads. All trails led to Cane Ridge. People poured in from Ohio, from Tennessee, and from every section of Kentucky. Age made no difference — the entire family, from the oldest grandfather to the youngest baby, was brought along. The frontier was alive with people on the march.

As the wagons rolled into camp, greetings were shouted to friends and relatives. Many were meeting for the first time in months or years. Soon the wagons were directed into position as the camp site was laid out in sections. Most brought their own provisions, but special wagons carried extra provisions for those who had not planned ahead.

While wagons, horses, and people arrived, many men were busy constructing platforms in various strategic places. They were rough stands erected for the purpose of preaching. In addition to these there was the meetinghouse, which was a permanent structure. Freshly felled logs also provided places for exhortation.

On Friday the preaching began. Methodist, Presbyterian, and Baptist ministers took turns exhorting; while some preached, others prayed. As the crowds grew, several preachers would hold forth simultaneously in different parts of the camp. Over twenty-five ministers were busily engaged. In addition many lay people also exhorted.

Soon people began to cry for mercy. The revival took hold as hundreds were confronted by their sins. All day the excitement mounted. When not shouting and praying, people and ministers sang hymns, and during the singing they often turned to their neighbors and shook hands indicating the right hand of fellowship.

It was an impressive sight to see a great mass of people swaying and pumping hands as they shouted in song:

"'Without Thy sweet mercy, I would not live here;
Sin soon would reduce me to utter despair;

But through Thy free goodness my spirits revive,
And He that first made me still keeps me alive.

" ' Thy mercy is more than a match for my heart,
Which wonders to feel its own hardness depart.
Dissolved by Thy goodness I fall to the ground
And weep to the praise of the mercy I've found.' "

Or, again, a favorite line in a hymn that had mighty effect on the people was:

"Take your companion by the hand,
And all your children in the band."

On into the night the revival moved, never ceasing. Some fell exhausted, others sought out their tents and wagons for a few hours' rest. But others were always up and about. Preachers took turns and gave each other rest. As the days wore on people continued to stream into the camp and participated in the movement. There was no letup.

Nobody knows exactly how many people attended. Probably it was between 12,000 and 20,000. No exact count of conversions was kept, but it was several thousand. Around 800 people were permitted to attend the great Communion service. Truly, it was one of the greatest revivals in the history of the Church.

How did it affect the people? The religion of the frontier was the same as the rest of frontier life. It was uninhibited, emotional, and extremely personal, lacking all formality. Because the people were under constant threats of danger and so under great emotional strain, their emotions were released with joyous abandon in their religious services.

To be convicted of sin meant to be struck down by the wrath of God. These were not idle words to the frontiersman; they were an actual experience. As sinners listened to the revival preaching they actually fell to the floor, sometimes with great sighs and moaning, sometimes in complete silence. Usually the person would utter a piercing shriek and fall to the ground. Others would follow until great numbers were so affected.

While lying on the ground some would be as stiff as logs, as if in a trance, not speaking and hardly breathing. Others would continue to shout and shriek until completely exhausted and no power remained to whisper. Still other convicted sinners while lying on the ground often began to preach in a loud voice and could not stop. They would keep on so shouting for hours without ceasing. One man testified that the finest sermon that he had ever heard came from a person so stricken. Other strange reactions were those of barking like a dog or jerking violently until exhausted.

All the English-speaking groups in the west were soon influenced by revivalism. It moved out of Kentucky and Tennessee north of the Ohio River and west into the great Northwest Territory. Everywhere in the west the camp meetings were being developed and used. A new way had been found to bring the gospel to the west.

Revivalism enabled the Churches to reach great masses of frontier people and to win them for their own. Nobody was automatically a member of the Church in America. Either each person or family was won to the Church and kept in it by persuasion or the Church had no members. There was no compulsory membership by state law; there was only voluntary membership by consent. The revivals and camp meetings became the means whereby the Churches won masses of people and turned them from indifference and infidelity.

The camp meeting was not only of religious significance, it also played another role in the frontier. It enabled people to gather together under a common program to share their deepest emotions and convictions. This, frontiersmen needed. For too many months they were shut off from friends and neighbors with little or no opportunity to share their experiences. Thus camp meetings were also an important social institution in the west.

Another result of the Great Revival was the emergence of one of the most distinctive features of American Protestantism. It was highly emotional, almost anti-intellectual. What was of most importance for the revivalist was a gripping emotional experience. If one deeply felt his conversion, if one shed tears, or one had been stricken down, or if one had been possessed by the jerks, then chances were that one was converted.

This stress on the emotions of the believers was vastly different from the religion that prevailed in the east. When Dwight and

Beecher carried on revivals they kept close control over the congregation. Yet the difference was one of degree rather than of kind. The average eastern clergyman, though well-educated, depended as much on the place of the emotions in conversion as did the frontier clergyman. The difference was that the former saw them as one part of a total religious life and expressed them in a more restrained manner while the latter was inclined to view bodily reactions as the very heart of the religious life.

There was something both good and bad in the emotionalism of the revivals. It was good insofar as it was the only possible religious approach for the frontiersman. It was of a piece with the rest of his life. It was not something foreign or forced. It was the genuine reaction of people deeply committed to the message they heard. It marked a full and complete response. There was little intellectual side to their faith because there was little intellectual life on the frontier. There was much theological disputation but little arbitration in terms of doctrinal consistency or proper Biblical exegesis.

The emotionalism was also very dangerous because it could easily be turned aside from a religious expression to a purely sensual expression. Ministers had to be careful at camp meetings lest rowdies and others would take advantage of the emotionalism and promote immorality. This, however, seldom happened. The real danger was that the stress on emotions could become so basic that all other sides of the religious life could be ignored. After all, the gospel spoke to the entire man, not just to part of the man. Revivalism could easily find that side of the frontiersman which readily responded, but could it carry him beyond his emotional state? The ministers attempted to do this through the tracts and books they distributed on the frontier, but their own inclination as well as the literature stressed the emotional and the moral aspects of the religious life.

Because revivalism reduced everything to a matter of simple choice — Christ or the devil, sin or goodness, infidelity or faith — it both answered the needs of western people and made it very difficult for them to pass on to a deeper understanding of the religious life. Faith was not always a simple matter of choice. One's whole past life formed one's decisions. To be sure, under the great emotional stimulus of the camp meeting one might be able to break through the past and to decide for God. But what happened when the emotional appeal was not present?

Simplifying the issues through emotional appeals made choices easier, but it overlooked many basic problems. It ignored the responsibility of the Christian faith to address current intellectual difficulties. It centered only on moral results. The consequence was that it was extremely successful in meeting the needs of the frontier, but it produced a spirit in American Christianity that made it difficult for Christianity to shift its emphasis in the face of new frontiers.

Thus its greatest success also produced its greatest temptation. The truly converted man was one who lived a moral life — this meant that he did not smoke, drink, dance, or swear. These were the great evils of the frontier. Whisky was almost as common as water. The little country store usually had a great barrel of whisky with a tin cup on a chain hanging on the side. It provided the refreshment.

Converted Christians gave up completely all those evils of the frontier life. There was no such thing as moderation in these matters. If one did them even a little, he was a sinner. So sin was identified with such things as drinking, smoking, and dancing; righteousness was identified with abstinence from such actions. The whole thrust of revivals was to get results in the moral life. This could be done only by converting individual souls. Thus revivalism was not concerned so much with theology or with the structure of society; it was concerned with personal morality and personal conversion.

The Great Revival spread across all denominational borders. Because it appealed to individuals and to morality it overlooked theological differences between different Churches; thus, it led to co-operation among all revivalist Christians. The revivals reached their peak by 1806 and slowly died out until the ember was kept glowing only by sporadic outbreaks.

But revivalism would not disappear from the American scene, and it would not be displaced. On a beautiful autumn morning of 1821 a tall distinguished-looking young lawyer, Charles G. Finney, slowly walked down the street of Adams, New York, on his way to the woods. His head was bent in deep thought as he turned the corner and disappeared down the country road. In the woods this proud young man fell on his knees and spent the whole time until dinner in prayer. He was going through the struggle of conversion.

As he trudged back to town, he still was not certain of his spiritual state. But that evening in the back of his law office he fell to his knees and wept a great flood of tears, uttering choked confessions of his unworthiness. He surrendered to the Lord.

When he returned to the front room, he said: " The Holy Spirit descended upon me in a manner that seemed to go through me, body and soul. I could feel the impression, like a wave of electricity, going through and through me. Indeed it seemed to come in waves and waves of liquid love; for I could not explain it any other way. It seemed like the very breath of God. I can recollect distinctly that it seemed to fan me, like immense wings."

Finney had experienced justification by faith. No longer depending upon his own merit, he threw himself on God's gracious forgiveness in Christ. As a result he determined to enter the ministry and to give up the practice of law. He had been retained as an attorney to represent a deacon in a law case. That very day he informed the man:

" Deacon B——, I have a retainer from the Lord Jesus Christ to plead his cause, and I cannot plead yours."

" What do you mean? " asked the astonished deacon.

" I have enlisted in the cause of Christ; I have a retainer from him to plead his case, so you must get somebody else to attend to your lawsuit," replied Finney.

After he studied theology under a local Presbyterian minister, Finney went out to preach. In a short time he was one of the greatest revival preachers in the nation. He swept through western New York in the 1820's, converting thousands. Soon a band of helpers worked with him in exhorting and guiding sinners.

Finney was a Presbyterian, but his methods seemed somewhat unusual even for the revivalists. He prayed for sinners by name; thus individualizing his appeal. The " anxious seat " was introduced. It was a bench in the front of church to which all sinners and those in the struggle of rebirth were invited. Furthermore, he allowed women to pray in public. All these things were highly irregular.

Though Finney had astounding results and an outpouring of emotional response, he never deliberately encouraged extreme feelings. His sermons were like the lawyer's plea. Using everyday language, hard logic, and a most persuasive presentation, he had no difficulty in converting sinners. In 1828 he invaded Philadelphia. All the other great eastern cities followed in order. Even New England, and Boston which had declared against him, accepted him. In New York City the Broadway Tabernacle was built especially for him, but within a short time he moved west to become the professor of theology at the newly founded Oberlin College. Later he was made president of that institution.

So revivalism came to the Church's rescue. It became one of the distinctive features of American Protestantism. It defeated deism and indifference, it overcame the problem of space and won thousands of members for the voluntary Churches. In revivals the Churches found an answer to the question of how to present the judgment and redemption of God, yet in so doing they also limited their message and bound it to emotionalism.

8

Dissension and New Churches

IN THE AUTUMN of 1803 the Presbyterian Synod of Kentucky was in session. Tension was in the air as a good deal of back-room discussion took place. All the enmity between those favoring and those opposing revivals reached a climax. For almost two years, several Kentucky Presbyterian ministers had warned against the extravagances and strange doctrines of the revivals. Many had replied favoring them. Thus, the synod was divided into the revivalists and antirevivalists.

Tension was great because two men, Rev. Messrs. McNemar and Thompson, were on trial as revivalists who, in the excitement of the camp meetings, had preached erroneous doctrines. As their examination proceeded it became evident that they were doomed; therefore, before the full proceedings could get under way they made a strategic move.

Joined by three revivalist brethren, Marshall, Stone, and Dunlavy, these men stood up before the synod and made a dramatic announcement. They condemned the actions of the synod and affirmed their independence from its jurisdiction, but they maintained that they were still in communion with Christ's Church in America. A great murmuring arose from the floor of the synod. Men jumped up and demanded to be heard. The moderator pounded for order, but the damage had been done.

What happened in 1803 was not surprising. The revivals not only brought great numbers into the Churches, they also brought violent disagreements. Not all ministers were in favor of such excesses as the jerks, the barks, or falling. Most men favored some type of revival, but the question was, What kind of revival? How could revivals be properly controlled? The synod argued that excesses certainly should not be encouraged. Furthermore, the teachings of the revivalists should be in harmony with God's Word and with the beliefs that the Church confessed in its creeds.

The five Presbyterian ministers proceeded to form themselves into a new presbytery called the Springfield Presbytery. They rejected all creeds or historic confessions of faith and held only to the Bible as the bond of fellowship. They received the name " New Lights " because of their adherence to the new revival methods.

Worship services were well attended. These men were looked upon as persecuted martyrs for the sake of truth. For a while the Presbyterian Church was in a bad way in some sections of Kentucky. It appeared as though the New Lights would sweep all before them.

The Springfield ministers stressed active, emotional worship services. They encouraged a free display of feelings. One of their favorite practices was taken from camp meetings, namely, shaking hands while singing hymns. This soon developed into a form of religious dance. As they grasped hands loudly singing, " ' Make me, Saviour, what Thou art: live Thyself within my heart,' " they would tremble, shake, and finally break into a leaping, twisting dance. This activity was similar to that of a movement called the Shakers.

In 1804 the presbytery dissolved itself by issuing what they called the " Last Will and Testament of the Presbytery of Springfield." " The Presbytery of Springfield, sitting at Cambridge, in the County of Bourbon, being through a gracious Providence in more than ordinary bodily health, growing in strength and size daily, and in perfect soundness and composure of mind; but knowing that it is appointed for all delegated bodies once to die, and considering that the life of every such body is very uncertain, do make, and ordain this our last Will and Testament. . . . We *will,* that this body die, be dissolved, and sink into union with the Body of Christ at large; for there is but one Body and one Spirit, even as we are called in one hope of our calling. . . . We *will,* that our power of making laws for the government of the Church, and executing them by delegated authority, forever cease, that the people may have free course to the Bible, *and adopt the law of the Spirit of life in Christ Jesus.* . . .

We *will,* that the people henceforth take the Bible as the only sure guide to heaven."

Many of the members of the independent Churches that came out of the Springfield Presbytery called themselves Christians. Barton W. Stone was active in promoting that name and urged that all congregations, in complete freedom, work toward the establishment of a truly united Christian Church.

Rather than unity, dissension arose even out of this move. Two of the original five ministers went back to the Presbyterian Church, two of them joined the Shakers, and only Barton W. Stone remained faithful to their original ideal. Indeed, the revivals produced many bad things as well as good things.

Trouble for the Kentucky Presbyterians was not yet at an end. No sooner had they overcome the blow of defection from the Springfield group than they were confronted with another schism. Again the source of the trouble was revivalism.

In December, 1805, a Presbyterian commission was sitting at the famous Gasper River Meeting House in Kentucky. It had the thankless task of trying to settle a dispute that had arisen in the recently formed Cumberland Presbytery. In face of the desperate need for ministers on the frontier, the Cumberland Presbytery had licensed several uneducated but gifted men to preach and catechize, and had appointed others as exhorters. These men were required to subscribe to the Presbyterian Confession of Faith only so far as they believed it agreed with the Word of God.

Some men in neighboring presbyteries were disturbed by these proceedings. They felt that men with wrong beliefs were permitted to act as exhorters and preachers. Also, they argued for a well-educated ministry which would be doctrinally sound and would understand and subscribe to the Confession of Faith.

The synodical commission clashed with the Cumberland Presbytery. Both claimed final jurisdiction in examining and passing candidates for the ministry. The moderator of the commission urged the suspect presbytery members to submit for synodical approval. The men on trial asked for a discussion recess.

Before they withdrew for conference, Mr. Stuart, one of the commissioners, stood up and delivered a sincere plea reminding all those present that the unity of the Church was at stake. His eloquence moved many to tears and created a solemn mood.

A short time later the suspect men — McGready, McAdam, Rankin, and McGee — returned. The assembly waited breathlessly as the question was asked: " Do the brethren wish to submit to the jurisdiction of the commission? "

A murmur of despair arose as they answered together: " No! "

Determined to uphold the supremacy of the synod in such matters, the commission suspended these men and twenty other licentiates and exhorters and prohibited them from performing their ministry. The young men were to be silenced.

The General Assembly upheld the Kentucky Synod's action and the independent Cumberland Presbytery was formed in 1810. It stood by the Westminster Confession of the Presbyterians except that it allowed some liberty on the doctrine of God's eternal election of some to salvation and others to damnation. Furthermore, it encouraged revival methods and employed camp meetings. The gift of the Spirit in the ability to preach sinners' conversion was felt to be more important than an educated ministry. The break was complete. Another Church was born out of the revival dissensions.

Disagreement within the Presbyterian Church did not cease with the New Light and Cumberland schisms. Rather, there was a continuous suspicion between the revivalists and antirevivalists. It included not only different views on emotion and education but also disputes concerning the true interpretation of the Christian faith.

Rev. Joshua Wilson was one of the leading Presbyterian ministers in the west. He was on constant guard against any false doctrine at work within the churches. In 1832 the famous Congregational preacher, Dr. Lyman Beecher, was called from Boston to become president of the recently founded Lane Theological Seminary in Cincinnati, Ohio.

Dr. Wilson immediately brought charges against Beecher and sought to prove him doctrinally unsound. The whole Church was astonished. Had not Dr. Beecher defended the truth against the infidels and Unitarians in New England? The trial commenced and raged back and forth for several days. Beecher was too able an opponent for Wilson to handle, and he was upheld and vindicated.

In vain did Wilson appeal to the synod and to the General Assembly of the Church — he could not defeat Beecher.

The Beecher trial was but a symptom of the grave unrest stirring within the Presbyterian Church. Other trials followed, but few were successful. Much of the unrest was due to the constant influx of Congregationalists under the Plan of Union. They were educated in New England, many at Yale under Prof. Nathaniel W. Taylor, and were thought to be very untrustworthy in doctrine. So, the Old School Presbyterians kept a close eye on them.

Meanwhile, another controversy arising out of revivalism shook the Presbyterian Church. It fed into all the other causes of discontent and made the tensions more acute. Charles G. Finney, the great Presbyterian revivalist of western New York, was the source and center of the controversy.

Finney was privately trained and self-educated in theology. His instruction was under his pastor in Adams, New York, a Mr. Gale. All the local pastors urged Finney to go to Princeton Theological Seminary, the outstanding Presbyterian training school. This he refused to do on the grounds that he did not wish to be trained as Mr. Gale and the other ministers in the presbytery. In spite of his dissatisfaction with the Princeton theology, he was licensed by the presbytery to preach the gospel.

As a result of Finney's background and training, his preaching was a good deal different from that of his Princeton-trained brethren. As he put it: " I was bred a lawyer. I came right forth from a law office to the pulpit, and talked to the people as I would have talked to a jury."

As a consequence Finney advocated speaking directly to the people as if one were appealing for an immediate verdict in favor of the Lord Jesus Christ.

" So it always is when men are entirely in earnest. Their language is in point, direct and simple. Their sentences are short, cogent, powerful. The appeal is made directly for action; and hence all such discourses take effect."

Furthermore, Finney directed his address to each hearer personally. He had no admiration for ministers who preach " about other people, and sins of other people, instead of addressing them and saying, 'You are guilty of these sins,' and, 'The Lord requires this of you.' . . . Now I have thought it my duty to pursue a different cause; and I always have pursued a different cause. I have often said, 'Do not think I am talking about anybody else, but I mean you, and you, and you.'"

Not only his straightforward sermons, spiced with illustrations from daily life, bothered his brethren, but even more his conduct of the service was attacked. Finney never intended to promote fanaticism and emotionalism; he actually tried to prevent it. The means he used for revival were "simply preaching, prayer, and conference meetings, much private prayer, and much personal conversation, and meetings for the instruction of earnest inquirers."

It was Finney's use of these last means which produced such opposition in the Churches. Out of it developed the "anxious bench" and the bands of converted exhorters. Those who were under the conviction of sin but had not yet experienced the release of forgiveness were urged to attend special meetings or to sit in a special place during the service.

The special meetings were usually conducted by the revivalist and some of his assistants in order to help those struggling for conversion. During the meeting the sinners would be prayed for by name. This was something different in that it put much more pressure on the sinners. To hear one's own name, to feel oneself as the special object of the prayers of the whole group was, indeed, an experience one could not take lightly.

Likewise, placing the "called" in the front of the church on the "anxious bench" so as to separate them from the converted and from the not yet called raised many problems. By placing them in that position it became psychologically almost impossible to escape conversion.

To all these new practices the antirevivalists objected. The objection was forthcoming not only from the Presbyterian Church but also from the German Lutheran and Reformed, from the Congregational, and from the Episcopal Churches.

The most telling criticism came from an outstanding German Reformed pastor and professor, Dr. John W. Nevin. In the early 1840's he wrote a treatise called *The Anxious Bench*. It was an at tack on the whole approach to revivalism. While he admitted that revivalism did much good, he insisted that it also did a great deal of evil. By its emphasis on conversion as a profound emotional experience, it tended to undermine the idea that many Christians are raised in the Church and gradually grow under the guidance of the Church to understand their faith and its meaning for life.

The religious system of revivalism, he argued, is different from the faith of the Presbyterian, Reformed, and Lutheran Churches. Rather than the sinner being captured by God's forgiveness in Christ through the regular ministrations of the Church and so being grasped by religion, revivalism insists that the sinner "gets religion." Feeling and not faith becomes the turning point of religious experience.

What Nevin wanted in place of emotionalism was "a ministry apt to teach; sermons full of unction and light; faithful, systematic instruction; zeal for the interests of holiness; pastoral visitation; catechetical training; due attention to order and discipline; patient perseverance in the details of ministerial work."

So the battle lines were drawn between those advocating the "church system" and those upholding the "revival system." Opposition to revivalism was on the march among the Congregationalists, Presbyterians, Anglicans, Lutherans, and German Reformed. Revivalism was not an unmixed good for American Christianity. In it the Churches found more light yet for attacking some of the most pressing problems. But in it they also found a source of schism and discontent. The foes of revivalism could do little to stop it. They could only stand as a corrective to it, reminding Christians that it was not the only nor the purest form that Christianity takes.

All eyes were turned to the speakers' table as President Andrew Jackson arose to propose a toast for the Jefferson Day Democratic banquet in April, 1830. Southern Democrats were in control of the program, and all speakers had been carefully picked to express the views of the Southern states' rights party.

Jackson raised his glass, turned and looked squarely at the Southern leader, John Calhoun, and said firmly and clearly, "Our Federal Union — it must and shall be preserved."

There were cheers and gasps from the crowd as it became clear that the President was opposed to all actions that would be detrimental to the liberty and welfare of the entire Union.

John Calhoun, not to be outmaneuvered, arose and responded: "The Union, next to our Liberty, most dear! May we all remember that it can only be preserved by respecting the rights of the states and by distributing equally the benefits and burdens of the Union."

The Churches were not the only bodies caught up in quarreling and dissension at this time. The entire nation was beginning to show the signs of sectional disagreement. Eastern states, developing manufacturing, wanted to buy raw materials cheaply but wanted tariff protection so foreign manufacturers could not undersell them at home. Infant industries had to be protected, they argued.

Southern states were agricultural and wanted to buy manufactured goods as cheaply as possible, whether from home or abroad; therefore, they were opposed to all tariffs which kept prices up. They wanted the best possible markets for their goods. The western states wanted to buy things cheaply, but they also wanted roads and canals to transport their goods east; therefore, they favored internal improvements paid by the Federal Government.

So each section battled and fought over taxes, tariffs, internal improvements, the annexation of new territories, the attitude of the Union toward England, France, and Spain, and many other things. Gone were the peaceful co-operative years immediately after the Federal Union was established. Jackson made clear that the welfare of the United States was more important than the selfish interests of any single part of the Union. But this did not settle the problem. From this moment forward the tension and disagreement between the various sections mounted until it coalesced in the slavery question and erupted in the Civil War.

Just as the whole nation was undergoing the serious quarrels of sectionalism, so the Churches, at this time, were also going through periods of argumentation. One of the most serious disruptions was that which occurred in New England — the rise of Unitarianism. It was a terrible blow to the Congregationalists as it stripped them of over half a million dollars' worth of property and over one third of their members in Massachusetts.

One man said of Unitarianism that "the protest began among a class of cultured men in the most cultivated part of America; with men who had not the religious element developed in proportion to the intellectual or aesthetic element."

The movement was firmly planted within the bosom of Massachusetts Congregationalism when, in 1805, Henry Ware, a decided Unitarian, who emphasized the unity of God to such an extent that it was difficult for him to maintain the traditional Christian belief in the divinity of Jesus the Christ, was appointed professor of divinity in Harvard University. Boston erupted in a heated controversy over this act. However, nobody was prepared to take any drastic steps.

Things were brought to a head by three separate events. In 1815 an article was printed calling the Boston Congregationalists "Unitarians." The name stuck. In 1819, Dr. William Ellery Channing preached a famous sermon in Baltimore entitled "Unitarian Christianity." And in 1820 the courts ruled that in Dedham, Massachusetts, church property belonged to the entire parish and not to the church as such. The parish was a geographical unit that contained both church members and nonchurch members; however, all qualified voters had a right to determine all questions pertaining to church property. Because the Unitarian Congregationalists were usually the leaders in the community and appeared to stand for a more common-sense and liberal position, they had little difficulty in obtaining the support of the majority in the parish and so gained control of the church property. Thus the wishes of the majority of the actual church members were often denied, so that a small group of Unitarians took control.

A bitter quarrel developed in Massachusetts. It was at this time that the Unitarians organized themselves into an association, in 1825. They numbered about 125 churches, which included the wealth, intellectual leadership, and energy of Boston. On the whole their wealth and social position led them to be extremely conservative in their politics and in their social views.

It was at this point that Lyman Beecher appeared on the scene and through revivalism stemmed the tide of Unitarianism. It never made much headway beyond the environs of Boston. There was a similar movement, however, which made a greater appeal to the common people and became widespread on the frontier. It was called Universalism.

During the late eighteenth century several preachers in New England insisted that God was not the kind of God who would punish man eternally. Eventually, they argued, God would save all men. Later, leaders such as Hosea Ballou and Thomas Whittenmore rejected the belief in Christ as the eternal Son of God, the belief in a personal devil, and any form of punishment after death. All punishment for sin, they argued, occurs during this life. All men are saved by God. Since they claimed salvation was universal they were called "Universalists."

The preaching of such beliefs caused controversy on the frontier and among the city churches. Peter Cartwright speaks of the prevalence of Universalism among frontier people. Some of his most heated arguments were with these people. While that particular Church did not grow greatly in numbers, its influence in conjunction with the Unitarian spread across the nation.

Meanwhile, contention and disagreement grew within the Protestant Episcopal Church as well. In 1811 two bishops were appointed and they came to represent two opposite tendencies in the Episcopal Church. Bishop Hobart of New York became the leader of what was called the High-Church party. They stressed Episcopal Prayer Book worship, the sacraments of the Church, and urged the necessity of ordination only by bishops, who were supposed to stand in line that went back to the apostles. This apostolic succession, they argued, was necessary in order to have a legitimate ministry.

Over against revivals and the conversion experience, High-churchmen upheld catechism, confirmation by the bishop, and a close direction of the spiritual life by the parish priest. They were certain that they held the true view of Christianity, and therefore they could not co-operate with other Protestant groups even in such things as the distribution of tracts.

Bishop Griswold of the New England diocese represented what was called the Low-Church party. This group also stood for ordination by bishops, but they did not feel that all other ministries were invalid unless so ordained. Furthermore, they did not feel that the Prayer Book was the only or highest form of worship. They held prayer meetings and classes for mutual edification. Even their preaching was different in that it was directed toward an immediate conversion experience.

These two groups were constantly in tension within the Anglican Church, but their differences never led to really profound disagreement. It was not until the 1840's that the disagreement reached a serious point. That was due to the introduction of a new factor into the picture. In England a movement centering in Oxford University, known as the Oxford movement or as Anglo-Catholicism, started in 1833. It stressed the continuity of the Anglican Church with the Catholic Church before the Reformation, though it repudiated Roman Catholicism. So it attempted to revive and emphasize many of the pre-Reformation forms of devotion and piety.

When this movement made its impact in the Protestant Episcopal Church, it coalesced with the High-Church party and stimulated heated opposition from the Low-churchmen or evangelicals. Several bitter disputes occurred, but both parties determined to remain within the Episcopal Church, and they did so.

Dissension of the period was reflected in the Lutheran churches as well. In 1820 a General Synod of the Lutheran churches was founded. It soon came to embrace a major proportion of the non-Scandinavian Lutherans until a fresh wave of German immigration in the 1840's brought several other Lutheran groups to America. However, the General Synod did not rest in peace and harmony. Chief among the new arrivals was the German group that settled at St. Louis and formed the Lutheran Church of the Missouri Synod. It upheld a strict doctrinal position and argued for a congregational polity. It was to become one of the two great Lutheran Churches in America.

Dr. S. S. Schmucker, one of the great leaders and professors at the Gettysburg Seminary, had been deeply influenced by the revival Churches. In the late 1840's and 1850's he and a number of friends began to urge practices common for revivalists but peculiar for the Lutheran Church. Furthermore, he advocated a departure from the historic Lutheran confessions of faith. In fact, he advocated a position that stressed moral activity with a minimum attention to doctrine and theology. This was unacceptable for many of his brethren. They insisted that the Church could not ignore its historic doctrinal position and that it had to be concerned with belief as well as with practice. A constant running battle emerged, which continued until the General Synod was torn by strife and finally split in the 1860's.

Meanwhile large numbers of German Lutherans and Scandinavian Lutherans began to arrive in America. As these were all foreign-language people, only their native churches could minister to them. Their pastors did a magnificent job of staying with these people. However, these groups introduced many new sources of dissension within growing American Lutheranism. It could not be helped. They brought not only national differences but also the lastest doctrinal arguments from their homelands. This was all reflected in the relationship of these new bodies to each other and to the older General Synod. American Lutheran churches could not escape the dissension of the period. The same was true of the German Reformed. Dr. J. W. Nevin, the opponent of Charles Finney the revivalist, became a storm center in that Church on the grounds that his advocacy of the " church system " was an importation of Catholic practices and beliefs.

Late one August night in 1834, the town of Charlestown, Massachusetts, witnessed the spectacle of fire shooting high into the air, of fire bells loudly ringing, and of great masses of people rushing through the streets. The Roman Catholic Ursuline convent was under attack by crowds yelling, " No papacy! " As the mother superior guided the children out of the rear entrance, a mob burst into the front and proceeded to demolish the building and put it to the torch. For several days Boston and its environs were in a state of unrest and imminent rioting. The violent outbreak against the Roman Catholics was under way.

Hatred against the Roman Catholics was based on the erroneous belief that they kept guns hidden in their churches and were awaiting the day when they could strike to capture America for the pope. Also, it was not to be forgotten that many people had fled to America to escape Roman Catholic tyranny, and the specter of Catholic growth appeared as a threat to democracy and religious liberty. Men harboring this fear organized themselves into various organizations. The most famous of these grew to become the Know-Nothing political party, which was active in national politics in the 1850's. Its purpose was openly a violent opposition to everything Roman Catholic.

Roman Catholicism had grown tremendously because of the arrival of hundreds of thousands of immigrants. At the close of the Revolution they numbered only a few thousand, but by 1830 they numbered over half a million. As they grew in strength and leadership, they began to exert their influence. They protested Bible-readings in public schools unless Catholic versions were used. In fact, they preferred to have their own schools so they could educate their own children. The United States had been colonized by men who were bitterly opposed to Roman Catholicism; thus, a good deal of ill will on both sides was almost inevitable. Only time could teach them to live together peacefully.

The strife that arose between the two groups was regrettable, but in a sense it was inevitable. The pity was that the disagreements could not have been limited to theological debate. The acts of church-burning and the activity of the Know-Nothing party were violently anti-Christian and greatly to be deplored. All Protestants must repent of them. It is true, but no excuse for the Protestants involved, that many other factors, in addition to religion, were responsible for the outbreaks of violence. Unrest was partially the result of the dissension of the age born of the suspicions of rising immigration and a changing spirit in the nation.

Meanwhile, in addition to the new Churches produced by strife and ill will, several new Churches were born out of the maelstrom of the frontier. They were another effort of Christianity to bring its message to the people of America.

In the fall of 1809 at Washington, Pennsylvania, a group of men under the leadership of Thomas Campbell met to form an association of Christians. This was to be not a Church but a dedicated group that would work for certain ideals, particularly that of unity, within the existing Churches. Their motto was, "Where the Scriptures speak, we speak; where the Scriptures are silent, we are silent."

They appointed Thomas Campbell to prepare a full statement of their beliefs and purposes. Campbell was a minister within one of the small Scottish Presbyterian bodies, but he was most unhappy in it and was having trouble. About four weeks after the Washington Association was formed, Campbell's official connection with the Presbyterian body was broken.

Thomas Campbell prepared a statement outlining the principles of the association as peace, purity, and unity. At the very time the elder Campbell was reading proofs on the statement, his son Alexander Campbell arrived in America. Within a short time the Washington Christian Association became a Church, it adopted adult baptism, and Alexander Campbell emerged as the real leader. The group associated with the Baptists in 1813.

Under the able leadership of Alexander Campbell new ferment was at work in the Baptist association. In the periodical he edited, he questioned such things as the relation between the old and new covenant, the function of reason in a believing faith, the steps in becoming a Christian, the full right of any layman to administer sacraments, and the extent of an association's jurisdiction over a local congregation. These questions involved Baptist beliefs and practices.

Campbell proved to be an outstanding debater and journalist. As he propounded his views and won many followers, dissatisfaction with the Baptists grew. Finally, around 1830, the gradually developing disagreement reached a peak and a break came between the Disciples of Christ, as the Campbellites were known, and the Baptists. The same year Campbell's famous magazine, *The Millennial Harbinger,* was begun. Its purpose was to prepare for the triumph of God's Kingdom on earth through promoting Christian unity.

In 1832 a union was effected between Campbell's Disciples of Christ and Barton W. Stone's Christian Church. While there could be no formal union because neither group had a formal synodical or associational organization, there was a full exchange of ministry and co-operation in revivals and evangelism. So the revivalistic Christians who split from the Presbyterians in Kentucky united with the ex-Presbyterian Campbells who had also come through the Baptist Church.

The group employed revival methods and met with great success in the border states. Under the leadership of many revivalist preachers the new Church moved out to the frontier, and made converts in Kentucky, Illinois, West Virginia, Indiana, Missouri, and Texas. Their battle cry was, " Back to Bible Christianity and unite all the Churches of Christ on the basis of that Christianity." While they sincerely preached and stood for these principles, they became, unfortunately, not a rallying point for unity, but one more denomination competing on the American scene.

Even the Methodists did not escape from the schisms and quarrels of this period. Under the circuit system and the plan of representation for conferences, neither the rank and file ministers nor the laity had much liberty. The laymen were not even represented and the clergy had nothing to say about the election of their presiding elders. There was constant agitation within the Methodist ranks to overcome these differences, but every such attempt was looked upon by the bishops as dangerous and radical. Finally, in 1830 a large number withdrew from the General Conference and founded the Methodist Protestant Church, which gave full rights of representation to laymen and refused to operate with bishops.

While the Methodist Church was having internal difficulties because of its Church government, it was making astonishing progress not only on the frontier but also among German-speaking peoples. In 1800 a German-speaking Methodist group, the United Brethren, was founded. In 1803 the Evangelical Association, centering in Pennsylvania, was founded as a German Methodist group. So Methodism gained among German-speaking peoples.

Revivals brought growth and strife to American Protestantism. In looking about to find ways of meeting the challenges of deism, the vast masses of unchurched peoples, the great space to be covered, the disintegrating morals, and the threat of financial collapse after the Revolution, the Churches found their answer in revivalism. It was nothing new in America. It was not turned to deliberately in order to meet these challenges. Rather, it was deep within the

Church and simply welled forth in the face of need.

The tragedy was that it brought so much strife and unrest as well as so much good. It placed a stamp upon American Christianity that remains to the present day — even in the form of Churches that split off as a result of revivalism. It was a blessing and a curse — the one could not be had without the other.

9

New Life in the Spirit

It was an overcast day in August, 1806, when several young men students at Williams College in Massachusetts set out to find a secluded spot for meditation and prayer. This was a common practice for those who had experienced conversion, but this meeting was to have unusual consequences. They found a quiet, deserted little grove close by the campus. There they began their devotions and mutual edification.

The one great concern that burned in their hearts was that of missions to the heathen. Since his conversion in 1802, Samuel J. Mills, the natural leader of the group, had desired to become a missionary. Wherever he went he talked about this basic task of the Church. Had not the Church received the commission to go and teach all the nations, baptizing them in the name of the Father, of the Son, and of the Holy Ghost? The other young men agreed with Mills.

In the midst of their devotions a thunderstorm struck and sent them scurrying for shelter to the lee side of a haystack. While the lightning flashed through the skies and thunder rolled and rumbled overhead, they reached just as earthshaking a decision. Mills proposed that they send the gospel to India, that they become personally responsible for the task. They all agreed that they could do it, if they wanted to.

This was no vague promise born of the emotion of the hour. Just as, three centuries before, Luther was struck down by a thunderstorm and entered the religious life, so these men determined to pledge their lives. The first step was the formation of a private society in 1808 that made formal the resolution of the haystack group. They drew up a constitution that made clear their purpose to develop a mission to the heathen. No members were to be admitted who, because of other commitments, would not be free to engage in foreign mission work.

The discipline and intent of the holy group was expressed in the words, " Each member shall keep absolutely free from every engagement which, after his prayerful attention, and after consultation with the brethren, shall be deemed incompatible with the objects of this Society, and shall hold himself in readiness to go on a mission when and where duty may call."

By 1810 several of this group were students in Andover Theological Seminary. Their interest in missions never ceased, and the faculty encouraged that interest. The British had set an outstanding example in missions which was eagerly watched by American Protestants. In June of that year the young men presented their concern to the Congregational General Association of Massachusetts. They felt that it was time for " New World " Christians to take up the work. A resolution was presented by students Judson, Hall, Newell, and Nott stating that " their minds had been long impressed with the duty and importance of personally attempting a mission to the heathen . . . ," and so they sought the advice of the Association.

A committee reported that a foreign missions board should be established and made responsible for finding " ways and means and adopting and prosecuting measures for promoting the spread of the gospel in heathen lands." The result was the formation, in 1812, of the American Board of Commissioners for Foreign Missions. Within a short time it raised substantial funds and found a number of men willing to serve on foreign fields.

In 1812, five men sailed for India and missions were established in Bombay, Ceylon, and later in Burma. These were the first outposts of American missions in the East, destined to become the first fruits of a rich outpouring of dedicated men and women who wanted to win the world for Christ. Within a short time the Presbyterians decided to co-operate with the American Board, as did the Dutch Reformed, with the consequence that the work was greatly expanded.

Though two of the men who sailed for India were on different boats, strangely, as they read their New Testaments, they came to similar conclusions. They determined to become Baptists. Then, when Adoniram Judson and Luther Rice landed in India they did not feel justified in retaining their connection with the American Board. Mr. Judson went up to Burma and became the founder of one of the greatest of American mission fields. Mr. Rice was compelled to return home.

Rice arrived home at the same time as the news of Judson's conversion and desperate plight. Here was a converted Baptist on the field waiting to act as the official missionary of the Baptists. What could be done? Luther Rice toured the South urging the formation of Baptist missionary societies to support Judson and others. He was eminently successful.

Baptists were noted for their fear of synods or any central Church authority; thus, many looked with suspicion on the formation of any national organization or agency to support anything. In the spring of 1814 a meeting was held at Philadelphia where a General Missionary Convention was established. A board of managers was elected, which was to meet annually. Also, it was determined to hold a General Convention triennially. They decided to retain Mr. Rice as an itinerant and voted officially to acknowledge and support Mr. Judson. This was not only the beginning of Baptist mission work, it also marked the beginning of the only national organization the Baptists were willing to construct.

Meanwhile, the Presbyterians were carrying additional mission work beyond the support of the American Board. In 1817 their General Assembly decided to join with several other Calvinistic Churches in forming the United Foreign Missionary Society. By 1826 they found it expedient to join forces with the larger American Board, so all their magnificent Indian work was united with that of the Board, and the Presbyterians worked as one with the groups supporting the Board.

All the American Churches turned their attention to foreign missions. Because of the presence of the Indians, American Protestantism always had an incentive for mission work. With the ever-expanding frontiers of the world, they received further stimulation to send men to such strange, remote places as Ceylon, India, Africa, and later China and Japan.

The Methodists and Episcopalians were not to be left behind. Both founded missionary societies and sent many men overseas. Because so much of the Methodist work was in reality home missions, their missionary society founded in 1819 made little effort to distinguish between home and foreign missions. In fact, it was not until the 1830's that the first Methodist missionary was sent overseas from America.

In the late 1850's the General Synod of the Lutheran Church founded a missionary society, but the first American Lutheran foreign missionary was C. F. Heyer sent by the Ministerium of Pennsylvania. This grand old man became almost a legend in India as he founded new fields and also built up the work started by earlier German Lutherans. He made several trips back to America, and after he had returned permanently to America he heard that the Lutherans were going to abandon their work in India; so, at the age of seventy-seven, he went back to the mission field. He traveled to his posts with his coffin, using it as a bed by night and as a cart on wheels by day. Finally, after his work was firmly established and held by younger hands, he made his final trip home to die in America.

Thus the mission spirit swept the American Churches. From whence did it come? It came largely from the impulses created by the revivals. People were made aware of their responsibility as converted Christians for the conversion of the heathen. They formed societies that cut across denominational lines. They collected pennies by the week to give to mission societies. The outpouring of God's Spirit brought new life to the Churches, and they saw their responsibility to shed abroad in the hearts of all men the light of the gospel.

In 1820, Peter Cartwright, Methodist western preacher, was passing through Kentucky on his way home. Saturday night found him in a region of the Cumberland Mountains, " where there was no gospel minister for many miles around, and where, as I learned, many of the scattered population had never heard a gospel sermon in all their lives, and where the inhabitants knew no Sabbath only to hunt, and visit, drink and dance."

Cartwright was forced to stay in a lodge where a dance was being held that night, and he determined to stay over so he could preach to these heathen people. He was a missionary to the godless. As he sat in a corner musing on the spiritual condition of the dancers, a young woman walked up to him and asked him to dance. Undaunted he seized upon this as an opportunity for evangelism.

"A beautiful, ruddy young lady walked very gracefully up to me, dropped a handsome courtesy, and pleasantly, with winning smiles, invited me out to take a dance with her. I can hardly describe my thoughts or feelings on that occasion. However, in a moment I resolved on a desperate experiment. I rose as gracefully as I could, . . . with many emotions. The young lady walked to my right side. . . . We walked on the floor. The whole company seemed pleased at this act of politeness in the young lady shown to a stranger. The colored man, who was the fiddler, began to put his fiddle in the best order. I then spoke to the fiddler to hold a moment, and added that for several years I had not undertaken any matter of importance without first asking the blessing of God upon it, and I desired now to ask the blessing of God upon this beautiful young lady and the whole company, that had shown such an act of politeness to a total stranger.

"Here I grasped the young lady's hand tightly, and said, 'Let us all kneel down and pray,' and then instantly dropped on my knees, and commenced praying with all the power of soul and body that I could command. The young lady tried to get loose from me, and I held her tight. Presently she fell on her knees. Some of the company kneeled, some stood, some fled, some sat still, all looked curious. The fiddler ran off into the kitchen saying: 'Lord a marcy, what de matter? What is dat mean?'

"While I prayed, some wept, and wept aloud, and some cried for mercy. I rose from my knees and commenced an exhortation, after which I sang a hymn. The young lady who invited me on the floor lay prostrate, crying earnestly for mercy. I exhorted again, I sang and prayed nearly all night. About fifteen of that company professed religion, and one meeting lasted next day and next night, and as many more were peacefully converted. I organized a society, took thirty-two into the Church, and sent them a preacher."

So the western missionary operated. Whenever the opportunity presented itself, he preached the Word and formed a church. The Methodist circuit system could be called one great home missions agency. It was set up in such a way that it could get the maximum service from each preacher in reaching the maximum number of people.

Yet the Methodist preachers did not have the support many missionaries received. They had little education, few books, and seldom more than fifty dollars a year income. As Cartwright put it, the Methodist preacher hunted up " a hardy pony of a horse, and some traveling apparatus, and with his library always at hand, namely, Bible, hymnbook, and Discipline, he started, and with a text that never wore out nor grew stale, he cried, ' Behold the Lamb of God, which taketh away the sin of the world! ' In this way he went through storms, wind, hail, snow, and swamps, swam swollen streams, lay out all night, wet, weary, and hungry, held his horse by the bridle all night, or tied him to a limb, slept with his saddle blanket, if he had any, for a bed, his saddle or saddlebags for his pillow, and his old big coat or blanket, if he had any, for a covering. Often he slept in dirty cabins, on earthen floors, before the fire; ate roasting ears for bread, drank buttermilk for coffee, or sage tea for Imperial; took with a hearty zest deer or bear meat, or wild turkey, for breakfast, dinner, and supper, if he could get it."

The entire Methodist organization tended to be a home missions society. Men were appointed to their area of work; they did not choose it. They chose only to serve the Lord; the Church through the bishops and district supervisory elders determined where they were most needed. The men were constantly shifted about so they could not become settled or stale. Of course there were great dangers in this practice in that a man never had the time to develop a full understanding ministry in any one place, but the system paid off in the numbers of people contacted and converted.

Under the missionary impulse and through the use of revivalistic preaching and methods, the Methodist Church experienced a phenomenal growth. At the end of the Revolutionary War, it was one

NEW LIFE IN THE SPIRIT 139

of the smallest Christian groups in the colonies. By 1830 they were surpassed in numbers only by the Baptists. Their growth occurred out on the frontier, in the west. In 1819 they founded the Methodist Missionary Society, but its work was primarily an extension of the mission work to the Indians and Negroes.

Meanwhile, mission work by other groups such as the Congregationalists, the Presbyterians, the Episcopalians, and the Lutherans was carried on in a more customary fashion. All these Churches advocated a settled ministry rather than an itinerant ministry; therefore, in order to expand and take the gospel to the frontier, they had to appoint and support home missionaries for the task.

The need for such work was impressed upon the Churches by the constant movement of population from the midst of settled communities with churches to the frontier with few social and no religious institutions. At first, local congregations tried to take care of the needs of their former members and friends. Soon the problem grew out of hand. It was at that point that societies for home missions were contemplated. Because of British opposition to any such groups, it was not until after the Revolution that they were begun.

The Connecticut Congregationalists formed one of the first local or state missionary societies in the 1790's, and it sent a number of men to labor among the new settlers in Vermont, New York, and Pennsylvania, and "New Connecticut" or the Western Reserve in Ohio. At the same time the Presbyterians recognized the need for a specific mission organization to carry their work to the unchurched. And so the pattern penetrated among most of the denominations. Missionaries were called with the specific task of going out on frontier tours in order to gather people into congregations. Later a regular pastor was sent. One of the great services performed by these local missionary society representatives was the survey of religious conditions in the west, which indicated the great need for Bibles, pastors, and literature for the frontier.

In addition to the work carried on by various Presbyterian synods, the General Assembly of 1802 formed a standing committeee on missions to handle the home missions problem. But the most important factor in the work of the Presbyterians and Congregationalists on the frontier was the operation of the Plan of Union of 1801.

Under it the two groups worked together in developing a frontier ministry.

Thus all the Churches recognized their responsibility to the people on the frontier. The question was what method should be employed to reach them. The Methodists with their circuit system and the Baptists with their lay preachers held a distinct advantage. But the Presbyterians and the Congregationalists were undismayed. They doubled their efforts to supply educated pastors and educational facilities as well as a simple gospel of conversion. This was no small task and was a real contribution to the development of American culture.

By 1820 the United States possessed all the territory west of the Mississippi to the Rocky Mountains with the exception of the California region and Texas, which were claimed both by the United States and Spain. To the north was Canada, and in the northwest was the Oregon territory claimed by United States and Great Britain. Having procured Florida from Spain, the young giant nation was beginning to take shape. Nationalism and patriotism vied with sectionalism as the nation continued to expand westward. Under President James K. Polk, Texas was annexed in 1845 and a war broke out between Mexico and the United States. As a consequence most of the California territory and New Mexico were added to the nation. Also under Polk, the Oregon territory was divided between Canada and the United States; thus, by 1846 the boundaries stretched from the Atlantic to the Pacific and from Mexico to Canada.

This was one great mission field facing American Protestantism. The Churches needed all the enthusiasm, manpower, experience, and organizational ability available in order to cope with the situation. It was not strange that the smaller local missionary organizations could not adequately meet the demands. Vast, well-organized national societies were required to handle the needs of such a tremendous territory.

Formation of the United Domestic Missionary Society was the first step in a fresh approach to home mission work. When founded in 1822, it drew into itself a number of smaller local groups and determined to pursue a new policy of missions. It wanted to go on record with the " earnest hope that the practice of employing missionaries to travel from place to place preaching here and there a sermon . . . and remaining at no one point long enough to accomplish anything likely to be permanent, will be universally abandoned."

Instead of supporting men who traveled from group to group, they determined to support ministers in local situations where the congregation could not yet afford to be self-supporting. When they reached that stage, national support was no longer necessary. The United Society felt that its object was to supply full-time pastors who did not have to depend upon some other job for support. Their men were to create permanent, stable churches which, in turn, would help to support other infant congregations.

At the urging of six Andover Seminary graduates of 1825 and at the entreaties of a number of clergymen, the United Society initiated the participation of interested Churches in the formation of an American Home Missionary Society. This was established at a meeting in New York in 1826. The Congregationalists and Presbyterians were the largest contributors. Here was a new experience at co-operation in the face of an overwhelming need. Within eight years it had 606 men on the field laboring in 801 congregations and districts. This was one way to face the national problem.

In 1824, a group of theological students at Yale Divinity School signed a compact " to go to the State of Illinois for the purpose of establishing a seminary of learning such as shall best be adopted to the exigencies of that country — a part of us to engage in instruction in the seminary; the other to occupy, as preachers, important stations in the surrounding country."

These men sent out by the American Home Missionary Society were known as the Yale Illinois Band. They established Illinois College in Jacksonville and became pastors in several key towns close by. In fact, they set somewhat of a precedent as other bands later went forth from seminaries. One of the most famous was the Iowa Band of 1843.

The spirit with which these home missionaries went forth was ably expressed by one of the Iowa Band when he said: " The under-

standing is among us all, that we go west not for a *temporary* purpose, unless the great Head of the Church shall make it so. We go
to remain *permanently* — to live and die there — and God grant us
grace to carry out this purpose."

The eastern Churches were well aware of their responsibility to
the people in the west. In fact, they looked upon the west as an area
to be saved from infidelity, Roman Catholicism, and antirepubli-
can sentiments. They felt that the minister had to do more than convert men from being sinners. The Church had to provide schools
and education, culture and learning.

The general instructions of the American Home Missionary Society to its missionaries stated: " Although the preaching of the
gospel holds the first and highest place in . . . the ministerial office,
yet there are a variety of subordinate measures, which . . . require
the diligent attention of every pastor and every missionary." They
were encouraged to establish Sabbath schools and Bible classes, to
promote education, to diligently instruct the church members, to
take a deep interest in both home and foreign missions, to promote
the various Christian tract societies and the temperance movement.

Lyman Beecher saw the importance of the west for the future of
America. While on an eastern tour seeking support for Lane Theological Seminary he delivered a famous address, " Plea for the
West." In it he stated that " if this nation is, in the providence of
God, destined to lead the way in moral and political emancipation
of the world, it is time she understood her high calling, and were
harnessed for the work." First one had to recognize that " it is
equally plain that the religious and political destiny of our nation is
to be decided in the west. There is the territory, and there will soon
be the population, the wealth, and the political power."

He saw the importance of the west in relation to the entire nation and so in relation to America's destiny of moral leadership for
the world. Thus the cause of missions for the west was of the highest importance. " It is equally clear that the conflict which is to decide the destiny of the west will be a conflict for the education of
her sons, for the purpose of superstition or evangelical light, of
despotism or liberty."

The one thing needful was to establish in the west strong colleges and seminaries, good Protestant churches, and plenty of well-trained ministers. Simply sending Bibles, tracts, and itinerating missionaries was not enough. Actual institutions had to be established. Beecher argued that democracy could not survive without a strong spiritual foundation. People had to be educated in their beliefs and practices. Freedom was everyman's gift but everyman had to grow in it and understand how to live it. When Beecher looked about the west he saw great masses of people untouched by schools and churches.

He thought that something had to be done, and it had to be done at once! He cried: "Whatever we do, it must be done quickly; for there is a tide in human things which waits not — moments on which the destiny of a nation balances, when the light dust may turn the right way or the wrong. And such is the condition of our nation now. Mighty influences are bearing on us and a slight effort now may secure what ages of repentance cannot remove away. We must educate the whole nation while we may. All — all who would vote must be enlightened, and reached by the restraining and preserving energies of heaven."

The urgency of the dangerous moment was made more acute for Beecher by the growing tide of immigrants who were ignorant of American principles. They were not to be turned away but educated before they could do any damage. Particularly did Beecher feel that the Roman Catholics were dangerous. He argued that they were ignorant of the principles of republican government and encouraged a superstition that was contrary to American institutions. He argued: "Whether Catholics are pious or learned is not the question, but what are the republican tendencies of their system?"

So Beecher closed with the plea that if "we do not provide the schools which are requisite for the cheap and effectual education of the children of the nation, it is perfectly certain that the Catholic powers of Europe . . . will do it." The west had to be saved from Catholicism, superstition, and atheism because in it was the future of a free America and so of a free world. Beecher's pleas did not fall on deaf ears. Many responded generously. Others came forward to plead the same cause.

Meanwhile many people in the west resented the implications of

Beecher's plea and others like it. They too believed that the future of the United States was in the west, but they were certain that they could provide well enough for themselves. There was no need of treating them as a field to be missionized by superior eastern brethren.

Peter Cartwright, the Methodist itinerant, disdainfully said, "About this time there were a great many young missionaries sent out to this country to civilize and Christianize the poor heathen of the west." He joked about their written sermons which they attempted to read to the people and remarked, "The great mass of our western people wanted a preacher that could mount a stump, a block, or old log, or stand in the bed of a wagon, and without note or manuscript, quote, expound, and apply the Word of God to the hearts and consciences of the people."

Many of the western frontier preachers resented the implications that their work had not been sufficient. They realized that a good deal remained to be done, but they wanted it clearly understood that they had labored to save the west for the Lord and that only their methods were the proper kind for the frontier. It was an affront to them to speak of the west as if there were not a godly people to be found there. The fact was that there was need for something besides the uneducated revivalist or the itinerant who conceived of his task principally in terms of fervid preaching and loud praying.

Spurred on by the revival preaching of Beecher, Finney, and a host of others, the east continued to pour out funds to save the west. There was not a territory overlooked. In the 1830's several missionaries of the A.H.M.S. made the long, tortuous trip to Oregon to undertake work among the Indians and the trappers. Frontiersmen were hard on the easterners who could not take the rugged western life, but they had only respect and esteem for men such as Marcus Whitman, Presbyterian doctor and missionary.

Dr. Whitman made his reputation with the frontiersmen when he removed a barbed-iron arrowhead from the back of the famous trapper Jim Bridger. A large crowd of trappers and Indians witnessed the operation, criticizing and giving advice. Nothing bothered Whitman. When the operation was over and Whitman remarked to Bridger that he could not understand how the trapper could have gone so long with such an object in him, the trapper replied, " In the mountains, doctor, meat don't spoil."

Furthermore, Whitman had another thing in his favor in the personage of his very attractive and friendly wife. She was a fine singer in addition to being a most beautiful woman. The trappers, who had not seen a white woman for years, were more than pleased when they met her. The Indians, who often wondered if there were any such beings as white women, were enchanted with her goddesslike beauty. They loved to strut and dance before her. Under the leadership of the Whitmans and the Spaldings the Oregon mission was started. Baptists and Methodists also had men and women on the scene.

So the Churches poured out men and money to win the west. They sent pastors by boat and wagon to California and the far west. The Dakotas and Montana were not overlooked. They passed on into the Rocky Mountains; they moved down into the southwest. All the denominations were conscious of their responsibilities — in the forefront were the Congregationalists, the Presbyterians, the Baptists, and the Methodists. Close behind but not so active were the Episcopalians, the Disciples, the Lutherans, and the various Reformed groups.

Opposition to the whole mission program, foreign and home, was particularly acute among the Baptists and the Disciples of Christ. The antimission movement was founded in the west and spread until it could claim almost 70,000 followers among the Baptists alone. When the Baptists founded their mission agencies in the General Missionary Convention of 1814 they met some opposition on the grounds that such a convention was an invasion of the rights of the local congregation, but such objectors though vocal and of considerable numbers were in the minority.

The real opposition to missions had a twofold basis — practical and theological. Most of the opposition was rooted in the former. Many of the Baptists' uneducated ministers resented the eastern treatment of the west as a mission field. One man was supposed to have said that he had no objection to sending foreign missionaries, " but what do they want to come among us for? We don't want them here in Illinois." He made his objection clearer when he said, "These missionaries will be all great, learned men, and the people will go to hear them preach, and we shall all be put down."

In addition to jealousy, fear, and distrust, some of the opposition to missions came from the fact that many looked upon them as an excuse to get money out of the Churches. When Luther Rice went among the Baptists to raise funds for missions he met with much selfishness and niggardliness. People grumbled about giving money for missions. Among the Disciples of Christ, still part of the Baptist Church, the opposition was voiced by none other than Alexander Campbell, their leader. He argued that this was an unscriptural way of carrying the gospel to the heathen. Later he reversed his view and became a firm supporter of missions.

The other argument against missions came from an extreme form of Calvinism. These men argued that since God had determined from all eternity those whom he would save and those whom he would damn, sending missionaries made no sense. God would see to it that all the elect were saved. Man could do nothing to aid or hinder it. So they were opposed to all missions. Yet, strangely, these men were not opposed to extremely emotional revival preaching which attempted to convert men from a sinful state. Although it caused serious trouble among the Baptists and Disciples, the anti-mission movement never made as much headway among the other denominations.

Missions were not the only new outpouring of religious life from the Churches. The tremendous energy tapped by revivals was released through a whole series of churchly activities. One of the most important areas of new life was that of education.

Sunday schools were largely unheard of in America until the Methodists introduced them shortly after the War of Independence. At first they met with opposition among some Churches but soon became popular. In a way, the idea of educating children in the faith was always part of the Puritan heritage. The Sunday schools set about to do this for all age groups under the direction of voluntary teachers; thus they were, in reality, only a continuation of an earlier ideal. However, in the absence of sufficient public schools, the Sunday schools were just as important in performing the service of teaching such basic knowledge as reading and writing.

Just as almost every Protestant movement in the early nineteenth century became national, so the Sunday school movement developed a national organization in 1824, the American Sunday School Union. Its purpose was to promote the spread of Sunday schools and to hold conventions in order to acquaint members with the basic problems to be confronted. By 1850 over half a million pupils were enrolled in Protestant Sunday schools.

Education at public expense was becoming the common practice in the 1830's and 1840's. Under the leadership of Horace Mann, the Massachusetts public-school system was thoroughly revamped, and the old practice of denominational religious instruction was eliminated in favor of instruction in universal Christian principles which were to be found in all denominations. Leading educators of the mid-nineteenth century agreed with Mann that religious instruction was essential to a well-rounded education. Later, opposition to this point of view developed both from those opposed to all forms of religious instruction in public schools and from Roman Catholics who upheld the right to instruct their children in their faith. This led to one of the most serious problems in mid-twentieth century America — the relation between religious instruction and public education.

Meanwhile other phases of education were not being neglected. As the Churches moved westward with the people they saw the need for providing colleges and academies so that true culture and godliness could be promoted. Hence great stress was placed on founding colleges. By 1800 there were only two genuine colleges west of the Alleghenies, but by 1830 that number had grown to twenty-six.

Most of the colleges remained small in comparison with the older eastern schools such as Harvard and Yale, but they did an outstanding job for the west. They became centers for the reform movements of the frontier, they poured men into the ministry, and they brought education to the west. Many of them failed, but great numbers of them survived to produce something unique in education, the small religious liberal arts college. One more gift of the Churches to the nation was the small college. In some midwestern states there are ten or fifteen such schools still performing an important function for the Church and the nation.

Also at this same period the problem of an educated ministry became more acute. Revivalism was partially responsible for raising the question. But as the nation grew and the Churches expanded they found theological training in the homes of individual pastors insufficient in quantity and quality. Therefore this age became the age of seminary building: the Church built schools where young men could go after college in order to be trained in theology and divinity. These were but one more example of the vitality and energy of nineteenth century Protestantism in America.

New York City was the scene of great activity in May, 1830. People gathered from near and far. Clergymen and laymen, both men and women, made for the big city. A great conference of all the various reform movements was being held. By that date America was swarming with benevolent societies.

There was hardly an evil that did not have a society organized to combat it. There were religious tract and Bible societies to publish and spread both the Bible and various religious pamphlets and books among the godly and godless. There were groups centering around the express purpose of saving the wayward girls who had succumbed to sin in the big cities. Sailors' rest centers were developed to keep the seamen out of evil saloons and to provide them with a place of worship. The temperance movement attacked the use of alcohol. There were prison reform societies, women's rights groups, world peace movements, and Sabbath observance organizations. All these, in addition to the home and foreign missions and educational agencies of the Churches, were expressions of the new life in the Spirit.

They were the products of the revivals and the reawakened faith of the American people. Charles Finney preached that sin was " a deep-seated but voluntary . . . self-interest " and that holiness or virtue was " disinterested benevolence." Conversion meant a turning from self-interest to " a preference for disinterested benevolence." Once converted to the cause of the Kingdom the believer " should set out with a determination to aim *at being useful in the highest degree* possible."

Thus the Great Revival of the early nineteenth century produced sinners converted to action, ready to lead the onslaught against the forces of evil. Just as Cromwell had cried out as he led his hosts against the enemy, so these soldiers of Christian morality shouted, "Let God arise, let his enemies be scattered."

A large share of the recruits for the reform army were volunteers from the Presbyterian, Congregational, and Unitarian Churches. These groups had long felt a responsibility for the total society. It was not enough simply to convert men from sin to faith. The Christian faith was of consequence for all of life. With the coming of religious liberty there arrived a basic problem for the Christian faith — how would it show its responsibility for all of society?

Men such as Beecher and Finney argued that converted Christians were to combine in voluntary organizations to combat all forms of civic and personal evil and to promote good. The Church could no longer interfere with the Government just as the Government could no longer interfere with the Church, but through voluntary reform groups the Christian citizen could, by moral pressure and a majority legislation, see to it that public morality was kept at a high level. As Beecher said, a moral influence " is needed distinct from that of the Government, independent of popular suffrage, superior in potency to individual efforts, and competent to enlist and preserve the public opinion in the side of law and order."

That is why in May, 1830, there met in New York City representatives of eight of the largest benevolence societies. Their delegates had gathered to review the year's battles, to plan strategy for the coming campaign, to check supplies and finances. In association was strength, so these societies drew on the strength of hundreds of thousands of members. Though there was no official connection between these societies and the Churches, the fact was that most of their members were drawn from the Churches. In a sense, they were the unofficial arms of the Protestant Churches. They had members from most of the larger Churches and were considered as a vital part of the American church life.

Beecher spoke for a vast majority of the American Protestants when he said that these groups " constitute a sort of disciplined moral militia, prepared to act upon every emergency, and repel every encroachment upon the liberties and morals of the State. By their numbers, they embolden the timid, and intimidate the enemy; and in every conflict the responsibility, being divided among many, is not feared. By this auxiliary band the hands of the magistrate are strengthened, the laws are rescued from contempt, the land is purified, the anger of the Lord is turned away, and his blessing and protection restored."

Thus the new life of the Spirit pulsating through the Churches was released by revivalism and poured through home and foreign missions and a vast number of societies for benevolence and reform. The Church was not forgetting its mission and message to all of life. Under the conditions of free voluntary Churches, the Christian faith found a new way of relating itself to life.

10

Source of Sects

EARLY IN 1805, three strangely dressed men set out on a journey from Mt. Lebanon, New York, to southern Ohio and Kentucky. They took nothing with them and traveled only on foot. They were ambassadors of the Shaker community seeking new converts. Whenever a revival was successful they were successful, so they turned their steps toward Cain Ridge and Gasper River.

As they traveled westward they recalled the story of the Shaker growth. In 1774, Mother Ann Lee, accompanied by her husband and seven followers, landed in New York. In England she had belonged to a group of radical Quakers who expressed their religious feelings through physical shaking; hence they were called Shakers. In America they quickly found several places in which to settle, but they had little success in winning converts.

In 1779 the revivalistic Baptists had a very successful revival in New Lebanon, New York, but the Shakers walked off with many of the converts. This was their first great triumph. Revivalism brought them increased growth. Many folks converted from a life of sin sought a higher, more satisfying experience than the regular Churches seemed to offer. The Shakers were similar to a monastic order that absorbed all those who wanted to live an especially strict life.

Under the leadership of Mother Ann Lee they worked out a position that was very strange for most Protestant Churches. They stressed the operation of God as the Holy Spirit. Mother Lee argued that in her the feminine side of God took flesh just as in Jesus Christ the masculine side became man. So God was thought of as both male and female, but God's last revelation was through a woman.

As a consequence, Mother Ann Lee felt herself to be possessed of God's Spirit, and she had visions and trances that revealed God's will for man. She was the first result of the new outpouring of God's Spirit, and when God's Spirit had finished his work, there would be a new heaven and a new earth just as the book of redemption promised.

Under the guidance of the Spirit of God who dwelt in man's heart, a person was driven to do God's will. Because the person was united with the Spirit, he or she could do no evil. A new spiritual life in full unity with God was lived. The Shakers were spirit mystics because they believed they were in union with God's Holy Spirit.

They developed a full program of twelve virtues to be practiced by all those dwelling in the Spirit. High on the list of these virtues was the abstinence from marriage, or from sexual relations on the part of those already married. The flesh had to be denied because the Spirit was in total opposition to the flesh. On earth very few people could attain to the perfection of the Shaker virtues, for they were God's elect, the forerunners of the life of perfection. Therefore, they were satisfied that their Church was not large. In God's own time all people would be saved; meanwhile the Shakers stood as a demonstration of what the saint was like.

In order to live the life in the Spirit, the Shakers perfected their community life and worship. Mt. Lebanon became the pattern for all their other groups. In order to guide and develop the spiritual life of the group, oral confession of all sins was practiced by those entering the group and periodically by members within. Strict discipline was maintained for all within the organization. Before one could enter such a strict life, he had to pass through a series of different stages of membership. Only the final stage, Senior Order, represented the full and complete membership. Anyone was free to remit the order or to be expelled at any time.

The Shakers lived a community life in which the membership was divided into various families that were responsible for doing the work of the group. Men and women worked separately, except where heavy work for women required male help, and they entered the church by separate doors. Though male and female were strictly separated, there was asbolute equality of the sexes, even in the ministry.

Their dress was very plain and practical, similar to that of the Quakers. Everything on the premises, from the buildings to the furniture, was of the utmost simplicity and practicality. Today many artists look on Shaker work as the forerunner of modern functional design. In their day the Shakers wanted to stress only cleanliness and practicality. Everything had to be neat, clean, and in place. Little pegs in the wall provided both coat hangers and a place from which to suspend the furniture while they scrubbed the floors.

The most peculiar side of Shaker life was their worship service. Prayer, preaching, song, and dancing made up the worship. Every medium of expression was employed. Their favorite practice was to form a series of concentric circles that moved in opposite directions as they chanted a tune. The motion would grow in intensity and violence as they danced and sang. At first these dances were quite solemn and subdued; later they became quite agitated. The important thing to note is that everything in life from their economic activity to their worship was centered in the community and not in the individual.

This was the type of life carried west by the Shaker missionaries. They met with huge success. Their membership went as high as 6,000, and they soon developed as many as twenty communities. One of their strongest settlements was to be in Mt. Pleasant, Kentucky. Revivals gave them fertile fields for growth. Several of the leaders of the New Light Presbyterian schism in Kentucky became Shakers.

Though their growth was astounding from 1800 to 1830, they developed no new communities after 1830, and they slowly died out. Because they had no children, their growth had to be through conversions or adoptions. As long as they represented a strict conversion position and offered moral as well as physical security on the frontier, they had appeal. But as soon as revivalism began to channel its effects into reform and humanitarian activity, it offered the possibility of a life of service and discipline.

Meanwhile, a number of other unusual religious groups developed in various places on the frontier, but none of them grew out of the revivals. However, in common with the Shakers, they also originated not on the frontier but in Europe, and they stressed community living. Whenever religious leaders and followers encountered difficulty in Germany or other European nations, they always looked to America for refuge. In the promised land there was freedom and plenty of rich soil and timber — a perfect place for a new Church.

In 1803, George Rapp, a German farmer, and his son sailed for America. They were the advance guard for six hundred German Pietists who were seeking a haven in America. Father Rapp, as he was called by his followers, located and purchased a large tract of land in western Pennsylvania. The next year his followers settled with him there.

The group were soon known as Rappites, and they had many beliefs similar to the Shakers. Under the strict guidance of Father Rapp, they introduced "communityism" and celibacy. All the people pooled their labor and resources to work for the common good. No longer was there private property or private welfare. In place of self-seeking and selfishness there was instituted the "community of equality." This was possible only on a strict religious basis, for only people committed to a common goal could so carry on their economic life. Furthermore, these strange Germans submitted absolutely to the control of Father Rapp. His sermons and advice controlled the group. Nobody could join except with his consent. All members confessed their faults to him. But under his leadership the group flourished and prospered.

In 1815, Rapp and his followers moved to New Harmony, Ind. There they repeated their Pennsylvania success. After a number of years they again moved, this time to Economy, Pennsylvania. Wherever they went, they made the ground produce rich and plentiful harvests, but the group were doomed to extinction. Because they were not interested in making converts and because they had no children, they had no source of new membership. They gradually died out.

The Rappites were not the only religious group transplanted to

America in order to find freedom to carry out their principle of holding all things in common. In addition to them there were such groups as the followers of Joseph M. Bäumler, who settled in northern Ohio and developed a very successful community called Zoar. Still others came from Germany to found the New Community, later called the Amana Society. First they settled in New York, but they later moved to Iowa.

So it was that American Protestantism of the nineteenth century witnessed the emergence and growth of many religious groups that did not originate in America. Nevertheless, they put into practice the principles over which many reform battles were waged. They may not have been large in numbers or influence, but they did represent one concern of American religious life — the need for moral fervor and reform.

Meanwhile, American religious life itself had brought forth several movements of similar tendency. It was not surprising that revivalism produced such fruits. It stressed the necessity of personal conversion from sin and the consequence of living according to God's will. The man converted from sin should sin no more. There was a possibility of becoming a perfect Christian, or so some thought. Perhaps one could not become absolutely perfect, but at least one could become as perfect as his talents and possibilities allowed.

But how could one practice the perfect moral life when society itself was evil? Men lorded it over women and considered them as inferior creatures. Economic and personal life were built on greed and selfishness. Only the person who sought his own selfish end could succeed. Money and power controlled the world. Human beings were only tools to be used in the game of gain. Against all this, revivalism protested. It cried for reform.

What a country to reform! Was not America a new land, with vast creative possibilities? Was not the Christian Church responsible to check the evil that was undermining the nation? So those converted from sin were made soldiers of the good cause fighting under the leadership of the Beechers and Finneys.

Out of the bubbling ferment of the revivalistic reform movements arose a series of American attempts to build God's Kingdom on earth, to achieve a genuine utopia where all the present evils would be overcome, where the first fruits of the new age would be visible. These different groups all had one thing in common. They were impatient with the regular reform movements trying to change society. They scrapped the society of which they were a part and started afresh by creating new communities which embodied the true principles of Christianity from the very beginning. That is what they believed, and on that conviction they staked their substance and their lives.

One of the first such ventures was the Hopedale community established in Massachusetts in 1841. Its leaders had been connected with the Universalist and Unitarian Churches. They undertook a joint enterprise which was not the same as common ownership but very similar. They wrote into their constitution support of all the great reform movements — equality of the sexes, temperance, chastity, peace, equality of all races, etc. They were opposed to " all things known to be sinful against God or human nature."

With the aim of a life of perfection as full Christian brothers, the enterprise got under way. Needless to say it failed, as did many others like it. Yet the failure was due not so much to the economic or financial arrangements as to a spiritual or moral failure. Somehow they could not re-create the pristine condition of man. Eden was not re-established. Hopedale was only one of several such attempts and failures.

The only really successful experiment to create a new society based on religious principles was that started by John Humphrey Noyes, a graduate of Dartmouth College, who was converted by Charles Finney in Vermont. When Noyes, a licensed divinity student, preached that conversion brought complete release from sin, his license was revoked. He went out on his own to think through his religious beliefs and came to oppose what he called the " Sin system, the Marriage system, the Work system, and the Death system."

He came to the conclusion that revivalism and socialism had to be blended in order to produce a new society based on Christian teachings. As his following grew he established a community in Vermont based on his new beliefs. Because of violent opposition from his neighbors, he was forced to find a new home, and the group settled at Oneida, New York.

There they found sufficient isolation to produce their own type of life. Everything was held in common — even husbands and wives. They practiced what was called complex life. Noyes argued that the love of one person for another produced jealousy and selfishness. All were partners holding everything in common, but nobody had to submit to another without his or her own full consent. Everything was kept under the strictest regulations of the entire community in order to guard against the abuse of freedom as well as the threat of selfishness.

The Oneida community became very successful financially. It turned from agriculture to industry. First, it became famous for producing steel traps. Later, it started the manufacture of knives and silverware. Today everyone has heard of Oneida Community Plate. But because of pressure from the outside the community was forced to give up the complex marriage system, and when this was surrendered the religious basis of the movement seemed to collapse. The community incorporated itself and became a very prosperous business venture.

So revivalism produced a new spirit that moved through staid old New England as well as through the rough new frontier. It encouraged zeal for reform and fanned the flames of hope for a new nation. Not only did it produce all the great missions and reform movements, it also produced strange and peculiar groups that sought to find more light yet in God's Word for nineteenth century America.

Strange, was it not, that as groups such as Oneida and Hopedale sought to follow God's will more completely they often appeared to go contrary to it in their zeal. In finding release from sin in conversion, many thought they had found release not only from their bodies but also from their every selfishness. And so the movements for perfectionism soon showed how far man was from perfection. They stood as condemnations against all halfhearted attempts to live the Christian religion. They also stood as condemnation against all illusions and pretensions that it was possible to live the Christian life without constant forgiveness or to live it in full perfection. The gospel had to grasp a man anew each day — the struggle between faith and disbelief was not settled once and for all in the blinding burst of the conversion experience.

It was a warm July evening in 1838 as Rev. Ralph Waldo Emerson, onetime minister of a Boston Unitarian church, stood in the small Divinity School chapel of Harvard University to address the senior class. Nothing appeared unusual about the occasion, but it was to be of great consequence for the Unitarian Church.

Ralph Waldo Emerson was deeply dissatisfied with the religion of his Unitarian brethren. He saw it as something dry and external. A collection of moral truths accepted only on the basis of a cold, hard reason. It had no life, no real vitality — it was, in short, worse than the so-called New England Calvinism against which it had protested. Boston Unitarianism was as lifeless and as formal as its opponents. It was bound to tradition.

Against the rationalistic arguments of his brethren, Emerson bid the young students turn within and find the divine at work in their own lives. Within the very soul of man is a noble and divine sentiment pointing him to what he ought to do. This inner reality is truly appealing, " a more secret, sweet, and overpowering beauty appears to man when his heart and mind open to the sentiment of virtue. Then he is instructed in what is above him."

Out of Emerson's protest against Unitarianism arose a new movement in American Christianity. This movement was called transcendentalism. It was so called because of its stress on the divine as being at the same time beyond man yet present within man's soul. As he put it: " Man is a stream whose source is hidden. Always our being is descending into us from we know not whence." Hence, man's knowledge of God is not confined to the operation of reason and the five senses but is primarily beyond them.

Because of the union between man as divine and God who is yet beyond all men, Emerson had great faith in the ability of man to cast off the shackles of the past, to realize the divine within, and to create a new, fresh life. He had given up his church in 1832 and proceeded to write and to lecture. He traveled around the country preaching his new message of man's divinity and limitless possibilities. He was not alone in proclaiming this message.

As early as 1836, a group of men in and around Boston had met in a Transcendental Club which discussed the works of recent German and English authors. In 1840 they published a magazine, the *Dial*, which, under the editorship first of Margaret Fuller, feminist and author, and then of Emerson, became the leading intellectual journal of America. It published poetry, criticism, articles, and book reviews.

Other outstanding members of the transcendentalist movement were such people as Bronson Alcott, one of the greatest lecturers America produced, Henry David Thoreau, naturalist and philosopher, and Theodore Parker, minister, outstanding reformer, and scholar. There were others too, but the number of the movement was always small, though its influence was tremendous.

One of the most famous of the group was the Unitarian clergyman Theodore Parker. He too broke from the Unitarians and urged men to find truth not in tradition but in their own personal experience as they confronted a changing political and economic order. He fought against slavery, he accepted women as equal even in expounding theology, and he preached the necessity of bringing the Kingdom of righteousness into fruition.

In addition to the belief in the ultimate perfection of man and the necessity of reform, the transcendentalists also founded a religious community. Brook Farm, their experiment in communal living, was founded largely under the inspiration and direction of George Ripley, a Boston Unitarian minister. But the whole group was interested in it and supported it through money and writing.

Brook Farm was completely democratic in organization. There was no John H. Noyes or George Rapp to control it. It was an attempt to realize through communal living the highest human virtues. It wanted to create a little world in which each individual could realize all his or her powers and gifts. Everybody was expected to do some work to help maintain the group, and all shared in every type of work, so there was no master and servant relationship.

The most remarkable aspect of Brook Farm was its school for children. Some of the finest families in New England sent their children. Education was largely through personal contact with some of the outstanding minds of America. Tutoring, learning through doing things, and participating in discussion, was the method of instruction. Thus the children were really part of a community given to cultural pursuits and learning. Their education was informal but very effective.

In 1845, Brook Farm changed its nature, when it was legally incorporated in order to become a new type of community. It joined the growing socialist movement known as Fourierism after its French originator. It became a local group of that movement and in a short time failed financially. Thus the transcendentalist experiment was sidetracked and disbanded. But transcendentalism did not die. It continued to flourish through literature and lectures. Even more important, it created a tendency in American Christianity which received expression in later years through a marked emphasis on the spiritual and ideal side of life over against the material and the actual.

While transcendentalism represented an intellectual effort to overcome the base material world with all its ugliness, meanness, and disorder, another movement arose among the uneducated which attempted to overcome the sinful reality of life by preaching the immediate coming of the Lord Jesus Christ and the end of the world.

Millenarianism was the belief that Jesus was coming soon to judge the world and to institute his reign. All evil would be put down, sinners would be judged, saints would be raised, and God would reign supreme in a new heaven and a new earth. This belief was widely prevalent in nineteenth century America and was almost universally accepted on the frontier. Sinners were urged to repent before the Day of Judgment struck.

Throughout the "burned-over" revival districts where various revivals had come and gone, strange beliefs persisted. Some men believed they had special powers of prophecy. Others had sticks they called divining rods with which they supposedly located lost treasures or received divine revelations.

In 1828 at a revival meeting in Vermont, a farmer, William Miller, felt the urge to get up and pour out his heart concerning his religious convictions, but he was afraid to do so. In 1832, after ten years of very intensive Bible study and of meditating and conversing with neighbors, he publicly spoke convincingly of the glorious coming of the Lord Jesus Christ. His congregation was appalled and fascinated. As his reputation slowly grew he was in great demand as a lecturer.

While lecturing in Boston he won a notable convert, a Baptist minister, Rev. Joshua V. Himes, who became director of the Miller schedule. Soon he was lecturing throughout the east. Several newspapers such as the *Midnight Cry* were published. William Miller was winning a large number of converts. His preaching was quiet, earnest, and sincere, but his message was dynamite.

In a letter of 1832 he wrote: " I am satisfied that the end of the world is at hand. The evidence flows in from every quarter. . . . Soon, very soon, God will arise in his anger, and the vine of the earth will be reaped. *See! See!* — the angel with his sharp sickle is about to take the field! See yonder trembling victim fall before his pestilential breath! High and low, rich and poor, trembling and falling before the appalling grave, the dreadful cholera.

" Hark! — hear those dreadful bellowings of the angry nations! It is the presage of horrid and terrific war. Look! — look again! See crowns and kings and kingdoms trembling to the dust! See lords and nobles, captains and mighty men, all arming for the bloody, demon fight! See the carnivorous fowls fly screaming through the air! *See!* — see these signs! Behold, the heavens grow black with clouds; the sun has veiled himself; the moon, pale and forsaken, hangs in the middle air; the hail descends; the seven thunders utter loud their voices; the lightnings send their vivid gleams of sulphurous flames abroad; and the great city of the nations falls to rise no more forever and forever! At the dread moment, look! The clouds have burst asunder; the heavens appear; the great white throne is in sight! Amazement fills the universe with awe! He comes! — He comes! — Behold, the Saviour comes! — Lift up your heads, ye saints — He comes! He comes! He comes! "

Little wonder that people were startled and frightened. To make things more compelling, William Miller was not alone in preaching such doctrines. Many people believed in the speedy return of Christ. But under the urging of his followers and after careful study, Miller took the fatal step of predicting the approximate time of Christ's return.

He said that " Christ would appear a second time in the clouds of heaven sometime between 1843 and 1844; that he would then raise the righteous dead and judge them together with the righteous living, who would be caught up to meet him in the air; that he would purify the earth by fire causing the wicked to be consumed in the general conflagration."

This was different! A possible date was set — the end was but a short time off. As 1843 drew to a close the excitement mounted. People began to question about the great day. Again Miller's followers urged him to select a date. He was reluctant to do so. He only insisted that the time was almost up and that believers should not give up the faith. Finally, the Millerites published the date — October 22, 1844, was supposed to be the last day of time!

Again excitement increased. By this time the Millerites had gained many followers and many sympathizers. When the great day arrived they went to their tabernacles and meetinghouses to sing hymns and await the Lord's coming. Nothing happened! Once again men had sought more light in God's Word and had misinterpreted it so as to produce delusion.

The newspapers had a field day. They told stories of Millerites climbing to the tops of trees and trying to fly to heaven to meet Christ — the result was, of course, disaster. They told of faithful followers, wearing white ascension robes, awaiting the end. Stories and rumors of suicides and murders by demented Millerites were passed about. But none of this was true. The movement did cause a good deal of stir and excitement, but it produced no such extremes.

The Millerites recovered somewhat from their great blunder. They did not become a large and powerful American Church, but they passed into two relatively small but flourishing sects called the Seventh-Day Adventists, and the Christian Adventists. Miller died a discouraged and forgotten man. Many leaders left their ranks. The doctrine of the Second Coming continued to be preached in American Protestantism, but the public was thereafter very cautious about taking it literally as to the day or the hour. The Millerites agreed

that the date selected for Christ's visible return was incorrect. No
man knows when that will occur. But they insisted that according
to the prophecy of Daniel, on October 22, 1844, Christ did cleanse
the invisible heavenly temple. They were right as to the time of
cleansing but wrong as to the where and how. Thus the movement
was consolidated and took its place in American Protestantism.

In September, 1827, the Smith family of Manchester, New York,
was greatly agitated by the actions of Joseph Smith. He had brought
home a mysterious box, which, he claimed, contained some golden
plates that he had dug from the ground at the direction of an angel,
Moroni. Furthermore, he maintained that two strange stones, the
Urim and Thummim, attached to a breastplate, accompanied the
golden plates. By peering into these stones he could translate the in-
scriptions on the plates.

Joseph Smith claimed that he was instructed in a vision to pro-
cure the plates and that an angel was to guide him in their use.
Now it so happened that this section of New York was part of
the "burned-over" revival district. Many strange stories and practices floated about. Previously, Smith and his father had worked
with a divining rod trying to find buried treasure. Necromancy,
mystery, and legend filled the air. The high hills and peculiar
mounds of the neighborhood mystified the local inhabitants. Many
claimed that they contained Indians who were buried there after
a tremendous battle in which thousands were slain in ages long past.
Others said that these Indians were the descendants of the lost tribes
of Israel of which the Bible speaks. In any case the mounds excited
curiosity.

In 1827, Smith began his translation of the golden plates. He sat
behind a curtain and dictated to scribes, among them a local teacher
named Oliver Cowdery. In 1829 the work was finished and in 1830
the Book of Mormon appeared. Joseph received a revelation from
heaven as to the price of the book.

What was the mysterious Book of Mormon? It was supposedly
the story of Nephi and Laman, the sons of Lehi, a minor prophet
of Israel who was not mentioned in the Bible, and of their coming
to America before the birth of Jesus. In America their groups di-

vided and fought. The sons of Nephi had scripture and divine guidance through prophets. After Jesus' resurrection he appeared to the Nephites and taught them all his doctrine, and among them he found his most faithful followers. A true Church was organized in which all things were held in common.

After two hundred years of peace, war broke out again until all members of the true Church were destroyed. Meanwhile this entire history had been kept on golden plates by the Nephite prophet Mormon and given to his son Moroni to complete and to hide in the earth, which he did. With the destruction of his people, the Church of Christ was no longer left on earth. It was God's purpose through Moroni the angel to make known the history of his true Church through the Book of Mormon and to use Joseph Smith as a prophet to start his Church anew. Thus a new age was to dawn, the millennium was to come, through a reconstituted Church into which all the saints would be called.

Joseph Smith received other revelations from heaven which instructed him on Baptism and the formation of the Church. He and a faithful little group were declared to be of the priesthood of Aaron, and he alone was declared prophet and seer. In 1830 the Church of Jesus Christ of the Latter-Day Saints was founded. Meanwhile, the Book was not selling too well, and Smith received a revelation to reduce its price over one half. But there were men out on the field winning converts. The Bible was not ignored; it was always read in the light of the Book of Mormon, which supposedly stated the same truths but in a clearer fashion.

By the early 1830's, Smith with his wife and family moved to Kirtland, Ohio, where they settled and prospered. Another group went to Missouri and settled near Independence. While in Ohio, Smith was full of prophecies and plans. Several other books of his revelations were published, and a temple was built. On the command of direct revelation he started his own bank, which failed miserably and lost the savings of many Saints. The people in Ohio determined to bring Joseph Smith to trial for violating the state banking laws, and he fled.

Meanwhile trouble was developing for the Mormons in Missouri. Their neighbors accused them of thievery and of planning to take control of the entire state. The Mormons responded that they were being persecuted for the sake of their faith. Several skirmishes were fought, and the Mormons moved to Clay County, Missouri. Smith joined his followers in Missouri, and by 1837 there were around 15,000 gathered Saints. Their missionaries went all over the world preaching the gospel of the reconstituted Church with free land for all the Saints.

Driven out of Missouri, the Mormons settled, finally, at Nauvoo, Illinois, in 1840. As they constituted such a large number and always voted in a block, Smith used this power to wrest from the Illinois legislature unheard-of powers for his town. The mayor, Smith, was a court in himself, and the mayor and council could pass any laws not repugnant to the liberties guaranteed by the constitution. They were even given the right to equip and put in the field their own private militia. Little wonder their neighbors feared them.

At Nauvoo the Mormons prospered. By 1844 this was the largest city in Illinois, larger than Chicago. Converts from England flocked to Nauvoo seeking the kingdom of plenty. Joseph Smith ruled supreme. He received a revelation that he should institute the practice of marrying women for eternity as well as for time. This meant that a man, if approved by the Church, might have several wives, and in some cases have the use of another man's wife. It is alleged that Joseph Smith married over twenty such women for eternity.

The enmity against and fear of the Mormons spread among their Illinois neighbors. Smith decided to run for President of the United States in 1844. Finally, due to the rumors over polygamy and the destruction of a press to silence opposition in Nauvoo, violence broke out. Joseph Smith, his brother Hyram, and two other followers voluntarily surrendered for trial in Carthage, Illinois. The trial never came off. On the evening of the twenty-seventh of June, 1844, Joseph and his brother were murdered by a mob in the Carthage jail.

This was a terrible blow to the Mormons, but they rallied under the leadership of Brigham Young and left Nauvoo for a long trek west. By the fall of 1848, a goodly proportion of the Mormons had settled in the valley of Salt Lake in Utah. No land was to be sold to the Saints; it was given to them — the only demand was that they be industrious and make it prosper. The timber and the mountain streams were the property of all, not just a few. Salt Lake City was laid out after a plan that had been revealed to Joseph Smith. Included in these plans was the center of life — a temple.

The Saints flourished; they made the desert bloom. Nobody could work only for himself — the community was as important as the individual. While a man was allowed to provide for all the needs of his family, he turned over everything above those needs to the group as a whole. And they did just that! Co-operative enterprises sprang up. Self-interest as the basic drive for economic life was replaced by concern for the Church of Jesus Christ of the Latter-Day Saints.

Another strange practice of the Mormons in Utah was polygamy. Brigham Young put into public practice what Joseph Smith received by revelation and practiced in secret. Not all could afford to practice plural marriage because the support of several wives and large numbers of children required the physical resources to maintain them. However, in the winning of the western desert the practice appeared to work quite well — it provided a large number of children to work the land and made use of all the excess women. The question of what it did to family relations is a difficult thing to determine.

Meanwhile, under the guidance of Joseph Smith's widow and son, a Reorganized Church of Jesus Christ of the Latter-Day Saints was founded with its headquarters in Independence, Missouri. It denied that Smith ever had more than one wife and was opposed to the doctrine of polygamy.

So the Mormons grew and prospered. In 1890 they were forced to give up polygamy by a law of the land, and when they did so Utah was finally admitted as a state. They became famous for their economic prosperity. Every year they sent hundreds of missionaries out to win converts, and they grew. They were one of the few new religions to develop in America. Mormonism was not an importation, not even a schism from another Protestant Church; it was the product of revivalism, the vast American frontier, the fertile imagination of Joseph Smith, and the dogged determination of the leaders and the Saints.

America is famous for its many strange and peculiar religious groups, yet it is not odd that they should have developed here. Under full religious liberty many kinds of religions could develop. But only two or three genuinely new Churches developed in America. Rather, America took all the offerings of Europe, all the oppressed, the peculiar, the strange, and here they were given an unmolested place to develop. Why not? The country was huge. It needed people who were willing to work and if they also wanted to test new principles, there was room to do so.

But American Protestantism did produce several strange groups of its own. Adventism is nothing new in history. William Miller can be understood as one among many men in history who thought he knew the date of Christ's Second Coming.

John Noyes was somewhat different. Here was a genuine product of American religious life. He actually succeeded in forming a community on principles absolutely contrary to the society around him. Yet those principles, for him, were only the logical consequence of the holiness produced by conversion. Zeal for reform could take unusual turns as well as the more common protests against injustice. Joseph Smith and the Mormons were also a peculiar American product. They sought to channel the results of conversion not into the spiritual life which denies the flesh but into the material world. It was in the use and manipulation of the material world that they sought the blessings of religion, and they found them in abundant crops, large families, and green, rolling hills. Strange that in seeking new answers to the religious quest of man these men distorted or perverted the gospel in a way that they could not see. It appears that the light may well have been hidden from them.

11

Slavery and Schisms

IN JANUARY of 1817 a large group of famous men met in Washington to discuss ways and means of dealing with the slavery question. The first slaves had been brought to Virginia in 1619. Since then they had increased steadily in numbers until in 1817 there were almost 3,000,000 in America. Many Americans were bothered by the buying and selling of human beings as if they were animals or any other kind of property. Among the men concerned with the problem were the famous Senators Daniel Webster and Henry Clay, and the President of the United States, James Monroe.

At the Washington meeting it was decided to form the American Colonization Society for the purpose of encouraging the emancipation of slaves and the transportation of freed slaves back to their homeland in Africa. The organization elected officers, hired missionaries, and published a newspaper. It received support from the North and the South. Clergymen preached sermons extolling the plans of the group.

But not all were happy with the Society. Many men, in both North and South, opposed it as an impracticable dream, a fantasy. How could the Society raise $300,000,000 to pay the owners for the loss of their slaves? Furthermore, the men in the deep South wanted to keep their slaves; they had no intention of losing their labor supply. Other men, in the North, opposed it as utterly unfair to the freed Negroes. Many of them had built homes and held jobs; they didn't want to return to Africa. It was argued that the Society was only an excuse to get rid of the colored people. It was only a salve for the white man's conscience. But enough people took it seriously so that Congress procured land in Africa and established the Republic of Liberia to be settled with freed slaves.

The activity of the Society, the opposition to it, and its inability to do much more than scratch the surface of the problem indicated how seriously slavery divided the American people. Christians and people of good will had long been bothered with the terrible evil in the midst of American life. Even Southerners such as Washington and Jefferson had been disturbed by it.

Among the earliest opponents of slavery were the Quakers. As early as 1671, when George Fox, their founder, visited America he spoke against it. But this did little good. As the eighteenth century opened, a number of Quakers as well as Puritans, Presbyterians, and Anglicans held slaves. Nonetheless, not many were kept in the North simply because it was not profitable. During that century, two great Quaker saints worked against the evils of slavery. John Woolman traveled from meeting to meeting among the Quakers to lay on their hearts the conviction of the sin of slaveholding. Anthony Benezet wrote and spoke against it and persuaded a number of outstanding people to oppose slaveholding.

Another early American Christian opponent of slavery was the follower of Jonathan Edwards, Samuel Hopkins. In 1776 he wrote to the Second Continental Congress, urging the members to take steps against this horrible evil. He argued that slavery is a social consequence of deep, depraved self-love, and that this could be overcome only by true holiness, which was a gift from God. True holiness was just the opposite of selfishness: it was selfless love, which poured itself out on all beings in general because they were the creatures of God. This meant Negroes as well as white men. In Christ all men were to be loved.

So, by the time of the Revolutionary War the Christian conscience was aroused against slavery. John Wesley wrote his treatise *Thoughts on Slavery,* 1774, attacking it as an evil. Few men in America were willing to defend it at that time.

Meanwhile another movement was exerting its power against the evil. In their attempts to understand their liberties which the British were attacking, the colonists asserted the theory of natural rights. This was the belief in certain rights and liberties which every man had by birth. Among them were such things as life, liberty, and the pursuit of happiness. No state or person could abrogate these. So the Declaration of Independence stated.

What then of Negro people held in bondage as slaves? Did they not have the same rights by birth as white men? Who had taken their freedom from them and cast them in chains to be shipped across the ocean in the foul-smelling, dank, hot hold of a ship? A number of men, in both North and South, saw that these freedoms applied to all men.

James Otis, one of the leading Revolutionaries, specifically included the slave as one who possessed all such natural rights by birth. Several New England colonial legislatures were confronted with bills, at this time, to abolish slavery as contrary to the laws of nature. In the 1760's, Arthur Lee of Virginia argued that freedom was the birthright of all men, Negroes included. But it was Thomas Jefferson who proposed the abolition of slavery to the Virginia Convention in 1774. Of course, the committee did not report the bill for action, but Jefferson was not alone in his sentiment.

A number of states had clauses in their constitutions upholding the inherent rights of all men but not specifically prohibiting slavery. Vermont in 1777 did specifically prohibit the holding of slaves. Pennsylvania made provision for gradual emancipation of slaves. In 1787, Congress prohibited it from the newly created Northwest Territory. At the time of the writing of the Federal Constitution it was determined to count slaves as two thirds of a person in computing the basis for representation. Furthermore, it was determined to abolish importation of slaves after 1808. Both Washington and Jefferson looked forward to the day when it would disappear from the nation.

Just when slavery seemed to be coming under control something happened that changed the entire picture! In 1793, Eli Whitney, a New Englander, invented the cotton gin, which made it possible to use a type of cotton that had not formerly been used, and which freed labor for work in the fields. Suddenly a new demand for slave labor was produced. The cotton gin made it possible to double, triple, and far surpass previous production. As production rose, greater supplies of labor were required. The older sections of the

South turned to the business of breeding slaves for the newer, more fertile fields of the deep South. What now was to happen to the antislavery movement?

Thus, when the American Colonization Society was founded in 1817 it was already facing a situation with which it could not cope. The Churches could easily stand against slavery in the days when nobody defended it, but now that it was the basis of the Southern economic empire what would they do? Many Churches had regulations against the holding of slaves, but the question of enforcement raised a real problem.

As a matter of fact, many in the South began to defend slavery as a positive good for American society. Suggestions for any radical solution of the problem, such as emancipation, had never been seriously considered, and now that slaveholders had the cotton gin, and cotton ruled as king of their economic life, they felt that they had to maintain slavery.

The first indication of the sensitive feeling of the South was evidenced in the debate to admit Missouri as a state. When it was proposed that slavery be prohibited by law before Missouri was admitted as a state, the reaction was immediate. Southerners defended slavery and claimed that Congress had no right over it. This was to be decided by every state. Furthermore, they argued that slavery was good for society. Northern representatives replied that it was contrary to the democratic principles on which the nation was founded, and it went contrary to the laws of nature and of God which were against all forms of human slavery. The result was the Missouri Compromise of 1820, in which Missouri was admitted without prohibition of slavery and Maine was admitted to the Union with an antislavery clause.

So the battle was joined. It involved politics, religion, economics, and all the vested interests of individuals and society. The political and economic arguments of the South stressed the fact that this was purely a state issue in which the Federal Government had no right to interfere. Also, Southerners argued that a slave society was the best form of society, and that " the division of mankind into grades, and the mutual dependence and relations which result from them, constitutes the very soul of civilization." Hence, finally, any attempt to undermine the system was an attempt to undermine the culture of the South.

The Southerner believed that he lived in a well-ordered society that was comparable to a body in which each living part played a certain role or performed a particular function. Somebody must do the dirty work or society would collapse. As one man said: " In all social systems, there must be a class to do the menial duties, to perform the drudgery of life . . . a class requiring but a low order of intellect and but little skill. Its requisites are vigor, docility, and fidelity."

There could be no real progress and security unless such a class could be maintained in society. This, they argued, the slave system guarantees. It allows freemen to work in trust at tasks of skill, and it permits the proper people to function as masters. This was supposed to be a government by the best people of brains, talent, courage, and virtue. Such an arrangement, they maintained, made possible the existence of free institutions. Only when all sections of society perform their proper functions can there be freedom. Only when the lower ranks of society are kept busy at their true tasks can the outstanding citizens find the security and time to work within free institutions. They said that " public liberty and domestic slavery were cradled together."

As politicians, publishers, and educators stepped forward to defend slavery so too did clergymen in the South. Some of the most able defenses of slavery were written by ministers. It was only natural that they would attempt to reply to the accusation that slaveholding was a sin in itself. Their defense could be one of two types. Either they could argue that slavery was at times an unavoidable evil but not essentially a sin. Or they could argue that it was not a sin but actually a positive good which was acceptable to God. They argued both ways. Great Southern churchmen such as Dr. James Thornwell, Presbyterian, Dr. Richard Furman and Dr. Fuller, Baptists, Bishop Stephen Elliott, Episcopalian, and Bishop James O. Andrew, Methodist, led the fight in favor of slavery.

The Southern churchmen based their argument squarely on Scripture. They pointed out that the Old Testament specifically advocated slavery both on the basis of sin and on the basis of relations with the heathen. These are the Scripture texts used:

" And he said, Cursed be Canaan; a servant of servants shall he be unto his brethren." (Gen. 9:25.)

" Both thy bondmen, and thy bondmaids, which thou shalt have, shall be of the heathen that are round about you; of them shall ye buy bondmen and bondmaids. Moreover, of the children of the strangers that do sojourn among you, of them shall ye buy, and of their families that are with you, which they begat in your land: and they shall be your possession. And ye shall take them as an inheritance for your children after you, to inherit them for a possession; they shall be your bondmen for ever: but over your brethren the children of Israel, ye shall not rule one over another with rigor." (Lev. 25:44-46.)

Thus, they argued that the Bible upheld the buying, selling, and possession of slaves so long as they were not Christian and of a different race. In vain did the Northern Christians argue that the passage applied only to the Jewish people in their particular condition. The Southerners replied that Jesus nowhere condemned slavery nor ever spoke a word against it. Paul went so far as to send a slave back to his master. If slavery was an evil or sin, would not Jesus or Paul have condemned it by name?

Other Christians argued that it was not necessary to condemn it by name as the whole spirit of Jesus' life and teaching was opposed to it. The basis of all Christian life was to love God with your whole heart, mind, and soul, and to love your neighbor as yourself. How could one love his neighbor as himself while he held that neighbor in slavery as a piece of property?

This did not stop the Southerners. They argued that full love of the neighbor as the self was not possible in this life. Because of sin there was inequality, and slavery was just one of the necessary forms of inequality. They never stopped to ask if some forms of inequality were worse than others, nor did they ever understand that man was constantly to strive under love to overcome all forms of inequality. The gospel gave nobody the right to rest in such terrible injustices, simply because there would always be some form of injustice.

Again the Southern men replied that slavery was not really an injustice but a good for the Negro. Did it not enable Christians to take heathens from barbaric conditions in order to civilize and missionize them? Furthermore, the Church had no right to try to overcome the evils of society, but it had every right to direct the personal relations between masters and slaves. So argued the Presbyterian, Dr. Thornwell. Only when masters and slaves acted toward each other as the Bible instructed, did God approve of it.

The relation between the two was patriarchal. The slaves were to obey the master as their elder or parent, and the master was to treat the slave in all justice as his dependent or child. The Church's task was to make certain that this relationship prevailed. Furthermore, the Church was to instruct and baptize the Negroes in order to make them Christian. It was the duty of the master to see that the slaves had the opportunity to become and remain Christian. Thus, both would understand and appreciate their relation to each other.

This type of life was approved by the Bible, argued the Southern churchmen. In this way alone could one express true love to the Negro as his neighbor. The Negro was created to serve in the ranks of slavery, and to tempt him to do anything else was contrary to God's will. But to care for the Negro in that station by instructing both him and his master was to express real love toward him. Thus, his bondage would be softened and lightened.

Ministers were convinced of this argument by the further assertion of the inferiority of the Negro. He did not have the capacities or the possible talents of the white man. He was not capable of thinking through any complex problem or of being trained to do difficult tasks. It was not by chance that the Negro was in this condition — he was so by nature, by creation. He was an inferior creature made to serve his superiors. Any attempt to discredit this was flying in the face of Biblical revelation and the findings of science. So the Southern pastors and educators argued. They alone understood the Negro and how he best could be assimilated into society — by means of slavery.

Meanwhile, Northern antislavery sentiment was on the march. It had a glorious precedent before it in the British example. Just as the many reform and benevolence societies of the British people provided a master plan for their American brethren, so their antislavery work stood as a challenge and a pattern. Step by step the evangelical churchmen in parliament had forced the retreat of the slave system.

Legislation was passed that was intended as preparation for the emancipation of slaves, but the slaveowners would not co-operate. By 1825 it became evident to the British reformers that only immediate abolition of slavery, by law, would extirpate the evil. In place of gradualism they advocated immediatism. Antislavery societies were founded with the express purpose of bringing about the abolition of slavery. Men and women poured money and effort into the project. Pamphlets and newspapers flooded the empire and descended on American shores.

The American reformers were not unaware of the British activity. They watched with great interest the progress of the British example. By 1828 a number of presses were pouring out literature condemning the slave system. Many of these were operated by Quakers. One of the most famous publications was the *Genesis of Universal Emancipation,* published by Benjamin Lundy.

In 1828, William Lloyd Garrison, Lundy's assistant editor, wrote a violent and uncompromising attack on slavery advocating the new British approach of immediate unconditional abolition. He was jailed when a Southern slave trader brought a libel suit against him in Baltimore. But in 1831 he started to publish his paper, the *Liberator,* in Boston. In his first issue he proclaimed his intent:

" I will be as harsh as truth and as uncompromising as justice. On this subject I do not wish to think, speak, or write, with moderation. . . . I will not equivocate — I will not excuse — I will not retreat a single inch — AND I WILL BE HEARD."

Garrison's activity met with little approval even in Boston. While New Englanders looked to Great Britain with respect, they could not understand the transplanting into the American scene of English slogans and phrases, born after years of frustrating work there. Garrison had no patience with anyone who disagreed with him, whether the Government, or the people. Either they followed his principles or they were wrong.

The consequence was that his paper had little influence in New England. It required men like Theodore Parker, the Unitarian minister, later to domesticate the antislavery sentiment in the Boston area. Ministers and Church reacted against Garrison's statement that they were "blind leaders of the blind, dumb dogs that cannot bark, spiritual popes — that they love the fleece better than the flock — that they are mighty hindrances to the cause of freedom."

While Garrison vented his wrath against slavery, the Colonization Society, and the Northern clergymen, another man, Theodore D. Weld, Presbyterian minister, was quietly building a vast reservoir of antislavery sentiment. While Garrison shouted what should be done, Weld quietly went about doing it. Of the two men, Weld was the one primarily responsible for the marshaling of the forces against slavery.

During one of Charles G. Finney's revivals near Utica, New York, an outstanding young student from Hamilton College was converted. The young man was Theodore Dwight Weld. He accompanied Finney as one of a "Holy Band," who labored with sinners under the pains of conviction during revivals. He was a magnificent speaker, a warmhearted, friendly man with boundless energy. He was easily interested in reforms of all types, and was not bound to conventional methods. One of his innovations was to give women equal right to pray and to exhort at a revival meeting. For a short time he also traveled about as a temperance speaker.

Weld became the leader of a whole band of Finney converts because of his natural abilities and his slightly older age. Though members of this band often worked in different parts of the nation, they kept in contact and agreed to attend a theological school someday. First, they all enrolled at Oneida Institute to complete their pretheological training. Then they all went west to the newly founded Lane Theological Seminary of which Lyman Beecher had recently become president.

Meanwhile the American Anti-Slavery Society had been founded. When the glorious news of British emancipation arrived in 1833, a number of New York reformers met and founded the New York City Anti-Slavery Society, which stood for immediate abolition, but they interpreted this differently from the way Garrison interpreted it. They recognized that preparation was necessary, so they urged immediate emancipation as a gradual process to begin immediately. As they put it, "In fine, it is *immediate* emancipation which is gradually accomplished." In December of 1833 a national organization, the American Anti-Slavery Society, was founded in Philadelphia, largely under Garrison's direction and domination.

At Lane Seminary, Weld soon won a position among the students almost equal to that of a faculty member, but his humility was so genuine and so deep that he disturbed nobody. Rather, he was slowly winning everybody to his side on the matter of abolition of slavery. In 1834 the student body met for eighteen nights in a revival atmosphere to discuss the pros and cons of the slavery question. When the meetings were finished almost the entire student body was converted to an antislavery position, and they determined to do something about it.

These young men were converted to the New York Society idea of gradual emancipation immediately begun, and they worked hard to help the Negro people in and about Cincinnati, Ohio. They urged people to love the Negroes as themselves. News of the Lane activity spread throughout the city, the state, and the whole nation. Beecher was faced with a problem that was aggravated by the trustees' harsh decision to ban all antislavery activity on the part of the students.

While Beecher was gone on a protracted trip, the board of trustees proceeded to enforce their regulations. A great proportion of the seminary's student body withdrew and went to Oberlin College. There they were allowed to pick their president, and they selected Asa Mahan, ardent antislavery pastor. They also brought John Morgan, a professor from Lane, to Oberlin with them. Finally, Charles G. Finney was induced to come as professor of theology. Colored students were to be admitted as equals in all things. Suddenly Oberlin grew from an unknown, almost extinct, struggling, backward college to an institution of international reputation. Under Finney and his converts it became the center of the antislavery movement and a host of other reform enterprises.

In the fall of 1835, Weld, commissioned as an agent for the national Anti-Slavery Society, proceeded to gather some of his band for an assault on Ohio. For several weeks he trained them in tactics. Then he visited Oberlin for three weeks, where he converted the entire community to the idea of immediatism.

Then the army marched on Ohio. Where Garrison had shouted in violence and had reaped hatred, they preached in love and reaped confidence and converts. Going was not easy. People were suspicious of all the talk about immediatism. But the young students endured " hard words . . . stale eggs and brickbats and tar." Nothing could deter their love and gentle spirit. They were heard in spite of Garrison.

Weld was the general and the leading spirit of the movement. He set the pattern for the others. Contrary to Garrison's methods and that of many easterners, he did not depend on the violent blast of an editorial or a single well-worked-out address. He used the method of the Great Revival. Just as at Lane, Weld used the technique of protracted meetings, in which he quietly and earnestly showed the evils of the slave system. Sometimes this took six or eight meetings; sometimes as many as thirty. His aim was to make clear the evils of slavery, to get people converted to oppose it as a sin, and to get them to take a definite stand against it.

Weld met with opposition wherever he went. He usually faced shouting, angry mobs, sticks and even stones. At times his audience would shout against him for hours before he could begin his address, but when a silence came he launched forth into his appeal. At the conclusion of his meetings he asked those who believed in immediate abolition to stand. Usually the entire audience would respond.

In this fashion he swept through Ohio, Pennsylvania, and New York, leaving behind thousands of convinced antislavery members who organized local societies. Perhaps it was impossible to do away with slavery by immediate legislation, but it was not impossible, nay, it was absolutely necessary, to repent of the sin of slavery immediately! This was what Weld and his followers preached. Against all the rationalization of the Southern clergymen they argued that buying and selling human beings was a sin against God. The first step was immediate repentance for the sin and a decision to work for its elimination. Before sin could be removed it had to be recognized as such and repented for. People were willing to do this whereas they were not willing to listen to the ravings of Garrison. Weld organized a band of seventy men to be sent by the national Society to employ his methods. This was not difficult for them because they too were converts from the Great Revival. With great astuteness, Weld saw that not New England or Boston but the rural west had to be won, so thorough attention was paid to that section. Under Weld's leadership pamphlets were written, petitions were sent to Congress, a deep-rooted, genuine agitation built on religious conviction ensued. John Quincy Adams presented to Congress the flood of antislavery petitions that poured in from the west. He made the right of petition a central issue through which to agitate against slavery. The South was furious. Weld later devoted his time to research for Adams and other antislavery Congressmen so they might be armed with powerful arguments in debate.

So the revivals produced the real opposition against slavery and provided the grass-roots strength to fight it. Men convinced of the sin of slavery could not be persuaded by the peculiar Southern Biblical arguments. Converts of revivalism clearly saw that the law of love, the highest demand and greatest gift of the gospel, was being violated by slavery. They had to act against it.

The Churches did not go unscathed by the slavery controversy. Almost every Church had a bitter fight over it, and the three largest and most influential groups split over it. The first schism occurred in the Presbyterian Church in 1837. On the surface this was made to appear as purely a theological and practical argument, but slavery also played its role.

For quite some time the Presbyterians had been agitated over the differences between the revivalists, called the " New School," and the antirevivalists, called the " Old School." Not only was this evident in the schism that occurred in Kentucky, but it was also a problem in their co-operation with the Congregationalists on the frontier under the Plan of Union.

The Congregationalists were largely products of Yale and Andover, both of which were strongly influenced by revivalism. They preached a doctrine that appeared wrong to the Old School Presbyterians because it seemed to deny God's absolute power in determining, apart from any human action, who would be saved and who would be damned. Revivalism appealed to the response of man in accepting or in rejecting salvation, but in reality, argued the Old School, God uses the regular means of his Church to effect salvation at any time he pleases.

In 1837 at the meeting of the General Assembly the Old School delegates were in control. They elected to break with the Plan of Union, to support only Presbyterian societies for missions and reform, and to cut off four large New School synods that they considered heretical. With one stroke the great Presbyterian Church was cut in two.

The slavery issue was kept out of the picture, but it had certainly played its part. The New School was the center of the antislavery agitation. It included men such as Charles G. Finney and Theodore D. Weld. Their methods and theology were those against which the Old School protested. So intent were the Southern delegates to avoid the appearance that slavery was involved that the Synod of North Carolina presented a resolution denying that slavery was involved.

New School delegates were shocked, but they wanted to remain within the Church, so they held a special meeting in which they voted to uphold the Plan of Union, maintained their orthodoxy, and determined to attend the next General Assembly.

In 1838 the schism was shown to be final. The New School had to organize separately into a Church of one hundred thousand members as over against one hundred and eight thousand Old School members. Within the Old School the slavery question could not even find a hearing. There was constant agitation but no discussion on the floor. This was to be expected as some of the great leaders of the Old School were Southerners, such as the famous defender of slavery, Dr. James Thornwell. After the start of the Civil War, however, the Southern branch of the Old School withdrew, leaving a Northern antislavery and Southern proslavery Old School Presbyterian Church.

In the New School, the slavery issue was constantly debated and discussed. Several strong resolutions were passed condemning slavery, and finally in 1857 a split between the Northern and Southern branches of the New School occurred. In 1836 there was one very large and influential Presbyterian Church in America in addition to several smaller ones, but by 1861 the large Church had split into four Churches.

The Baptist was the second of the great Protestant denominations to split over the slavery issue. The only way the Baptists could separate was through their missionary conventions. As the work of Weld and the Lane band spread throughout the North, a number of Baptist ministers and a large number of Baptist laymen became convinced of the need for immediate repentance of the sin of slavery.

In 1836 the Maine Baptist Association declared slavery a vile sin and questioned whether they should retain relations with slaveholders. Southern Baptists, on the other hand, defended the institution of slavery and attacked the Northern abolitionists. The officers of the mission boards wanted to avoid all such controversy so the mission work of the Baptist churches would not be impaired. They determined in 1840 not to discuss the question.

The Northern antislavery men kept agitating, and the Southerners set out to make certain of their safety. The moderates and Southerners combined before the triennial convention of 1841 to keep the slavery question off the floor and to replace a Northern abolitionist board member with a Southern proslavery man. Victory appeared to be theirs.

Agitation continued among the Baptists until the next national meeting of the convention in 1844. Once more the moderates controlled the sessions, but this time some Baptists were growing uneasy at the method of handling the problem. Everything was left to the decision of the mission boards. The Southerners still were not certain of the good faith of their Northern brethren, so they proposed a Southern slaveholding pastor for an appointment as a home missionary. After protracted debate, the board turned him down. The Southerners immediately withdrew their support, and turned their attention to the foreign mission board. They asked outright if the board would appoint a slaveholder as missionary, and they were told no!

In the spring of 1845 the Southern associations gathered together and formed a Southern Baptist Convention to carry on the benevolent and missionary work of the Southern Baptist churches. The second great American Protestant denomination had split over slavery.

The third large Protestant denomination to split over the slavery issue was the Methodist. In their early days the Methodists had stringent rules against slaveholding, but by the early nineteenth century they had shelved those regulations. Meanwhile a large number of Methodists, particularly in New England, were influenced by the abolition movement. They published an abolition newspaper, the *Zion Herald,* and a number of Methodist antislavery societies developed. By 1836 a large number of Methodist pastors and people were convinced abolitionists.

At the General Conference of 1836 it became evident that no definite action for or against slavery could be taken, though the subject provided a good deal of heat and discussion. The battle scene then shifted to the local annual conferences where various antislavery resolutions were introduced, but they were ruled out of order by the presiding bishop and a " gag rule " was applied. The consequence was the withdrawal of some antislavery men.

By the time of the General Conference of 1844, held in New York, opinion in the North had coalesced against the gag of silence placed on the slavery question. Many felt that such action only evaded the real question and drove good Methodists into schism. So when the conference met, a new spirit was evident. Furthermore, the case of Bishop James O. Andrew of Georgia, a slaveholder, came up. Could a slaveholding bishop who had to preside at conferences all over the nation preside at a New England conference? After long debate and many discussions it was decided that he could not perform the functions of a Methodist bishop.

During the dispute the question of separation became acute, and after the decision against Andrew a committee of nine was given the task of drawing up a plan of separation in case it became necessary. In perfect good will and harmony they presented the plan. Two years later the Southern brethren followed the plan, separated, and formally founded the Methodist Episcopal Church South. The break was inevitable.

However, some Northern men were dissatisfied and declared the action unconstitutional, and when the next General Conference met in Pittsburgh, in 1848, they declared the act null and refused to accept the Southern fraternal delegates. Legal warfare over property, press, churches, and institutions resulted. Hatred and bitterness reigned supreme. Cases could not be amicably settled, and the courts of the nation had to decide. In the border states between North and South, the dispute was particularly bitter. Separation appeared inevitable, but in place of a peaceful settlement of differences, there resulted a heated battle that largely ignored Christian charity and forbearance.

So the Churches of the nation were torn by slavery. Not all separated, but all felt its effects. The Episcopalians met as separate Churches during the war. The Lutherans split after the war had started. Even the Roman Catholic Church experienced some unrest, but it could not split because of its allegiance to the pope. One diocese could be proslavery and another antislavery. The Disciples of Christ had no national organization to rupture. The Congregationalists had but few Southern members and so did not have the necessary conditions for a schism.

Protestantism in America was capable of producing a new spirit in missions and reform, but it could not hold the Churches together when the nation was divided over slavery. Feelings ran high. It was the old question of the gospel against entrenched social evil. Many men thought they knew the will of God for the moment. Each group felt that it had found more light yet in God's Word either to defend slavery or to condemn it.

It is good that some men in the Church such as Theodore D. Weld could attack the evils of slavery and yet maintain a Christian spirit of compassion and mercy toward both master and slave. It was not a simple matter of standing up and self-righteously condemning an evil which one actually never had to face. It was, rather, a matter of both sides standing under God's mercy and judgment.

The pity was that Northern churchmen were so intent on attacking the obvious sin of their Southern brethren that they did not see their own pharisaical sins of self-righteousness and vindictiveness. The consequence was that a deep cleavage was produced between Christians, Northern and Southern, that is not completely healed even to this day.

12

War and Reconstruction

A TALL, GAUNT MAN stood before a convention of Republican delegates at Springfield, Illinois, in June, 1858. As Abraham Lincoln spoke, he uttered words of prophecy which few people understood. Everyone recognized the seriousness of the slavery crisis, and many talked of the disaster it would bring, but few seriously considered the possibility of outright war. The Republican Party was new, dedicated to the principle of keeping slavery out of all the new territories of the United States.

Ever since the Missouri Compromise of 1820, the nation had been agitated by the slavery controversy. Time after time solutions were sought. In 1850 a compromise on the new territory won from Mexico was worked out. But each time a territory presented itself for statehood both sides wanted to claim it. In 1854, the Kansas-Nebraska Bill was passed allowing the sovereign citizens to vote on the matter. This set aside all previous compromises, and the two sides rushed settlers into the Kansas Territory in order to get a favorable vote.

So Lincoln stood before the Springfield convention and pointed to the necessity of understanding the past in order to comprehend the gravity of the present when he said: " If we could first know where we are, and whither we are tending, we could better judge what to do, and how to do it. We are now far into the fifth year since a policy was initiated with the avowed object and confident promise of putting an end to slavery agitation. Under the operation of that policy, that agitation has not only not ceased but has constantly augmented. In my opinion, it will not cease until a crisis shall have been reached and passed. ' A house divided against itself cannot stand.' I believe the government cannot endure permanently half slave and half free. I do not expect the Union to be dissolved — I do not expect the house to fall — but I do expect it will cease to be divided. It will become all one thing or all the other. Either the opponents of slavery will arrest the further spread of it, and place it where the public mind shall rest in the belief that it is in the course of ultimate extinction, or its advocates will push it forward till it shall become alike lawful in all the states, old as well as new, North as well as South."

In 1860, Lincoln was nominated to carry the Presidential banner for the youngest of the American political parties, the Republican. He campaigned on the principle of no immediate interference with slavery in the states where it already existed and absolutely no extension of slavery into any territories. As he put it: "Wrong as we think slavery is, we can yet afford to let it alone where it is, because that much is due to the necessity arising from its actual presence in the nation; but can we, while our votes will prevent it, allow it to spread into the national territories, and to overrun us here in these free states? If our sense of duty forbids this, then let us stand by our duty fearlessly and effectively."

When the November election was over Lincoln had won, but he could not take office until March, 1861. Throughout the campaign, Southerners had boasted that they would not accept a "black Republican" as President, and four days after the election, South Carolina called for a convention to consider withdrawing from the Union. In December it took the fateful step, and by February of 1861 five states followed in secession from the Union.

All attempts to reach a peaceful settlement were smashed by the bombardment of Fort Sumter in April of 1861. The Civil War was on! The Confederate States of America rallied under the leadership of Jefferson Davis. Lincoln shrewdly played to hold the border states on the Union side. Of one thing he was absolutely convinced — the Union must be preserved.

Not only had slavery split the Churches, it had split the entire nation. Yet there was a good deal more than slavery involved. There was the fight between state rights and the preservation of the Federal Union. There was the competition between the cotton-growing agricultural South and the rapidly growing industrial might of the

North. There was the constant agitation over the status of new territories. Little wonder there was civil war!

All the Churches, North and South, sprang to the defense of their respective causes. Both prayed for the blessing of God for their side, and both were certain that divine favor would bring them victory. Chaplains were provided in large numbers to accompany the blue and the gray. Services were held on battlefield, in hospital and camp. Even while men fought they were reminded of God's judgment and his mercy.

For some time the final outcome of the struggle was in grave doubt, but as the Union armies won victories in the west, particularly in Missouri and Louisiana, the Northern Churches were confronted with two problems. What was to happen to the Negro? What was to be done about the disloyal Southern pastors who held their pulpits or who fled and left no religious services?

The answer given to both of these questions during the war set the pattern that prevailed during the period of reconstruction. With regard to their attitude toward the Southern Christian, many Northern churchmen looked upon the whole South as a mission field to be won from the slaveholders. As the Union armies moved into Southern territory, the Union chaplains wrote home telling of the religious needs of the South. A number of Methodists and others responded to these letters by saying that it was the duty of missionary boards to handle the problem.

In 1862 the Methodist Bishop Ames got permission from Secretary of War Stanton to take over and use the churches of the Methodist Episcopal Church South for Christian services. The American Baptist Home Missions Society and the Presbyterians received similar privileges. Large numbers of Northern missionaries were sent south to occupy Southern pulpits. The Southern churchmen rightly resented the highhanded attempt to seize their churches and people under the protection of the Union armies.

Lincoln had better sense than Stanton or the Church leaders. He clearly saw that the Government had no right to interfere with church life by giving Southern churches to the Northern " missionaries." He also saw that this would lead only to bad results for the nation and the Churches. Many churchmen could not see it this way, and so the Churches became the forerunners of the "carpet-baggers" that descended on the postwar South.

Again with regard to the slaves Lincoln showed better sense and truer Christian insight than many of the ministers of his day. As soon as the Union forces proved victorious anywhere the Churches demanded the immediate emancipation of all slaves. In 1862, General Frémont went directly against Lincoln's will and declared all slaves in Missouri free. Lincoln overrode his order because he saw the harm it would do to the Union cause in the border regions.

So clergymen began to attack Lincoln and to uphold Frémont. Many wrote to Lincoln or visited him with advice as to when to free the Negroes. Almost every minister who came thought he knew the will of God for the situation. Only Lincoln was sufficiently humble to realize that he didn't fully know or understand God's will.

He replied to a committee representing various Protestant denominations asking for immediate emancipation in 1862 by saying: "I am approached with the most opposite opinion and advice, and that by religious men who are equally certain that they represent the divine will. I am sure that either the one or the other class is mistaken in that belief, and perhaps in some respects both. I hope it will not be irreverent for me to say that if it is probable that God would reveal his will to others on a point so connected with my duty, it might be supposed he would reveal it directly to me; for I desire to know the will of Providence in this matter. And if I can learn what it is, I will do it."

Thus Lincoln, a Christian who did not feel fully at home in any of the Churches of his day, had a fuller grasp of the will of God than the churchmen who were so positive that they knew God's will. Lincoln was willing to say that it was possible that he did not fully know God's will, that he always had to weigh carefully each situation to discern God's hand in history; thus, he was more apt to find it than the clergyman who bluntly stated that he was positive at all times what the will of God really was.

In a short meditation Lincoln revealed a deep insight into the Christian notion of the will of God, an understanding that enabled him to act with a breadth of wisdom in political matters unparal-

[eled in American history. He said: "The will of God prevails. In great contests each party claims to act in accordance with the will of God. Both may be, and one must be, wrong. God cannot be for and against the same thing at the same time. In the present civil war it is quite possible that God's purpose is something different from the purpose of either party; and yet the human instrumentalities, working just as they do, are of the best adaptation to effect his purpose. I am almost ready to say that this is probably true; that, God wills this contest, and wills that it shall not end yet. By his mere great power on the minds of the now contestants, he could have either saved or destroyed the Union without a human contest. Yet the contest began. And, having begun, he could give the final victory to either side any day. Yet the contest proceeds."

Here was a man who understood that God works in mysterious ways to bring his will to pass. There was no attempt to hide the stark tragedy of life, no tendency to stand up and shout, "I know the will of God." There was only a humble, sincere effort of faith to discern God's presence in every act of history and so to open himself fully to all the possible means God might be using to work out his purpose. This did not paralyze Lincoln from acting; it enabled him to act with wisdom and discernment not possible to a fanatic or a bigot.

So he watched as the war slowly dragged on. At the proper time he pronounced the emancipation of the slaves, and the Union was not weakened by it. He attempted to work out a peaceful settlement with the South, but he recognized that the time had not yet come — it did not yet seem to be God's time.

It was in his second inaugural address, in 1865, that Lincoln clearly laid out the policy he hoped to follow when peace came to the nation. With his profound insight into the ways of Providence in history, he could not take a vengeful attitude toward the South. Lincoln knew that both sides read the same Bible, that both appealed to the same God, that both were under God's judgment, and that "the judgments of the Lord are true and righteous altogether."

Thus he appealed to the people of the victorious North to set aside their hatred and triumph in order to face the herculean task of rebuilding the nation. "With malice toward none; with charity for all; with firmness in the right, as God gives us to see the right, let us strive on to finish the work we are in; to bind up the nation's wounds; to care for him who shall have borne the battle, and for his widow and his orphan — to do all which may achieve and cherish a just and lasting peace among ourselves and with all nations."

In that same year the most bloody war in the nation's history ended and the life of its great leader, Abraham Lincoln, was taken by an assassin's bullet. If only more of the Northern Churches would have breathed the same spirit of charity and mercy and would have sought to bind up the nation's wounds! Rather, many of them pronounced blessings on those statesmen who wished the vengeance of the victors on the vanquished. The war was over but the peace was not won. Slavery had been stamped out, but the slave was not yet really free.

During the war far-reaching changes were taking place in the nation, changes that were vitally to affect the task of the Churches. The North was composed of a combination of agricultural states in the west and industrial states in the east, and in both radical shifts occurred. The threat to the Union and the necessity of financing a huge war tended to center more attention and power in the hands of the Federal Government. This was absolutely necessary that the Union might be preserved.

No sooner had the war ended than a swift stream of immigration again poured into the nation. Between 1860 and 1900, 14,000,000 people came to America. They fled from terrible living conditions, from persecution, from military service, and they sought freedom and plenty. The northern European people flocked to the midwest to the rural areas and farms. The Irish and later southern European peoples stayed in the big cities. How would the Churches reach these people?

After the war America was a nation of terrible contrasts. The rich grew richer, and the poor grew poorer. The South was prostrate, struggling to recover and attempting to relate itself to the recently freed Negro. The west was booming with excitement and expansion. Great ribbons of steel stretched across the nation tying one section to the other. Financiers fought pitched battles for possession of the railroads. The cities were teeming with life and activity. Sprawling factories belched forth smoke and soot as they ground out a never-ending stream of products and machines.

It was a raw, raucous age which was low on morals and high on enthusiasm. Corruption and scandals were widespread. In 1872 a terrible scandal rocked the Grant Administration. Some Congressmen had gone into partnership with some financiers to milk the profit out of the construction of the Union Pacific Railroad. Shares and profits were distributed among Republican Congressmen to assure co-operation. Later one of Grant's cabinet members was involved in a corrupt deal. In New York City the infamous Tweed Ring had fleeced the city of twenty million dollars through control of city politics. In 1869, Jay Gould and his financial associates almost got a corner on the gold in the nation and forced the closing of the banks. So the nation came through the war and entered the period of reconstruction.

During the war itself the Churches faced a problem that accompanied them until the present day — what were they to do with the Negroes who had been so unjustly treated for almost two centuries? Before Lincoln's emancipation act many generals had simply turned Negroes over to the Army chaplain to take care of them. Some were placed on land to till; others were employed as cooks or orderlies. The problem became so acute that a department of Negro affairs was created in the Army.

Soon the various missionary agencies of the Church heard of the Negroes' plight, and they responded by forming private agencies to care for the freedmen. In March of 1865, Lincoln saw to the establishment of the Freedmen's Bureau to assist the Negroes in making the transition from the slave to the free state. It was under the direction of General Oliver S. Howard, a Presbyterian. Churchmen were instrumental in getting it started and in urging its support on the Federal Government.

One of the most helpful things for the Negro people was the establishment of large numbers of schools and colleges in their behalf. Almost all the Protestant Churches, both North and South, participated in this, but the Congregationalists did the lion's share of the work. They were the primary group in the American Missionary Society, which started such famous Negro schools as Hampton Institute, Fisk University, Tougaloo, and Atlanta University in Georgia. Also Howard University, in Washington, D.C., was the result of Congregationalist inspiration.

The Negro people made remarkable progress from a condition of slavery to responsibility, and this against great odds. Many white folks still insisted that Negroes were inferior people doomed to second-class citizenship. The South tried to keep them under control by denying them the vote. Constitutional amendments prevented this, so they sought ways to escape the requirements of law. Northern politicians and businessmen went South and sought to use the Negro to their own advantage. But slowly and steadily the Negro people moved forward.

One of the greatest boons to them was the growth of Christianity among Negroes. Within the Churches they found freedom and responsibility, though they found this most fully within their own Churches. A huge Negro Baptist Church was developed as well as a fairly large Negro Methodist Church.

The regular denominations began to lose large numbers to the Negro Churches because within them the Negro found greater freedom. Often those most anxious to free the Negro from slavery were more reluctant to accept them as fully free members within the Church. They were willing to give money for them, willing to pray for them, but not willing to sit next to them in church. This shows the depth of the social evil produced by the slave system — it could not be eradicated by war, sermon, or prayer. But the Churches did not surrender entirely; they kept working at the problem.

Another proof of the energy of the Church immediately after the war was to be seen in its work among the Indians. By 1870 there were only 278,000 Indians left in the entire nation, yet they presented a problem for both nation and Churches. The curse of the white man applied here as with the Negro problem — he felt his color so superior and his civilization so much better that he could not share it in fellowship. The land-hungry white men constantly encroached on Indian territory and pushed the Indians from place to place.

Originally the Federal Government paid for missionary societies to educate the Indian children, but this questionable practice was abandoned during the 1880's. Nevertheless, the Churches did not give up their work among the Indians. It was difficult to Christianize a pagan people, unsettled, always on the move, exploited by the white man, open to his vices and diseases.

But the Churches carried on bravely. The American Board of Commissioners for Foreign Missions undertook Indian missions as did most of the major Protestant denominations. It was exceedingly slow and painful work. How could the Indian trust the white man, who brought disease and destruction? Yet he did, and before the First World War one third to one half of the Indians belonged to Christian groups.

As more and more people swept westward, pushing the Indians before them, the Church was one of the few forces trying to prevent their exploitation. This indicated a real vitality in the life of the Churches. The Quakers had the responsibility, for a time, of nominating Federal Indian agents and other supervisors. But in spite of their fine work, the Churches never persuaded the nation to accept Indians as full brothers in Christ with all the rights of free people in a free land.

While Indian and Negro work was carried on as an aspect of the Church's home mission task, the regular home mission work did not slacken a whit. The Northern Churches, especially Baptist and Methodist, invaded the South as a mission field. All Churches expanded their home missions throughout the nation. But nationwide work was sporadic until the railroad had spanned the nation; then the Churches spread everywhere.

New Protestant agencies were developed to cover the west with Churches. Railroads often gave free land for churches in order to encourage the building up of the prosperous communities. Again the circuit system of the Methodists and their use of lay leaders stood them in good stead. Their Church Extension Society was one of the most active agencies in the west. The Lutherans were also active in forming midwestern rural congregations among the more recent German immigrants.

Meanwhile the reform activity of the Church was not dead. The golden age of reform, the 1830's and 1840's, was long past, but there was still much benevolent activity. In face of the urban needs too great for any single denomination, thirty-some Protestant mission societies sprang up after the war to work exclusively in the cities.

The city was a new challenge for the predominantly rural Protestant Churches. But they drew on their zeal and experience from the earlier part of the century to develop the activities of their tract societies into something of a wider interest. This marked the beginning of the care for the bodily needs of the down-trodden. It was but a short step from passing tracts to destitutes to passing clothing and food. Buildings for the work were provided by the vacant churches left by wealthier people who were moving out of the disintegrating sections of the city.

Something of that type had to come if the Churches were to work effectively in the big cities. Before the Christian message could reach the dispossessed and destitute, they had to be fed and clothed, they had to be shown that somebody cared for them. That is what the newly organized city mission groups and brotherhood organizations provided. They served both the body and the soul of the needy.

In the autumn of 1865, a group of almost 120 outstanding Protestant ministers and laymen met in Cleveland, Ohio, to consider joint efforts for city mission work. They established a permanent committee for action called the American Christian Commission and appointed two secretaries to make a survey of the situation. They found deplorable conditions in the cities. Church attendance was falling; corruption, vice, and greed were rampant; housing conditions were terrible; and pauperism and crime were on the increase. The cities were real mission fields.

One of the consequences of the new emphasis on city work and works of mercy was the fuller use of women's talents. Many of that day thought it highly improper for women to engage in religious work, but the outstanding service of nurses during the war helped to change things. An additional factor in Protestantism was the introduction of deaconesses patterned after the German Lutheran program. It was only a matter of time until women took their place in doing full-time Christian work.

Another institution that greatly aided in doing city mission work was the Y.M.C.A. and later the Y.W.C.A. The first American Association was founded in Boston in 1851, but the movements mushroomed during the war, and the Y's became one of the leading social institutions after the war. They originated with the purpose of providing young people in the cities with Christian fellowship and of keeping them away from evil temptation. Part of their program was evangelism and part was educational. They led in the establishment of Sunday schools, missions, and stations of mercy. Without their outstanding work, the Protestant ministry to the cities would have been greatly impoverished.

While the Churches were busy creating new agencies and institutions to handle the new problems of the city, they were not overlooking their regular activities in reform and publication. The religious press became one of the most important institutions in American public life. In 1850 there were 191 religious papers and in 1870 there were 407. A religious weekly such as the *Independent* became, under the editorship of Henry Ward Beecher, one of the most influential journals in America. In it, all the pressing moral issues of the nation were discussed. Also, the various publication houses of the denominations grew in this period.

Home missions, reform, city missions, and religious publications all pointed to the vitality pulsating through the Churches. But if one really wishes to note the life of the Churches, he has to see the fruits of the foreign mission program. Two things were important about it. First, through the creation of women's missionary societies the women were able to find one more area through which they could work. Secondly, this period marks the beginning of the modern mission movement, when America began to supply a large proportion of the world's missionaries and money for the spread of the gospel. Christianity was very lively and strong in America.

However, not all was peace, plenty, and growth in American Protestantism at this time. It was also a period of disagreement and

theological argument. One of the first groups to reveal the theological tension was the Lutheran. As America passed beyond the
Civil War, large numbers of German and Scandinavian peoples
came over. The Lutherans in America did a magnificent job of col-
lecting them into their native churches, but they brought not only
opportunity for growth but also dissension.

In face of the trend away from the German language and the
theological confessions of the historic Lutheran Church, a large
group of men protested. They did not want to dissolve Lutheranism
into a general revivalism interested only in moral action. They insisted that how one believed was vitally important and affected what
one did. As a consequence of this argument, one group of Lutherans
advocated a strict adherence to the historic Lutheran confessions
of faith and the other group advocated the modification and play-
ing down of these confessions. The result was a split in the Lutheran
General Synod in 1867. The newer Lutheran groups, such as the Missouri Synod, still speaking European languages, sided largely with
the more conservative General Council, but they would not join it.
Thus the basis for Lutheran disunity in the twentieth century was
laid.

While theological battles were being waged in Lutheranism, the
general unrest over theology was evident in the reception of the two
greatest mid-nineteenth century American preachers and theologians. Henry Ward Beecher and Horace Bushnell were both greatly
admired and respected, yet both were under attack for preaching
strange doctrines.

In 1831 at a revival in Yale College, a young tutor, Horace Bushnell, was converted. Yet this conversion was not simply the result
of the revival. For quite some time the brilliant young student had
intellectual doubts about the Christian faith. How could one believe doctrines that reason said were impossible? Teachers at Yale
gave him little comfort.

While reading the English writer and theologian Samuel T.
Coleridge, one of the most influential Christians in England and
America, Bushnell was persuaded that religious truth was not
grasped primarily by the mind but by the response of the whole
person centering in the heart and moral nature. Religious truth

cannot be proved like a mathematical demonstration; it has to be deeply felt in the heart. When Bushnell had trouble with the doctrine of the Trinity he said, " My heart says the Bible has a Trinity for me, and I mean to hold by my heart."

He did not feel that man's reason was to be ignored. On the contrary, he had the highest respect for intellectual training and the reasonable formulation of Christian truth. He argued that religion was open to reason with a plus. The plus was the sum total of man's deepest aspirations and apprehensions.

In 1833 he took a parish in Hartford, Connecticut. There he early distinguished himself as a mediator between opposing points of view. He upheld reason but only in conjunction with the emotions. He was suspicious of revivals, but admired the conviction they inspired. He was against slavery, but feared the excess of abolitionism.

In 1846 there appeared his first work to get him in serious difficulty with his Congregational brethren. *Christian Nurture* was an attack on the evils of the prevalent revivalism. The trouble with revivalism, he argued, was that it encouraged Christians to act as if there were no such things as Christian homes and churches, or growth in the Christian life. Though a child was raised in supposedly Christian surroundings, the assumption was made that he remained completely a " child of wrath " until under the pressures and promptings of revivals he suddenly found himself converted to be a Christian.

Against revivalism's taking "every man as if he had existed *alone,*" Bushnell argued that " the child is to grow up a Christian, and never know himself as being otherwise." No longer should the Churches urge that " the child is to grow up in sin, to be converted after he comes to a mature age; but that he is to open on the world as one that is spiritually renewed, not remembering the time when he went through a technical experience, but seeming rather to have loved what is good from his earliest years."

Though Bushnell did not ignore the fact that all men are naturally self-seeking or sinful and though he felt revivalism had a place, especially among those never exposed to Christian training, he was bitterly attacked by his Christian brethren. It was not until the twentieth century that the movement of religious education championed his ideals over against revivalism. Meanwhile the Lutheran, Anglican, and some Reformed groups carried on church life under the practice of Christian nurture rather than revivalism.

But his attack on revivalism was not his greatest or most important contribution to American religious life. Bushnell became one of the leading controversial figures in nineteenth century American Protestantism because of his upholding a new method for theology. Both revivalism and strict nonrevivalistic orthodoxy upheld their beliefs by a rigid adherence to the words of the Bible. What the Bible said was literally true!

The trouble was that the Bible said many things in many different ways. Which was right? Each group insisted that its interpretation alone was correct and that all others were wrong. The Roman Catholic Church finally solved the problem by saying that what the pope said was true was that which was right, for he could never make an error in pronouncements on faith and morals.

Over against all attempts to prove truth by a literal quotation from Scripture or by an appeal to an infallible leader, Bushnell argued that the difficulty arises from language itself. Words never convey the exact spiritual truth they are meant to convey. Both through actual use and through an inability to carry the full meaning of a truth, words always convey a meaning that is partly false and partly true.

Therefore, Bushnell argued that " all formulas of doctrine should be held in a certain spirit of accommodation. They cannot be pressed to the letter, for . . . the letter is never true. They can be regarded only . . . as badges of consent and good understanding."

The response was a violent attack on Bushnell and though his health was broken he applied his theories to the doctrine of the Trinity and to the atonement on the cross. His sermons and writings during the 1860's set the pattern for large segments of educated Christians. Here was an attempt to hold honestly to the beliefs of the Christian Church and yet to be open to modern advances in science and in the rest of the world.

Another great figure of postwar American Protestantism was Henry Ward Beecher, the son of Lyman Beecher. Not primarily a theologian, Henry Ward Beecher was first and foremost a preacher and writer. His Plymouth Congregational Church in Brooklyn was built to suit his gifts. It was a plain auditorium with perfect acoustics, and it provided a speaking ramp that jutted out into the congregation. No pulpit for Beecher! He wanted to stand face to face with his 2,500 listeners so he could get his full message across.

Early in his ministry in Indiana, Beecher learned that in order to get results from the pulpit the preacher had to speak the language of the people in a clear, simple, and direct way. The purpose of the sermon was to elevate man's moral life. This Beecher did as no other preacher of his generation. Though he passed for an orthodox preacher, he was interested not so much in correct doctrine as in correct living. So he was a child of the revival.

Yet Beecher had one side that revivalism lacked. Not only was he interested in all the reform movements, he was one of the greatest antislavery preachers. He was also interested in the intellectual life of his day. He read widely in the literature and politics of his day, and all was grist for his mill — all was to be used to show forth the love of God to man and the regenerative presence of the everliving Christ. He was the first outstanding American minister to be receptive to the idea of evolution.

Beecher's name was common in the war-era household. His magazine and newspaper articles were read throughout the nation. Large secular papers in New York, Chicago, and Philadelphia reprinted in full many of his sermons each Monday. Under attack from his Congregational brethren for supporting strange views, he was without definite connections with that Church the last five years of his life.

Perhaps the greatest post-Civil-War preacher was the towering Anglican Phillips Brooks. This was an age of truly great Protestant preachers in America, but none overshadowed Brooks, and his influence was keenly felt in college and university circles as well as in other denominations. Against the opposition of the High-Church party, the Episcopal Church selected him as bishop of Massachusetts. Beecher and Brooks were household names in nineteenth century America, and their fame was eloquent testimony to the influence of Protestantism in contemporary American life.

So American Protestantism emerged from the Civil War. Split between North and South but still vigorous and alive, it turned its attention to the new problems arising from the cities, from industrialism, and from changing intellectual life. Christianity constantly sought more light yet in God's Word, and great preachers such as Bushnell, Beecher, and Brooks felt that they had found new light that enabled them to remain faithful to the Christian message and at the same time honestly to face up to the new findings of science. They performed a great task for their age, but in their day they were in the minority. The real strength of the Church was still in revivalism, and this was not something new cast up to face the postwar challenge. It had been the very heartbeat of a large proportion of American Protestantism since 1800.

13

A Fresh Outpouring

YOUNG DWIGHT L. MOODY had recently moved to Boston to work as a shoe salesman for his uncle. He was converted to Christ under the instruction of his Sunday school teacher, Mr. Kimball, but he had trouble with his faith. He sought the help of his aunt, to whom he said:

" I like the pastor, and Mr. Kimball; but these rich and pious folks at Mt. Vernon make me sick and tired."

" Never mind, Dwight, the Church is the Bride of Christ."

" But the young folks are so lofty and proud. Is that Christianity ? "

" Lad, we are to fight the fight of faith. Do you love the Church ? "

" Well, I guess I do! "

" Then forget the rest."

Even after he was converted and when he had accepted the advice of Aunt Typhenia, Moody had difficulty with his religious life. Somehow he could not speak of his experience to others. Again he sought his aunt's advice.

She asked him, " Do you love Christ ? "

" Well, I guess I do! "

" Then don't worry, lad, over how you talk; just try to tell the people what he has done for your soul, and he'll do the rest."

In 1856 this stocky young man arrived in Chicago determined to make $100,000 in the business world and then retire. Eager to be a success, Dwight Moody easily secured a job as a shoe salesman. His lively and pleasant manner made him an outstanding salesman, and he never lost the ability to " sell " the cause of Christ. He quickly joined a church, rented several pews, and filled them with boys he had rounded up off the streets. But this was too much for the very prim and proper congregation.

Seeking more favorable surroundings elsewhere, young Moody found a weak and struggling Sunday school in the Chicago slums. Within a short time he had collected so many boys for classes that the building could not hold them. First he hesitated to teach, but finally he accepted a class. So fast did the school grow that it had to move to different quarters and spread into an additional building. Every Sunday morning Moody could be seen riding toward Sunday school on a pinto pony carrying a full load of children.

Matching his success as a Sunday school missionary was his business career. In fact, he was well on the way to becoming a leading business figure in the shoe industry, but something stopped him. He could not serve two masters. A break was certain to come.

One day, one of his fellow Sunday school teachers, deathly ill, called on Moody to inform him that he had to return home to die, but before he went he wanted to set things right with the girls of his class. He was sure he had not converted a single person. Moody had had an experience teaching this class. "They laughed in my face." He agreed to accompany the teacher in visiting the girls.

Marvelous results followed. Moody, for the first time, prayed directly for the salvation of a person, and his prayers were answered. One by one the girls were converted by the dying teacher and the shoe salesman. Finally, after a wonderful meeting together, the teacher prepared to leave.

Moody told the story as follows: "The next evening I went to the depot to say good-by to that teacher. Just before the train started, one of the class came, and before long . . . they were all there. What a meeting that was! We tried to sing but we broke down. The last we saw of that dying teacher, he was standing in the rear car, his finger pointing upward, telling us to meet in heaven."

Shortly thereafter, Moody gave up his job to devote himself fully to the Lord's work. From this time, 1860, until 1870 he was a whirlwind of activity and energy. When a speaker failed to show up at a Sunday school convention, he undertook his first public exhortation—over 60 were converted. He was active in Y.M.C.A. work;

he did chaplain work for Camp Douglas, a prisoner of war camp just south of Chicago; he carried on his regular Sunday school work; and he started Sunday evening services.

One man observing Moody in action at this time remarked, "I never saw such high pressure; he made me think of those breathing steamboats on the Mississippi that must go fast or bust: a keen, dark-eyed man with a shrill voice, and a thorough earnestness."

But by 1867 he felt himself preached out. Somehow his message was not what he thought it should be. Several things happened to make another great change in his life. He went to England and heard the famous Baptist preacher Spurgeon. There he also met Henry Moorehouse, who returned to America with him and gave a series of sermons on God's love. As a consequence Moody gained a new respect for Biblical preaching and for the concept of God as love. He turned to the Bible and saw it in a new light. He studied it with a concordance and traced the word "love" from Genesis to Revelation. Henceforth, he was to be strictly an expositor of Scripture.

In 1872 just before departing for England he had a renewal of his conversion experience. As he walked the New York streets one November night he cried out: "O God, why don't you compel me to walk close to thee, always? Deliver me from myself! Take absolute sway! Give me thy Holy Spirit!"

He fled to a friend's room nearby and experienced such an outpouring of God's spirit in his heart that he could not speak of it. He knew only that God's love was completely filling and overflowing his heart. Before that happened he was as one trying to pump water out of a dry well, but after that experience his heart was like an artesian well that never ran dry.

Off he went to England with a singing partner, Ira D. Sankey, whom he had met at a Y.M.C.A. conference and had persuaded to return to Chicago. What a team they made in England! Moody a short, barrel-chested, huge man, well over two hundred and fifty pounds, with a bushy beard and flaming eyes; Sankey, a somewhat taller, rather distinguished-looking, man with a sweet, full, baritone voice.

They landed in 1873 and took England and the British Isles by storm. At first there was much opposition to them, but all was over-come by them. The people heard them gladly. Publishers were be-sieged with orders for gospel hymnbooks and Bibles. Though the mass of their thousands of listeners came from the uneducated lower class, even the learned heard them and not without some approval.

When Moody, who had had a very inadequate education, was once chided for his poor grammar, he responded: " That's all right, brother. What little grammar I have, I use for the Lord Jesus Christ. What do you do with yours? "

Moody and Sankey returned to America as conquering heroes. Everybody had heard of their fame; newspapers and magazines had spread the good news. Their American revival started in Brooklyn in October, 1874. Five thousand people filled the building three times a day. On they swept to Philadelphia, where 13,000 heard them in each meeting. For ten weeks they held forth in New York City while 500 ushers tried to handle long lines of people who came to hear. Over 1,500,000 had heard them by that time. Special taber-nacles were built to house the audiences.

Truly this was a fresh outpouring of the Spirit through revival. Before Moody's life was ended he was supposed to have converted over 1,000,000 to Christ and many millions had heard his message and Sankey's songs. This was the beginning of a new era in Ameri-can Protestantism, a resurgence of revivalism, but a new kind of revivalism.

Moody was to the religious world of the hectic '80's and '90's what Rockefeller was to oil and Carnegie was to steel. He dealt with huge masses of people, he exhibited all the daring, the certainty of con-viction, and the tireless energy that marked the captains of business. But he was a captain in the Lord's legions.

Moody and Sankey popularized the place and function of the gospel hymns in revival meetings. Their hymnbook sold millions of copies, and though sold cheaply it brought in handsome sums in royalties. Not a penny of this remained in Moody's pocket — all went into his religious enterprises.

Another novelty widely used by Moody was the inquiry room, where those distressed of soul repaired for advice. This was similar to the older anxious bench but was private and gave an opportunity for personal contact between the preacher and the convert.

His business acumen was evidenced in the care with which he mapped out the strategy of his revivals. Every detail was cared for. He was one of the first to use advertising as a medium for informing the people of his services. Children of the Sunday school distributed thousands of pamphlets, and billboards carried notices of his meetings. But all was in good taste. Though he was unordained, he had a church of which he was minister in Chicago; but he always urged converts to join their own Churches. Men were not converted to float about from Church to Church.

Moody's message was dynamic, simple, and straightforward. He had no doubts as to the literal accuracy of every portion and part of Scripture, but he had a leniency about him that was not evident in many another revivalist. One of his closest friends was the great naturalist and upholder of evolution, Henry Drummond. Dwight Moody always respected him.

What did Moody accomplish? He created a series of institutions to carry on Christian work: First, there was his church, and the Moody Bible Institute in Chicago. In his home town of East Northfield, Massachusetts, he founded a girls' school and Mt. Hermon, a boys' school, which have become outstanding educational institutions. Into all these he poured his money, and they stand as monuments to his activity.

In a sense, Dwight L. Moody represents the end of one phase of American Protestant life. He died in 1899, but his revival methods continued to play an important role in American life. Under his guidance revivals became for the huge new cities what they were formerly for the smaller towns and country — they were ways of winning members for the Church.

Toward the end of his life, Moody complained that church members crowded in to hear him preach and so kept away the unconverted. This was a real problem for revivalism, yet it started a fresh impulse in American life. Moody became the symbol and the center of the movement. American Protestantism was not anxious to give up the method of soul-winning that proved so fruitful under a spiritual giant such as Moody.

Giants are usually followed by men of lesser stature, and so it was with Moody and his successors. He set the pattern for the revivalists accompanied by the gospel singer, and he set the pattern for the inquiry room and advertising. Many who copied the pattern lacked the master's touch. Where he was free and generous, they were often narrow and niggardly.

Many wondered why Moody did not attack the theory of evolution or Biblical criticism; he obviously did not believe in either. He was too full of sweetness for such attacks, and he recognized that good Christian men such as his friend Drummond held them with no ill effects for their faith. Later revivalists considered these the twin devils of the modern world, to be attacked with zeal and hatred. Moody only felt that intellectual training was of no help in understanding salvation, but they took the next step and glorified ignorance as conducive to the operation of the Spirit.

There was no lack of evangelists after the death of Moody. Their numbers were legion. Dr. Reuben Torrey was Moody's successor in the Chicago and Northfield, Massachusetts, enterprises. One of the real eye catchers was B. Fay Mills, who introduced a number of innovations in revivalism. Under him revivalism became big business. Each city was thoroughly canvassed beforehand, and committees were put in operation in every district. He had a complete organization from musicians to financial director. No offering was accepted until the last day, and all knew this and prepared for it.

Mills developed special days, such as " Good Cheer " days and " Midweek Sabbaths," during which all the secular business in a city would close down for a day. Thus everything in town revolved about the revival. Finally came the use of pledge cards. When the congregation was fully prepared to accept Jesus, assistants in the crowd would quietly pass out pledge cards, on which a convert had only to sign his name to a pledge to " follow Jesus " and to " live a Christian life."

Early in 1909 Boston was seething with religious fervor and excitement. The former stronghold of the Puritans and the Unitarians, now dominated by the Roman Catholics, was anxiously awaiting the arrival of J. Wilbur Chapman and the gospel singer Charles Alexander. For weeks everything built up to the great arrival. Protestant Churches systematically evangelized their parishioners. Teams of laymen went about arousing interest. Preachers prepared their flocks.

Boston was ripe for a great revival. It had not experienced a genuine thoroughgoing awakening since Moody's last visit. People were in a humble and contrite spirit as the result of a financial depression in 1907. Everything stood ready; the fields were white unto the harvest.

The great day dawned and thousands of people poured into Tremont Temple, while other thousands milled around outside. So the revival bandwagon was set rolling to the songs and hymns of Charlie Alexander. J. Wilbur Chapman took over with his exhortation. This was to be no wild-eyed, rousing meeting; rather, it was a systematically planned, carefully calculated program of evangelism. Chapman spoke in a sincere, direct, dignified manner. Of course emotions were tense and at times tears flowed. This was inevitable when one " got religion."

All over the city prayer meetings, hymn sings, and night marches were held. On the fourth day, 166 outlying churches took up the campaign, but all roads led to Tremont Temple. There was the heartbeat of the revival. Even Harvard students participated in some meetings. Evangeline Booth of the Salvation Army turned out to help with a unit of the Army band.

The final meetings were held in Mechanics Hall, where 10,000 people pushed in each evening while an equal number, disappointed, milled about outside. Surrounding New England towns sent special trains into Boston. When all was finished over 2,500 had pledged to lead new lives in Jesus. Nobody knows exactly how many actually remained within the Church, but this was one of the last great Moody type revivals.

Meanwhile, revivalism continued to play an important part in American Protestantism within the larger Churches and also as a fruitful source of smaller " holiness " groups. Revivalism was fully supported by the three great Churches — Methodist, Baptist, and Presbyterian. Congregationalists also gave their support in certain areas, but some of them, along with a few Presbyterians, doubted the wisdom of such an extreme emphasis on revivalism. Only the Anglicans and Lutherans were thoroughly opposed to revival techniques. They felt that it dissolved a real sense of God's Church and placed all the emphasis on man's feelings of the moment.

The fact was that not even the larger Churches that approved of revivalism made sufficient use of it to appease considerable numbers of people. At this time, around the turn of the century, there arose in America a large number of smaller Churches, such as the Pentecostal groups, the Assembly of God, and others, that relied fully and completely on the extremely emotional revivalistic gospel and the swing of gospel hymns.

Some were called in derision " Holy Rollers " or " Holy Jumpers." Their meetings were usually held first in large tents as were many revivals. People would crowd in to sit on benches spaced about five feet apart. Between the benches and in the aisles were sawdust and hay. As the meetings progressed a great bass drum beat out the rhythm of the hymns until the whole crowd, caught by the rhythm, began to shout, clap their hands, and go into furious motions. They believed themselves possessed of the Spirit. No regular Churches could provide them with sufficient outlet for such emotion, so there were many independent organizations started.

Up and down the nation through towns and villages traveled the revivalists. The big tent, the sawdust trail, and gospel hymns became commonplace in religious life. In came the revivalist to hold forth for several days or several weeks. And often he left with pockets full and spirits high. He was bringing Christ to the multitudes. Anybody who could exhort, who appeared sincere, and who had a plan for organization could become a revivalist. It was a good business for many; it was a sincere effort on the part of others.

One of the last of the line of these revivalists was William ("Billy") Sunday, famous baseball player for the old Chicago White Sox. Converted, he served for a while under Chapman and then hit the sawdust trail. He had an efficient organization which surveyed the field of labor, made a definite financial agreement with the local churches, handled the advertising — which was terrific — and trained the ushers and musicians.

Billy Sunday was a salesman for Christ, and so he looked upon himself. He seems to have been an accomplished " ham " actor who appealed to the instincts of the crowd. Always attacking something, he posed as a fearless fighter against the devil, evil, liquor, cards, gambling, wicked women, Huns, Bolsheviks, and Roman Catholics.

His message was one of hatred, fear, and violence as he scared sinners out of hell. A trail of smashed chairs and shattered tables was left behind him. He was fighting for the Lord, and in doing it he built up a handsome purse for himself. Billy Sunday produced plenty of excitement at his revivals. He would get on the floor and pound, calling on the devil to come up and fight him, and when the devil did not appear he stood before the crowd, arms raised, as the defender and champion of the faith. Perhaps he was looking for the devil in the wrong place.

But not all forms of revivalism degenerated into such extremes of exhibitionism. In 1880 the Salvation Army was introduced into America. In the London of 1878, William and Catherine Booth, ex-Methodists, organized a religious group along the lines of an army in order to fight for the souls of the downtrodden in slum areas. They did not stop with a simple preaching of the gospel; they also fed, clothed, and trained the men they had rescued. The object was to rehabilitate the outcasts of society.

In America the Salvation Army engaged in street preaching, entered saloons to conduct meetings, and sought out the poor and destitute in the worst slums. Their uniforms and bands became a common sight in the poorer districts. Many Churches disapproved of their tactics and refused to co-operate with them. For a while, internal dissension threatened them, but after 1886 the Booth family took command of the situation and built a strong, successful organization.

The Army accused the conventional Churches of a tendency to lapse into social clubs that were not really concerned with the total welfare of their fellow human beings. Revivalists, on the other hand, were interested only in saving a man's soul, and they assumed the body would take care of itself if the soul was right with God. Who could minister unto the needs of the modern, homeless, lost city dweller? That was the job of the Salvation Army.

The Army was accused of being undemocratic and of being like a Roman Catholic order because of its armylike regulations and organization. In a sense it was a closely knit, carefully disciplined religious order. Only in that way could it meet the needs of modern urban masses. Many thanked God that some group in Protestantism saw the great need and ministered to it.

But the organization was not really autocratic — it just possessed more order and discipline in its ranks than the regular Churches, such as the Methodist, Congregational, and Presbyterian. These and other Protestant Churches looked on the Army as a mere sect. Slowly the Army won popularity by meeting a need that no other group did. It founded institutions of rescue and rest, the slum brigade and slum settlement homes, nursery schools, orphanages, shelters, and war-relief work. It sought new light in God's Word for the people in the slums of modern cities and found sufficient insight to revolutionize the city ministry.

It was a hot summer, in 1861, when 251 students from colleges and Y.M.C.A.'s gathered at Mt. Hermon, Massachusetts, for religious stimulation and edification under the leadership of Dwight L. Moody. For twenty-six days the students met together and saw the conference take a turn which they had not planned. It became a full discussion of the mission problem.

It was not strange that their talk should turn to missions. One of the finest effects of Moody's work was its stimulation of mission work. Under the impact of his movement seven Cambridge University men offered themselves as missionaries to China, and in 1885 one of them visited American colleges to tell their story. And in 1880, the Interseminary Missionary Alliance was formed among college students. Twenty-one of the men present at the Mt. Hermon meeting planned to go to the foreign field.

During the meeting one of the addresses was "All Should Go and Go to All." No longer was the problem who should go; the question now was what sufficient reason could a student give for not going into foreign missions. America was full of Christians and could well spare men. As the days wore on, more and more men pledged themselves to the missionary task. Before they were finished, almost eighty more men declared themselves available.

Out of this meeting came the Student Volunteer Movement for Foreign Missions, one of the most important contributions of American Protestantism to world Christianity. In 1888 the permanent organization was formed under the chairmanship of an outstanding young American who was present at the Mt. Hermon meeting, John R. Mott. Within a short time this became the most important movement in American student life, bringing large numbers to its conferences.

The purpose of the S.V.M. was to enlist students for foreign mission work, and its slogan, "The Evangelization of the World in This Generation," spoke of their zeal and determination. It became the source of the vast reservoir of missionaries who went from America at the turn of the century.

The urgency of the group was expressed by Mott when he said: "Every reason for doing this work of evangelization at all demands that it be done not only thoroughly but also as speedily as possible. The present generation is passing away. If we do not evangelize it, who will? We dare not say the next generation will be soon enough."

These men were not starry-eyed idealists unaware of the difficulties involved in their slogan. They faced them but countered by saying that if the first generation of Christianity could accomplish so much, then certainly they could, under Christ, accomplish the evangelization of the world in their generation. They reminded critics that this had been the same goal for every generation of Christians; the S.V.M. was simply the first group to adopt it officially as a slogan. As Mott put it, "The watchword has exerted a most helpful influence in the lives of individual Christians. By emphasizing Christ's command, it furnishes a powerful motive."

The movement with its slogan was to have vast consequences throughout the world. Between 1899 and 1914 it rallied 4,521 missionaries to leave American shores to work in China, India, Africa, and the Pacific islands. As a consequence America took over the leadership in the foreign mission enterprise both as to funds and manpower.

Another important consequence of the S.V.M. was its impact on England and the European nations. Out of it came the Student Christian Movement in Great Britain and Ireland, the primary source of English missionaries. This organization grew in world proportions until it included a number of lands in the World's Student Christian Federation, 1895. Thus revivalism was productive of one of the truly creative movements in modern Christianity. In this organization college and university students studied the meaning of their Christian faith in relation to the problems of the modern world. They received inspiration through conferences and literature. They were presented with the challenge of directing their lives to a Christian faith that was vital for the whole world.

Students were only one source of the vigorous new missionary life that pulsated through the bodies of American Churches. In order to carry on the work money was needed, and efficient organization had to be supplied. It was at this point that the good women of the Churches stepped forward to provide the devotion, talent, and time to play the Martha for the large numbers of students willing to leave all as did Mary and follow the Lord whithersoever he might lead.

Another important step in creating support for the missionary enterprise was the Laymen's Missionary Movement, founded in 1906. Before the mission program could have real utility it had to have the support of large numbers of church people. The only way possible to do this was through the laity. The laymen's organization did just that. It arose out of the inspiration of the S.V.M. and drew into itself businessmen and others interested in providing funds for the work. Most of these men were influenced by revivalism.

The Y.M.C.A. was also an important source of foreign mission workers. In 1889 the North American Y.M.C.A. formed a foreign division and made plans to develop associations in foreign fields. Under the leadership of John R. Mott, who remained a layman, the "Y" had a phenomenal growth in foreign lands. Truly this foreign work was an accurate indication of the vitality of American Protestantism. Never before had it been so vigorous and active both at home and abroad.

While all this activity was taking place within the Church, world events were so shaping up that it was possible and almost inevitable for Christians to take up anew the challenge of missions. The late nineteenth and early twentieth century was the age of colonialism and imperialism. France, England, and Germany engaged in a race for the domination of the raw materials and also of the peoples in Asia and Africa. Continents were divided into spheres of influence as vast segments of land were parceled out among the great powers.

The remarkable thing was that the missionary enterprise partook of such a small degree of imperialism. By and large it was the only movement from the West that did not seek to exploit colonial peoples, and wherever it was sufficiently strong it forced governmental officials to deal more justly with the native peoples. But the missionaries could not avoid the fact that they were often present in foreign lands only because their own nation or some other Western nation was in control. If they sought no advantage from this arrangement, they could overcome their initial handicap. When they sought extra protection and privileges, they destroyed their effectiveness.

In 1898 the United States went to war against Spain and emerged with the Philippine Islands, Puerto Rico, and a protectorate over Cuba. The war was caused as much by the excitement built up by the American press and pulpits as by the misconduct of the Spanish. Their treatment of those possessions was little different in 1898 from what it was in 1798, yet in 1898 a war resulted. The consequence was that America found itself catapulted into the arena of foreign affairs.

The pulpit and religious papers were solidly in favor of the war, and after the war they promoted the American retention of the territory in order to prepare the natives for freedom. The first step to freedom was to bring them the gospel as interpreted by Protestantism. Here was a chance for American Churches to operate on a foreign field under American control. They did not pass up the opportunity. As a result new work was undertaken in the Philippines and Puerto Rico, and in light of America's enhanced position in the Far East mission work in China and Japan became of greater importance. The foreign mission movement entered a new age.

The fresh life in the foreign mission movement had consequences for religious life not only in foreign lands but also in America. With unprecedented numbers entering foreign service and with ever-increasing funds being raised for missions, it was inevitable that it was to have some effect on American Protestantism.

For one thing it made Americans in general and Christianity in particular aware of different peoples and customs. Though missionaries went only to preach Christ and him crucified, they constantly faced the question of how this could be done. They at first simply ignored the whole foreign culture to which they preached, but they soon found this was impossible. They had to find the best means of making the gospel relevant, and so they took a new interest in other religions and cultures.

Furthermore, while working on the foreign field, they found that needless competition between various Protestant groups only stood in the way of evangelism; therefore, they were forced to seek cooperation with one another. This had consequences not only on the foreign field but also on the Churches at home in America. They had to reappraise their common faith as well as their differences.

Finally, the increased use of laity both in the Churches and in the colleges made for a Christianity of greater life and vitality. It made all Christians feel responsible for spreading the gospel. This was not simply a job for hired pastors or professionals. The great leaders who left businesses remained laymen while they led the missionary enterprise. Dwight L. Moody, Robert E. Speer, and John R. Mott are examples. So the expansion of foreign missions brought the layman into a new position of importance in American Christianity.

Meanwhile, going hand in hand with the increased tempo of revivalism and the redoubled efforts at foreign missions was a fresh impetus to reform. This took the form of the Sabbath movement and the temperance movement, both of which had long been dear to the hearts of revivalistic Christians.

All those coming out of revivalism were greatly disturbed by the slow distintegration of the strict Sabbath. They felt that it should be a day devoted exclusively to religious activity with absolutely no merrymaking. Large numbers of German, Scandinavian, and southern European immigrants thought otherwise. To be sure, the religious among them started the day with church, but the remainder of the day was to be spent in recreation and relaxation. God made the day for man's recreation. So they made merry, sang, laughed, and even drank.

Against this view of Sunday the revival Christians protested with all their vigor. Sabbath clubs and organizations were founded to enforce laws against the merrymakers. But the full weight of their wrath was let loose on drinking. At first the temperance movement in America was purely a voluntary society that aimed at temperate use of milder alcoholic beverages. In the 1840's it developed into a movement that was opposed to all use of alcohol as a beverage and advocated law to prevent its usage.

Immediately after the war, in 1865, a National Temperance Convention was called. The battle lines were drawn between the brewers' and distillers' industry and the revivalists. In between was the mass of people not quite certain which way to turn, but most of them preferring their glass of beer. In 1869 the National Prohibition Party was founded on the principle of putting all alcoholic beverages under the ban of law.

Though the revivalistic Churches supported its program, it met with little success. Again the ladies had to take over and promote a cause. In 1874 the Women's Christian Temperance Union was founded, and in 1895 the Anti-Saloon League of America. Miss Frances E. Willard became the leader of the W.C.T.U. They started a vigorous campaign, using revival techniques to convert the nation to total abstinence by choice and through law. They were not to succeed for almost twenty years, but then they were to gain a temporary victory.

So a rich new energy was brought into the Churches through revivalism. It was the time-tested source of strength whereby American Protestantism sought to meet the new problems it faced in the big cities, the colonialism of the century, and the rising scientific thought. Revivalism produced great preachers and giants in leadership and organization. It produced a certainty and conviction that could not be stopped. It won millions for the Churches and imbued all with a new moral fervor. Revivalism brought fresh impulses into student life, rallied the women and young people into many societies, poured out thousands of missionaries, produced new groups to work in the slums, created institutions of mercy and charity.

But the very certainty of conviction and the very intenseness of zeal were to prove its undoing. It was so sure of its grasp of truth that it quickly became the Pharisees praying, " God, I thank thee, that I am not as other men are, extortioners, unjust, adulterers," and continuing with drunkards, card players, or dancers.

Those who were converted behaved in a certain way. Those who did not so behave were not Christian. So the revivalists' question, " Brother, are you saved? " was a " loaded " question. One was " saved " only if he acted as the revivalist said he must. Christianity was too easily identified with a series of negative actions — a series of things that one did not do.

Furthermore, in its strong emphasis on individual conversion it often overlooked God's Church as a channel through which God reaches man. All one needed was a certain kind of experience, and that would automatically provide a complete answer for the Christian life. What of those who quietly grew up in Christian homes and never had such an experience and yet lived the life of repentance, sacrifice, and love? That was the question Bushnell asked of the revivalists. They never answered it. They were too busy winning souls.

What of the great injustices in society, in economic life, in politics? Convert the individual and all else will follow, was the revivalists' answer. Or, better still, replied another group, these things don't count; only eternal souls matter. Soon the world will end anyway. Something was wrong with such a view. Surely the Church as the fellowship of believers must act in concert against great injustices that violate God's law. The dream of the Puritans had been lost. The soul of the Christian was divided from his body.

Not only did revivalism divide man's soul from his body, it also tended to ignore his mind. Moody, Chapman, Mills, and Sunday were opposed to all attempts to relate the latest findings of man's mind to the deepest insights of his Christian faith. They cried out that the Bible and conversion were enough, man needed no more.

But had not the Church given birth to the universities? Had it not founded the earliest schools in America? Was not the mind of man also created by God? Did not the faith relate to the whole man and the whole of his society? Revivalism tended to ignore these basic questions as it concentrated on one great problem: Are you saved? In so doing it helped to promote Christian faith in America, but at the same time it de-emphasized the role of the Church by concentrating on an individual experience, and it also made Christianity a stranger to large segments of American intellectual, cultural, and political life.

14

Battles Over Beliefs

IN 1859 a bombshell burst in the field of world academic scholarship and scattered its fragments into every area of life. European reaction was immediate, and the American response came after the Civil War. Charles Darwin's *Origin of Species* was important not only for scientists but also for all men interested in the origin, nature, and destiny of man. Not the least affected was theology.

No sooner had theology made a partial adjustment to the new theories of geology than it was confronted by a more serious threat concerning the very origin and descent of man. Through the patient work of Sir Charles Lyall and others, geology proved that the earth was millions of years old, and that it had been formed through a slow process. This was in direct contradiction to the Churches' generally accepted beliefs based on a literal reading of certain books of the Bible.

For centuries the Churches had taught that the creation of the world occurred exactly as it was described in the book of Genesis. In six dramatic days packed with marvelous actions, the Creator had formed the world and placed all living beings in it. Furthermore, by adding up the ages of the various Biblical figures backward from Christ to Adam, and by adding that sum to the years since the birth of Christ, many Biblical scholars believed they could determine just how old the world actually was. Indeed, some thought they could fix the exact day and hour when the Creator began his work. On this basis they figured that the world was around six thousand years old.

Little wonder that clergymen were shocked by the geologists' claims that the world was millions of years old, and that it had taken a long time to be formed. But not all was lost! Nobody could say how the process started and how the various adjustments during the process took place; therefore, the clergy seized upon the idea that the six "days" of the Genesis creation stories referred not to a literal day of twenty-four hours but to indeterminate periods of time. Did not Scripture say that "a thousand years in thy sight are but as yesterday"? They also maintained that the various changes in mineral, vegetable, and animal life were due to the invisible direct intervention of the Creator at different points in the process.

So the case rested until Charles Darwin. His was a theory that claimed to provide an answer to the how of creation as well as to the when. Building on the findings of geology that gathered specimens of various animal and vegetable forms that had been preserved in rock formations, Darwin had no difficulty in showing that the forms in the older rock formations were simpler than those preserved in the more recent formations; therefore it proved that there had been a slow development from simpler to more complex forms. Also, there were definite resemblances between structures of various animals showing that there was a continuity from the more simple to the more complex types.

How then did these forms develop from the simple to the complex? Darwin argued that all depended upon the survival and adaptation of the most fit specimens. Those forms which proved most adaptable to their surroundings survived and made adjustments that enabled them to survive. These adjustments were passed on from generation to generation until the forms became ever more complex and better able to live in their surroundings.

Man stood at the apex of the movement. He was not created at a definite point in history. No, said Darwin, he evolved from the most simple form of life through the various stages of lower animal life, through the mammal form, until he arrived at where he now stands — on two feet!

A wave of indignation swept through the Churches. How dare some little scholar dispute the statements of the Bible? If Adam was not created by God and if Eve was not taken from his rib, then the Bible was wrong. And if the Bible was wrong and full of errors, how could one believe that God's nature and will was revealed in it? Charles Darwin was wrong because his theory explained the origin of life in a way contrary to Biblical revelation.

Within a short time his theory was labeled atheistic, that is, that it did not believe in God or have a place for God. The first call to the attack centered on that front. As one minister put it:

"Founded by atheism, claimed by atheism, supported by atheism, and exclusively in the interests of atheism, suppressing without mercy every jot of evidence for the divine existence, and so making a positive rational faith in God wholly impossible, the doctrine of evolution may well be set down as not only a foe to theism, but a foe of the most thoroughgoing sort."

This was what really bothered the fearful churchmen. If one destroyed the Genesis story of creation and substituted the gradual emergence of different forms as they struggled for survival in their environment, then one destroyed the entire argument for the proof of God from the evidence of creation. Where then did God fit in the picture? How could one speak of the magnificence of creation as it came from the hand of God? God as the great, wise creator was blotted out by a slow process of change.

The famous Dr. Charles Hodge of Princeton Seminary pointed to this when he said that in Darwinism "species owe their origin, not to the original intention of the mind; not to the special acts of creation calling new forms into existence at certain epochs; not to the constant and everywhere operative efficiency of God, guiding physical causes in the production of intended effects; but the gradual accumulation of unintended variations of structure and instinct."

All the fears of the clergy were realized when in 1871 Darwin published *The Descent of Man,* in which he traced the origin and development not of the general forms of life but of man himself. Reaction was immediate! Now the battle was completely joined. The theologians sprang to the defense of man as having by birth the capacities and gifts of freedom, virtue, and immortality. But Darwin argued that there were no such spiritual inborn powers. Man had developed these as habits.

Some argued that Darwin tried to do away with God and to transform man into a gorilla or ape. As one put it, "The man of this philosophy is nothing but . . . a worm of the millionth generation, or a monkey with some enlargement of the brain, set upright, tail removed, the forearm shortened and the hand perfected by natural selection."

Others insisted that such a theory meant the end of the Christian religion. One defender of the faith said, "If man and monkeys, magpies and mackerel, mosquitoes and moles are all alike the descendants of the earth and sea, then is our religion vain and we are without hope and without God in the world." The president of Princeton University said, "It logically involves an utter denial of Christianity and of all else properly styled religion."

Tempers were unleashed. Churchmen and scientists vied with each other to compose the most extreme denunciations. Both sides had much to be ashamed of. One of the great preachers in an outburst of wrath against the scientists was supposed to have said: "It makes me sick to see these literary folks coming down the aisle with Darwin under one arm and a case of transfixed grasshoppers and butterflies under the other arm, talking about Huxley's protoplasm and natural selection . . . lithping with an exquithite lithp, and calling all common men fools."

The controversy grew in intensity and bitterness, but warning voices arose occasionally to remind the theologians that they had best let science alone or at least not despise it so completely. Many were worried over both the spirit and the method of the Christian defense. The ministers were reminded that the real problem was a genuine reconciliation of Christianity and science that would recognize the proper basis and spheres of each.

Many clergymen were astonished when President McCosh of Princeton University came out for a truce in the fight and suggested that the Church should not side in scientific disputes. Others followed with warnings. Henry Ward Beecher gradually came to adopt the theory of evolution. He insisted that men must be ready to meet God wherever he reveals himself, "where he moves in the providences of the world, where he is at work in natural laws, when he is living in philosophical atmospheres, when he is shining in

great scientific disclosures . . . you are bound . . . to meet the
Lord, to welcome him, to accept him in all the new garments that
he wears."

Beecher called evolution "the teaching of the divine method of
creation as gradual." It would be useless to "throw the Bible at it"
because such action would accomplish nothing. He recognized that
"a greater change has taken place within the last thirty years, probably than ever took place in any former period of five hundred consecutive years." That was due to the doctrine of evolution, which
was a radical shift in the belief in creation. Beecher approved of it.

Slowly but surely numbers of clergymen swung about to accept
and support the theory of evolution. They made another compromise. God was the one who established the process of evolution, set
it into motion, guided it, and governed it. Only in that way, they
argued, could one account for the origin of life and the direction
that was evident in the unfolding forms of life. This was a new
way of looking at God's creative activity. Many accepted it gladly.

With Beecher setting the pace, a number of men not only made
peace with the theory of evolution, they also used it as the basis for
a new theological method. Lyman Abbott, Beecher's successor at
Plymouth Church, wrote and preached a theology that stressed
evolution. God was no longer viewed as the one who created the
universe by his will and was separate from it. Now God was a presence throughout all of nature, all of life, sustaining and constantly
bringing forth new forms.

As Abbott put it, "My little grandchild sat next to me at the table
one day, and said to me, 'Grandfather, how can God be in Cornwall and in Newburgh at the same time?'"

Abbott touched him on the forehead and said, "Are you there?"
"Yes."

The minister touched the child on the shoulder and asked, "Are
you there?"
"Yes."

Then he touched him on the knee and repeated, "Are you there?"
"Yes."

"That is the way that God can be in Cornwall and Newburgh
at the same time."

God was a great soul present throughout the universe, giving it direction and meaning. Gone was the view of the Fall, of man's sin, of the uniqueness of Jesus the Christ, and of God's final judgment over history. In its place was the belief that man had been slowly brought forth from lower barbaric forms to higher, more spiritual, forms. Just as the bodily and animal forms were subject to a law of progress so were the spiritual qualities of life.

Sin was the blocking of the spiritual progress of man by a turning backward or downward to the lower physical things. As Beecher put it, sin was a conflict " between the lower element of human nature and the higher." Abbott called it a " downward tendency " which came from the subjection of man's spiritual powers " to the lower elements of our being."

Thus the prophets of evolution had a new outlook on God, man, and history. Life was a struggle, to be sure, but the struggle pointed to the constant emergence of good as victor. Behind man lay the dark shroud of hundreds of centuries from the slimy ooze of the primeval forest to the first civilization. Ahead was a glorious future of ever greater development.

" Excelsior! " became the cry of the new theology — ever onward and upward. Temporary defeat, slight backsliding, death, and all other hindrances were but temporary. Beginning in struggle and bondage, carried along by constant opposition, the brute animal nature of man had slowly been refined in the fires of history until the spiritual qualities emerged, slowly gaining ascendancy and control.

What then could stop this progression? Nothing! It was God himself working out his scheme of redemption in history. As one Christian thinker put it, man would be " indefinitely perfected and raised to a totally different plane than that on which all life had hitherto existed." The good of each generation was passed on to its children, so that each generation was morally superior to the previous one. Said Dr. Atterbury of Princeton University, " Men know more now, think better, have higher natures than those of earlier stages of civilization."

The peacemakers in the Churches were in the minority, however, and the proponents of a synthesis evolution and Christian faith were but a handful. Great names such as Beecher and Abbott had to be reckoned with, but the mass of the clergy and the vast preponderance of the laity remained hostile to the theory of Darwin.

Most believers still maintained that evolution denied the Christian religion, threw out the Bible, and did away with Christ. They wanted no part of Beecher or Darwin. In the South, stronghold of revivalism, the warfare against evolution continued unabated until the 1920's, and among a majority of the Southern clergy and laity it is still unacceptable. Only the east and the university centers of the midwest were hospitable to the theory of evolution.

So it was that both sides appeared to present a part of the Christian faith. Somehow those opposing the evolutionists sensed that Christian faith was not simply the belief in a relentless upward climb of man toward a perfection on earth. Sin was something more than and different from a heritage from man's barbaric origins.

But these opponents of evolution could not come to terms with the evidence for evolution, they could not reinterpret the Christian faith for the modern scientific mind. They could only stand firm on the old ramparts, in an attempt to hurl back the onslaught of the scientists. While they were busy repulsing the handful of scientists, the world quietly marched by the ramparts, not bothering with attack or defense. The average man either inconsistently accepted both the Genesis story and the Darwinian account, or he was indirectly influenced by the spirit of the age and succumbed to the common belief of the relentless progress of mankind. Why not? Was not America the peak of civilization at this point in history?

At the opening of the twentieth century German universities were pulsating with life. Great scholars probed and examined the history and literature of the Christian Church. Never before had so much been discovered about any religious movement in history. The finest minds of Europe were bent on discovering the exact text of the Bible. Men searched for new manuscripts, and by scientific analysis they helped to establish the most accurate version of Scripture.

Scholars were not satisfied only with producing the most accurate text of the Bible; they also wanted to know how the Bible came into being, when its various parts were written, the total surroundings in which the various books were written, and the consequence of all this for an understanding of the Christian faith.

The same tests applied to the date and authorship of Homer's poems were applied to the Bible. The results were shocking for many Christians. Scholars such as the German professor Wellhausen pointed out that the various books of the Pentateuch exhibit different strands of writing, indicating that the present books were not written at one time by a single author such as Moses. Each is a collection of several earlier accounts. Other scholars worked on the dates and authorship of the books of the New Testament. Still others studied the early history of the Church, and applied the evolutionary idea of development to the Church long before Darwin worked out his theory.

As they produced magnificent pieces of research, the German universities drew students from all over the world. Shortly after the Civil War, American ministers and theologians beat a well-worn path to the German lecture halls. There they drank deeply from the well of scholarship. They filled themselves and their flagons and set out for the long trip home. In America they began to teach these new ideas.

Reaction was immediate! Here was another attack on the faith of the Church! Just as Darwin had undermined the belief in creation and in God, so these men destroyed faith in the Bible. How could one believe anything the Bible said if something in it was incorrect? Did not the Church teach at all times that Moses wrote the Pentateuch, that Matthew was the first Gospel written, and that Paul wrote the Epistles to Timothy?

In vain did the followers of the historical study of Scripture argue that the Bible nowhere says that it has no mistakes in it or that the usually accepted authors of the books of the Bible actually were such. Much of this had been traditional in the Church. But some sensed that this was an attack on the authority of the Christian faith. The Bible could not be touched.

On January 20, 1891, Rev. Dr. Charles A. Briggs was placed in the newly endowed chair of Biblical theology at Union Theological Seminary, New York. He delivered an address entitled "The Authority of Holy Scripture." As a consequence he was accused of being a heretic in the Presbyterian Church and charges were pressed against him. Dr. Briggs was found guilty in 1893 and suspended from the Presbyterian ministry, but he continued to teach at Union and became a clergyman in the Episcopal Church.

What did Dr. Briggs say that was so dangerous? He upheld the new discoveries of Biblical scholars and insisted that such a genuine and honest criticism of the text and authorship of the Bible could not damage the Christian faith. Furthermore, he insisted that the sources for divine authority were threefold — the Bible, the Church, and reason.

This was what bothered many ministers. Not only did Briggs uphold Biblical criticism, he also argued that the authority for religious truth was not found in Scripture alone. This was not exactly new, and yet it was. Even those who insisted that Scripture alone was the basis of truth also interpreted it in light of their Church and their reason. To say that all three together were equally the source of authority was to some an attack on Scripture.

Dr. Briggs attacked this idolatry of the Bible as *Bibliolatry*. He said that such men treat the Bible " as if it were a baby, to be wrapped in swaddling clothes, nursed, and carefully guarded, lest it should be injured by heretics and skeptics." But the Bible needs no such protection. It is " the greatest treasure of the Church." No longer can the " self-constituted defenders . . . retain a monopoly of the Word of God and exact conditions of all who would use it. It has already been taken from them by Biblical criticism, and it is open to all mankind, without conditions."

He was not the only minister and teacher to defend the newly discovered scientific study of the Scriptures, nor was he the only one to be tried for it. The Presbyterian Church was the scene of many accusations of heresy and of several trials. Professor Henry Preserved Smith was found guilty of deviating from Presbyterian doctrine and became a Unitarian. Another Union Seminary professor, Dr. A. C. McGiffert, was hounded by his opponents until he found refuge in the Congregational Church. So the battle raged. One side felt they were defending the truth of God's Word. The other side insisted that they were the genuine defenders of God's Word because they freed it from all human idolatry so God could speak through it.

The shifting winds in the field of belief stirred up other new tendencies. While some great preachers, some students, and some professors made their peace with historical criticism and evolution, other developments in religion were taking place. All these new tendencies went under a common name — liberalism. The various liberal movements were united in the belief that the old creeds and beliefs of the Church hindered modern man from understanding God's nature and will. Changes were necessary in order to make Christianity meaningful for modern man.

Some wanted to do this by using the old language of the creeds and by pouring new meaning into them. Others wanted to use completely new language while trying to retain the same old concern as the creeds. They wanted to construct a new set of beliefs which grew out of an appreciation for the past. These more radical men were known as " modernists."

This was not without effect on the daily life of the Churches. Though such beliefs were not widely prevalent in the Churches, they won a new avenue of communication in the rapidly expanding field of religious education. The Sunday school movement was always strong in nineteenth century American Protestantism, but under the impact of liberal theology it was to be of even greater importance, especially after the First World War.

If the religious life is one of a gradual growth toward maturity in faith, then the various agencies of the Church should be used to promote such growth. No longer did most of the public schools have Bible-reading or religious instruction. How were the young to be guided in the growth of their religious convictions? Church schools and better programs in those schools was the answer of religious education.

So closer attention was paid to the teaching and the materials used in Sunday schools. Uniform lessons for all the Churches were advocated. National organizations were established to promote the development of good religious education in the Churches. Some

Protestant groups, particularly the Lutheran Church of Missouri Synod and its affiliates, felt that such part-time training was insufficient, and they developed parochial schools.

While the Protestant Churches were facing mounting battles in beliefs and while many were attempting to reinterpret the faith in the light of modern demands, one thing continued to mark the American scene. A number of new religious groups developed in America or revolted in dissatisfaction from the older Churches.

Before genuine liberalism appeared on the scene or before Darwin made any impact on the American Churches, a vigorous new faith had developed in the face of a dissatisfaction with the general Protestant beliefs. Christian Science had its origin in the late 1860's, but really did not make an important impact until the 1880's and 1890's.

In 1875, Mary Baker Glover Patterson, a New Englander who was to become known after her third marriage as Mary Baker Eddy, published *Science and Health,* the basis of the Christian Science movement. Having been healed of ill-health by one Phineas P. Quimby, a hypnotist and healer, Mrs. Eddy became a devotee of faith healing. She took lessons from him and received a copy of his writings called *Questions and Answers.*

In the 1860's she became a teacher of the new principles and while writing her book she and a young assistant, Richard Kennedy, engaged in faith healing. Her book first made little impact on the American religious scene. It was not until she and her students moved from Lynn, Massachusetts, to Boston that she found a ready hearing and success.

In Boston she continued to teach her theories in her school, and in 1892 saw the Mother Church of Christian Science founded. It was by then another full-fledged religious group on the American scene. Based upon the absolute belief in the primacy of the spirit, it taught that only spirit is truly real; consequently such things as evil and pain really do not exist.

The tremendous appeal of Christian Science was to be found in its claim to healing power. No doctors or medicines were needed, only absolute trust and faith plus a full knowledge of the spiritual powers in life. As Mrs. Eddy said, " The physical healing of Chris-

tian Science results now, as in Jesus' time, from the operation of
divine principle, before which sin and disease lose their reality in
human consciousness and disappear as naturally and as necessarily
as darkness gives place to light and sin to reformation." Again she
pointed out, " If one turns away from the body with such absorbed
interest as to forget it, the body experiences no pain."

Here indeed was a strange doctrine. Its book was put forth as a
new revelation supplementing and completing the Bible. While
Darwin and others were discovering the very processes of life working through matter, Mrs. Eddy was insisting that matter was not
real apart from mind which brings it into being. Most Christians of
the day felt uneasy with both theories. One seemed to deny the
Creator by divinizing matter and the forces of nature, and the other
appeared to deny the Creator and the goodness of creation by insisting that only mind and spirit are good and real. This led some
to say that the movement was neither science nor Christian. But
under the leadership of the Mother Church in Boston local churches
were founded throughout the nation. It was especially popular
among women and the upper classes.

Around the turn of the century there arose a host of movements
similar to Christian Science yet differing in several important respects. All of them emphasized the superiority of the spiritual and
the necessity of suppressing, controlling, or denying the material
side of life. Some advocated healing by spirit, all advocated control
of mind over matter, and others spoke of the contact with the departed spirit world. None of them had close relations with the
Christian Churches, and they attacked Protestantism as but a
childish understanding of the religious life. The Churches accused
these groups, such as Unity, New Thought, Theosophy, Spiritual-
ism, and others, of gross distortion of the truth and a denial of
Christianity. All these movements grew but never seriously threatened the position of the Christian Churches. Strangely enough,
those groups which denied the importance of the material side of
life, including Christian Science, appealed largely to people who
were richly blessed with the world's goods.

On all sides the Church, creeds, and beliefs were under serious
attack during the late nineteenth and early twentieth centuries. Not

only scientific thought and historical scholarship but also peculiar cults and leaders pressed the criticism. Men such as the famous lawyer Robert Ingersoll traveled about the nation preaching belief in no God and accusing the Bible of grave inconsistencies and numerous errors. His writings and lectures were to be found in a number of homes, indicating that this type of thinking was not uncommon.

Though under attack on what it felt to be the very heart of its faith, the Church was not a dying or a weak institution. On the contrary, this was one of the most vital periods in the history of American Christianity. This was the day of vigorous student volunteer activity and of unprecedented growth in foreign missions. It was the hour of expanding Indian missions and of new churches being opened in Alaska. Certainly the Churches were not disintegrating.

While many ministers argued that evolution had undermined the Bible as a source of Christian insight and practice and while others argued that the new historical critical approach destroyed all reverence for the Book, a history-making event occurred. In 1881 the first complete new translation of the Scriptures since the King James Version of 1611 appeared. The result of combined English and American scholarship, it was an immediate success.

In 1901 there appeared the complete American Standard Revision, embodying the preferences of American scholars who had worked on the 1881 edition. This was one of the fruits of the new interest in Biblical scholarship. It was an attempt to translate the Bible into modern language, using the additional manuscripts that had been discovered and employing the latest findings of scholars. Such activity could not have destroyed the value of Scriptures, for the new revision sold out its first printings and there was a tremendous demand for it.

In addition to the lively activity exhibited in Bible revision, in scholarship, and in translation, the Church did not slacken its interest in reaching the public through printed and spoken words. Though the camp meeting was still widely employed, it gradually became a means of education for Christian laity.

In 1874, Bishop John Vincent brought together a group of Sunday school teachers for a combined two weeks' training course and recreational period at an old camp meeting ground on Lake Chautauqua in New York. So successful was this that it soon developed into a national institution offering lecture courses and correspondence courses on a variety of religious and cultural subjects. Each summer the greatest orators and teachers were brought there to lecture to thousands of people. Similar institutions, largely under the leadership of Churches, sprang up throughout the nation. They took the place of the old-fashioned revivalistic camp meetings and became the new nerve centers for reform activity.

Reform grew during this period. Especially important was the reorganization and strengthening of the prohibition movement. The Women's Christian Temperance Union continued its activity, and through the Chautauqua meetings recruited ever larger numbers. In 1895 the Anti-Saloon League developed a national organization, and the Churches were organized in a great crusade against the use of alcoholic beverages. The Methodist, Baptist, and Presbyterian Churches provided the bulk of the leadership and membership for the fight. Politics became the arena in which the battles were to be fought. Law and indirect or direct pressure were the weapons whereby " demon rum " and the " evil saloon " were to be destroyed.

During this period the Church caught the eye as well as the ear of the public. It continued to be an age of religious journalism. Weekly papers and monthly magazines of interdenominational origins were as common on millions of American tables as the national dailies and weeklies. As long as men such as Henry Ward Beecher, Lyman Abbott, and T. DeWitt Talmage wrote, they would have huge audiences. In these papers the Christian believers read opinions on politics, science, literature, and art. Through them the Churches and preachers made known their reactions to all the major issues of the day. In that way they served as a means of organizing and crystallizing Christian opinion on important questions.

So the Churches in America faced many battles in beliefs as well as struggles in the face of new social and economic conditions. Protestantism could not ignore the recent discoveries of science pertaining to the origin of the world, the nature and origin of man, and the operation of nature.

Uncertain in the midst of the swift-moving events, it first reacted defensively to the " religious revolution." On second thought, many adopted completely both the results and the methods of science. Their problem was how to remain identified with the Christian religion. In their eagerness to accept the new discoveries, they failed to remain critical of both method and results. So identified were they with the new cause, that they had difficulty both in relating themselves to the old and in pronouncing the ever-needed word of judgment on the new.

Those who reacted in a purely defensive way failed to grasp the truth in the new scientific discoveries and set the mind and heart of the Church against the truth recently discovered. They made it difficult for the Christian faith to relate itself in a word of judgment and redemption to the newly developing culture and intellectual life of America. They spent so much time and energy defending the indefensible that they failed to make truly relevant the deepest insights of the faith.

But the Churches did not wholly fail in this age. They were alive and vital, expanding, entrenching, inquiring, and proclaiming. Out of the battles in beliefs was to come a new spirit in many circles of Christianity — a spirit of search and inquiry, a spirit of seeking more light yet in God's Word.

15

Justice in Society

ONE NIGHT in 1897, during the depth of a depression, all New York was buzzing about a magnificent ball given by one of the fabulously wealthy men of the age, Mr. Bradley Martin. True to the taste of the day, everything was copied after the glorious days of the splendid French monarch, Louis XIV.

In order to have the proper surroundings the famous Waldorf-Astoria Hotel was completely redecorated to appear as the French palace Versailles. Rare and expensive pictures and tapestries set the tone. The guests represented various countries while Mr. Martin walked about as Louis XIV. One gentleman wore a suit of armor marked with gold inlay of ten thousand dollars' value. Beautiful and expensive jewels were as common as corsages. Altogether it was a magnificent display.

Yet there was nothing extraordinary about this party. It differed from many others only in degree. Wealthy men vied with each other to produce the most startling and extraordinary parties. Some held dinners eaten on horseback; at one party cigarettes were wrapped in one hundred dollar bills. Animals were brought in for amusement, and some pets had collars studded with diamonds and had special valets to care for them. This was the gilded age!

The age of big business had dawned with a vengeance. New, powerful factories had been built during the Civil War and expanded at the turn of the century. Thousands of millionaires were produced, and at one time only one tenth of the people controlled nine tenths of the wealth of the nation. How could this be? Fortunes were built on speculation, shrewdness, luck, and sheer determination. There was little or no control over the actions of these men so long as they stayed within the limits of a very lax body of laws.

This was the age of expanding productivity. Mines, agriculture, manufacturing, transportation, communication, packing, food processing, and finance — all offered opportunities to amass huge fortunes. Labor was cheap and plentiful, making high wages impossible and leading to a terrible exploitation of the men, women, and children.

Meanwhile, the Carnegies, Rockefellers, Vanderbilts, Hills, Fisks, Drews, Dukes, and others built up their fortunes. They found a ready-made defense in the Darwinian theory of evolution. As they surveyed the mass of struggling mankind, firm on the pinnacle they had achieved, they complimented themselves as having triumphed because they deserved to. Economic life was supposedly ruled by certain unchangeable laws such as supply and demand, but the basic law was that of absolutely untrammeled competition and survival of the fittest.

In the struggle of competition the men truly fit survived and became wealthy, but those who were not so fit went down to destruction. Government was to stand aside and let competition reign supreme, seeing to it that certain minimum rules prevailed. Yet, while these men talked glibly of freedom of competition and no Government interference with their activities, they felt perfectly free to use the Government to favor their own enterprises.

Government was used to build huge tariffs to protect their industrial products from foreign competition. It was used to promote mass immigration so as to provide cheap labor, and it was also used to put down strikes and labor unrest against the rising business empires. While they talked of freedom, they practiced control through government wherever it benefited them. Responsibility was something they seemed seldom to have heard of. Indeed it had to be learned.

Charles Francis Adams, scholar, gentleman, and an ambassador to England during the Civil War, remarked in 1871 that the years after the war "witnessed some of the most remarkable examples of organized lawlessness, under the forms of law, which mankind

has yet had an opportunity to study. . . . These modern poten-
tates have declared war, negotiated peace, reduced courts, legislatures, and sovereign states to an unqualified obedience to their
will, disturbed trade, agitated currency, imposed taxes, and boldly
setting both law and public opinion at defiance, have freely exercised many other attributes of sovereignty."

The "robber barons," as the great lawless industrialists and financiers were later called, moved toward even greater control over large
segments of American economic life. Out of the struggle between
individual companies there arose through absorption and truce the
great corporations and vast trusts that moved steadily toward
monopolistic control of a given commodity or service.

The Churches were immersed in all this activity — they could
not escape it. Large city churches in New York, Washington, Philadelphia, Chicago, and San Francisco had many of the great businessmen in their congregations. Also, as church buildings grew
larger and the programs were expanded, the Churches, like any
other corporations, had to be concerned about budgets and solvency.
The rich man was respected and admired, and it was only when he
was definitely caught in an unlawful act that he was suspected.

Acquisitiveness was the mark of the age, and the Churches were
not the ones to lead a crusade against it. On the contrary, they defended it and attempted to channel its results in what they felt was
the proper direction. Most Christians felt that God had given
wealth to the great figures of business. The most sacred thing in
material life was property. President James McCosh of Princeton
University said in 1892 that it was theft "to deprive us of the right
to earn property or to use it as we see fit."

Along with the sacredness of property, the Churches defended
the gain of riches by frugality and industry. Christians were encouraged to follow John Wesley's advice to get all they could, to
save all they could, and to give all they could. Men were urged to
gain wealth in order that they might use it for the benefit of their
fellow human beings. While many did feel responsible to society
and to their fellow human beings, what was to be done with those
such as Bradley Martin with his Waldorf-Astoria party, or with

those who purchased a fifty-thousand-dollar collar for a pet? Was property more sacred than the health and general welfare of great masses of human beings?

The fact was that while a comparative few were building vast fortunes by every means conceivable, great masses of laboring people were being denied even the fair return of their efforts. They worked long, unbearable hours under dangerous and unsanitary conditions. No distinction was made between men, women, and children except as to wages. They lived in filthy slums bereft of every comfort and convenience of life, having little they could call their own, and enjoying but few relaxations or luxuries. Some churches collected rent from the slum properties in which these people lived.

One religious journal in 1874 expressed its view of the place of labor in society when it said: "Labor is a commodity, and, like all other commodities, its condition is governed by the imperishable laws of demand and supply. It is all right to talk and declaim about the dignity of labor. . . . But when all has been said of it, what is labor but a matter of barter and sale?"

Even the great Horace Bushnell turned a deaf ear to the pleadings of women for protection by law against unbearable working hours and low wages. Said the leading liberal spokesman: "Again, it is nothing that women, sewing women for example, are not helped directly in the matter of their wages by legal enactment, any more than men are not—there is no such possibility as a legally appointed rate of wages; market price is the only scale of earnings possible for women as for men."

In other words, said Bushnell, the employer can pay only the kind of wages that the market allows. The Government has no right to interfere. Where were the laborers to find bread in this wilderness? All of society seemed intent on defending the principle of unrestricted liberty in the economic sphere. Nobody seemed willing to admit that liberty easily became irresponsibility and license. The one thing the Churches seemed to offer was advice to work hard and become rich and then to give liberally of one's vast stores of wealth. Almost everybody seemed agreed that if each pursued his untrammeled economic interests without any interference, some kind of automatic harmony would prevail throughout society.

The only alternative open to the oppressed was to organize into groups and to find strength in numbers. It was at this time that the labor union movement started. In an attempt to get better wages, better and safer working conditions, and protection from arbitrary bosses, the unions employed the strike as their major weapon. This always led to violence, because the employers were determined to break the unions. They were looked upon as a threat to the law of competition; therefore, the bosses hired detectives, ex-convicts, and thugs to attack the picket lines and to open the lines for production.

In 1877 the nation witnessed one of the bloodiest strikes in history, the infamous railroad strike. To be sure, it was a violent outbreak, but little wonder that it was so. The railroads treated their workers in a shameful fashion, justice was unknown in dealing with the workers, and the public remained indifferent to their plight. Faced by a strike, the railroads determined to break both it and the unions. State militia were called out to support the thugs and detectives employed by the railroads. In Pittsburgh, during a battle between laborers and strikebreakers, the roundhouses, station, and hundreds of freight cars went up in flames. Finally Federal troops were called out.

It is difficult to condone violence, but in many cases it is understandable, and in all cases it should lead men of good will and discernment to seek out the reasons for it. Not so with the Protestant Churches of the day. They immediately sided with the railroads against the " wild beasts turned loose upon society."

One of the leading religious journals had this to say:

" If the club of the policeman, knocking out the brains of the rioter, will answer, then well and good; but if it does not promptly meet the exigency, then bullets and bayonets, canister and grape — with no sham or pretense, in order to frighten men, but with fearful and destructive reality — constitute the one remedy and the one duty of the hour. . . . Napoleon was right when he said that the way to deal with a mob was to exterminate it."

Henry Ward Beecher, living very comfortably, attacked the railroad workers for their inability to live on their wages:

" It is said that a dollar a day is not enough for a wife and five or six children. No, not if that man smokes or drinks beer. It is not enough if they are to live as he would be glad to have them live. . . . But is not a dollar a day enough to buy bread with? Water costs nothing; and a man who cannot live on bread is not fit to live. What is the use of civilization that simply makes men incompetent to live under the conditions which exist? "

So, many of the clergy and Churches reacted against the laborers without ever posing the question of justice or the love of one's brother as oneself. The Churches, it is true, urged arbitration to settle disputes rather than the use of strikes. But only two equal sides can arbitrate if an equitable solution is to be arrived at. The very thing businessmen detested was sitting down at a table to arbitrate with labor unions as their equals. Nobody could dictate to or bargain with business on the running of the business. Strange that the Churches never attacked this self-glorification of the employer!

Rather than systematically trying to understand the unions and the needs of the workers so arbitration could be possible, the Churches condemned the unions and cried for arbitration. *The Christian Advocate* called trade-unions " despotic and revolutionary in tendency," argued that they contained " communism," and called on the nation to " legislate trade-unions out of existence."

During a coal strike in 1902, George F. Baer, president of the Reading Railroad, still had the audacity to say, " The right and interests of the laboring men will be protected and cared for not by labor agitators but by the Christian men to whom God in his infinite wisdom has given control of the property interests of this country."

By that date religious and public opinion had changed so drastically that Mr. Baer was laughed out of court. But such a view was prevalent in the 1880's and still common in the early 1890's. Slowly, however, the Churches began to review their relation to the laboring classes and their responsibility for justice in society. Relations between capital and labor were not so simple as they appeared in the 1870's. Perhaps there was too much dishonesty and arrogance in the field of business. Perhaps it was even impossible to handle these problems purely on an individualistic basis of keeping a dollar-a-day family man from smoking and drinking.

Meanwhile, the Churches could not ignore the increasing social problems in the large cities. Immigrants were pouring into America by the millions and settling in already overcrowded city slums. Workingmen were utterly at the mercy of an economic system that paid pitifully low wages and offered absolutely no security. For those who could fight their way up into the professional or business classes or even into the ranks of foremen, life could be pleasant enough. For those who were never that fortunate or aggressive, there was only a life of constant fear and uncertainty. Removed from all personal contact with their employers, they were as parts of a huge impersonal machine that went clanking on and on.

In the face of the immense human need and misery produced by this system in the cities, the Churches continued to work through their agencies established earlier in the century. The Salvation Army expanded its work of offering a hand of mercy to the sick, needy, hungry, and unwanted. The early tract and missionary societies enlarged their work of rescuing human wrecks of economic competition, and they began to pay more attention to the immigrant through language classes and employment agencies.

One of the truly creative answers developed by the Churches was that of the institutional churches. They had developed in the 1880's, especially among the Congregationalists and Episcopalians, and in the 1890's their numbers rapidly increased. One of the most famous of these was St. George's Episcopal parish in New York under the pastorate of Dr. W. S. Rainsford.

The institutional churches were nearly all alike regardless of their denominational origin. Usually they were located in what was once a "better part" of New York or some other large city, which had been taken over by recent immigrants. Members of the church council or vestry were often outstanding businessmen who found the institutional church a means of exercising Christian stewardship. For example, J. P. Morgan underwrote a large part of the financial program of St. George's, and that of St. Bartholomew's was underwritten by Cornelius Vanderbilt and his mother.

The center of the church life was a huge parish house which provided facilities for lectures, art work, athletics, dances, and other recreation. The churches were kept open not just on Sundays but every day of the week. Furthermore, there was no pew rent to be paid. The staff of the church was greatly expanded to include several ministers, directors of religious education, directors of music, and others. Often the church would have eight to fifteen on its staff.

The program of the institutional church was planned to meet the social and cultural as well as the religious needs of the neighborhood. Rather than fleeing from a rapidly changing neighborhood, the church changed its program so that it could minister to the new people. In this way men of wealth felt they were dealing with the problems of human want which emerged from economic competition. In a sense they were, but in doing this they were only scratching the surface. It was fine that the Churches went even that far, but something more drastic than a sedative for pain was needed. A true diagnosis of social evils and an attempted cure for social injustice was the real need of the hour.

Another response of the Churches and people of wealth to the needs of the immigrant and poor laborer was the settlement house. Patterned after English examples, American colleges founded settlement houses in the midst of blighted areas in order that college students might go into the area and, through service experiences, learn at first hand the needs of these peoples. This provided service for the poor and much-needed experience for wealthy young collegiates. Jane Addams' famous Hull House in Chicago as well as Graham Taylor's Chicago Commons were along the same lines.

Just as the Church never failed in its works of charity, so it was never completely blind to the social evils and economic injustice of the day. There were always some who were dissatisfied with the devotion paid to greed and the blessings placed upon acquisitiveness. A few always recognized that the task of the Church was not to uphold the *status quo* as the best of all possible arrangements, but to pronounce judgment wherever the laws of God were broken.

One such outstanding preacher was Washington Gladden, pastor of a number of important Congregational churches, the most famous of which was his pastorate in the First Congregational Church of Columbus, Ohio. In pastorates at North Adams and Springfield, Massachusetts, he had large numbers of diligent, sober, hard-working laboring men who were utterly at the mercy of economic caprice. He saw that economic problems were also moral problems in that they brought despair and injustice to many innocent people. Furthermore, he had accepted the doctrine of evolution and believed that God was working through all men and nature in order to realize his goodness. Anything that distorted or perverted the work of God's Spirit was of concern to the minister; therefore, he was vitally concerned with economic inequalities.

Gladden was one of the first ministers to recognize the rights of workingmen to organize into unions, yet he felt they should never employ force or violence to attain their ends. As he put it, " The law gives to capital an immense advantage in permitting its consolidation in great centralized corporations; and neither law nor justice can forbid laborers to combine, in order to protect themselves against the encroachments of capital, so long as they abstain from that use of violence and rely upon reason and moral influence."

Later he came to see the complexity of the problem of strikes and violence, though he always insisted that the Golden Rule, love to the neighbor as oneself, was the basis for all social and economic actions. He held that true co-operation was the best possibility, and he thought history was moving in that direction. Gladden felt that this was still to be done primarily through the persuasion of individuals to the Christian point of view, but the results would mean a change in the structure of society — an overcoming of ruthless competition by enlightened self-love, co-operation, and sharing.

Though the Church always started with the individual, that individual was in society. As he said, " no man can be redeemed and saved alone; no community can be reformed and elevated save as the individuals of which it is composed are regenerated."

While Washington Gladden thought and preached this way from the early 1870's onward, he was not a solitary figure in the Church. During the same period other prophets of Protestantism announced their dissatisfaction with the ethics of big business. No longer were all preachers willing to tell laborers to wait in patience for wrongs to be righted or to exact no real justice until heaven. The new theology emphasized the presence of God within the very stuff of nature and man, and it insisted that this presence be allowed to manifest itself through co-operation and good will. Avarice, greed, and uncontrolled acquisitiveness were not to be condoned.

Discussion of the new situation was in full swing. The Church did not know quite what to do in this new situation because it had no real basis on which to act. Of one thing most Christians were certain, the answer could not be found in the new European prophet, Karl Marx, nor in the more peaceful socialists.

" Workers of the world, unite! You have nothing to lose but your chains! "

With this cry, Karl Marx and Friedrich Engels launched a world-shaking movement in a little pamphlet, the *Communist Manifesto,* in 1848. Europe has never been the same since that time. Marx argued that there would be no peace or justice in the world until the proletariat, or laborers, rebelled against all Governments as masks behind which the businessmen ruled. The revolution would usher in a new age where the workers would be the only class and would own everything through the state, because they were the state. Each would be given according to his need and so each, getting a full share of the world's produce, would be willing to work. It took several decades before this message found large numbers of adherents.

Much more cautious than Marx were those socialists who argued that labor would have to organize politically into trade-unions. Through peaceful democratic means plus the regular labor instruments such as the strike and boycott, labor would have to see to it that the great essential public means of production and transportation, necessary for the health and welfare of the entire nation, were owned and operated not by a few selfish men for their own benefit but by the state in behalf of the public. They also stood for shorter working hours, abolition of child labor, payment of wages in cash, and compulsory education.

In 1879, Professor Hitchcock of Union Theological Seminary, New York, wrote a book, *Socialism,* in which he attacked it as a system detrimental to America and religion. Professor R. Ely, economist of Johns Hopkins, also spoke against it. Most of the alert ministers as well as the scholars admitted that socialism had correctly analyzed the situation, but they all argued against its solution.

Meanwhile, ministers continued to be dissatisfied with the nation's economic inequalities and they searched for a firm basis on which to build a criticism and a constructive program. All such men expressed dissatisfaction also with the current orthodox theology which tended to talk only about conversion and the life to come while the great social evils of the present were ignored. As Protestant ministers were groping about for a solution that would embrace both a personal and social reality, a brilliant Lutheran theologian, J. H. W. Stuckenberg, worked out a solution in terms of the New Testament teachings of Jesus as related to all of life. For some reason his excellent book, *Christian Sociology,* passed largely unnoticed.

As growing numbers of ministers and teachers began to speak a word of judgment against the society of their day, a movement arose at Grinnell College, in Iowa, crying for the complete reconstruction of society on the basis of the New Testament teachings. A magazine, *The Kingdom,* a prophet, George D. Herron, and an organizer, Dr. George Gale, president of Grinnell, were the powers of the movement.

More than anything else, this "Kingdom movement" challenged the Churches and society of the 1890's. Wherever Herron appeared he made a lasting impact. The Nebraska governor publicly challenged him. Through retreats and schools as well as in lectures, the message of Christ as king and his Kingdom as the goal of society was spread throughout the nation. Though Herron failed in leadership and the movement quietly disappeared into a broader stream by 1900, it did give birth to an attempt at a colony in Georgia that published a paper entitled the *Social Gospel.* The name came to signify all those people and groups working in the interest of social Christianity.

During the last several years of the nineteenth century a new theological basis was worked out for an entire reconstruction of society on the basis of Christianity. Men such as Professor Shailer Mathews of the Divinity School of the University of Chicago and Professor F. G. Peabody of Harvard published works pointing to the source and norm for Christian action. Jesus had been rediscovered by modern scholarship as a prophet and teacher. No longer was his work as divine Saviour and atoner on the cross stressed.

Rather, he was the one who through his sublime life of service and teachings of love revealed to man God's will for society and individuals.

The teachings of Jesus became the basis of their message, and the heart of that message was the Fatherhood of God and the brotherhood of man. God was a God of love, who willed the children of his Kingdom to live not in strife and competition but in brotherhood, each loving the other as himself. Every human being, according to Jesus' teaching, was of infinite worth in the eyes of God. Any social structure that treated human beings as a commodity or as impersonal ciphers was a denial of Jesus' teachings. On this basis these men called for the application of those teachings to the social and economic order and the reformation of all social life on a new basis.

In 1896 this was dramatized in one of the most widely read novels of history, *In His Steps,* by Rev. Charles M. Sheldon. The story recounts what happened to fifty people when they tried to base every decision of their lives on the question, " What would Jesus do? "

The story opened in a swank Protestant church where at the conclusion of the service a poor, unemployed, shabby young man got up and told his story of unemployment to the startled parishioners and ended by saying: " You can't all go out hunting up jobs for people like me, but what I am puzzled about when I see so many Christians living in luxury and singing, ' Jesus, I my cross have taken, all to leave, and follow Thee,' is what is meant by following Jesus? I remember how my wife died gasping for air in a New York tenement owned by a member of a church. I suppose I don't understand, but what would Jesus do? "

That was the question! What would Jesus do? How could Jesus accept those living in ill-gotten luxury wrung from the toil, sweat, and tears of helpless men, women, and children? What would he do? Over twenty million copies of the novel have been sold, and it is still selling. It did for the masses of Christians what Mathews, Peabody, and others did for the ministers and educators — made them aware anew of the moral demands placed on Jesus' followers.

In 1907 all these strivings and yearnings were caught up in a dramatic book written by a Baptist minister and professor of Church history, Walter Rauschenbusch. In his *Christianity and the Social*

Crisis he highlighted the demand of the hour: "The cry of Crisis! Crisis! has become a weariness. Every age and every year are critical and fraught with destiny. Yet in the widest survey of history Western civilization is now at a decisive point in its development."

Here was a new prophet of the social gospel! One who spoke from the depth of a ministry in New York's infamous Hell's Kitchen and from the breadth of training in German universities, he was ideally suited to interpret the theological basis or direction of social Christianity. The deep social crisis he saw was not something the Church could ignore, for if society continues to disintegrate, he said, "the Church will be carried down with it."

He called upon the Church to "repent of the sins of existing society, cast off the spell of lies protecting our social wrongs, have faith in a higher social order, and realize in ourselves a new type of Christian manhood which seems to overcome the evil in the present world, not by withdrawing from the world, but by revolutionizing it."

Jesus had provided the means whereby society would be constantly and progressively transformed — the Kingdom of God. It was in this idea that Rauschenbusch propounded the appeal and the power for the social gospel. This was the center of Jesus' teachings, and it was being discovered and applied to modern life. Rauschenbusch said that "this doctrine is itself the social gospel."

With Jesus the Kingdom "got its first foothold in humanity." He received the Kingdom and transformed it to mean the reign of God as "the organized fellowship of humanity acting under the impulse of love." This fellowship is at work in society as a historical force and energy carrying the believers to a fuller realization of God's will of love. Redemption means standing within the Kingdom, living the life of love and sacrifice here and now as a present reality as well as a future hope. It is not something simply religious, but it embraces all of life insofar as all forms of life embody the spirit of God's law and love. As he said, "the Kingdom of God includes the economic life, for it means the progressive transformation of all human affairs by the thought and spirit of Christ."

In his great systematic work, *A Theology for the Social Gospel,* 1917, Rauschenbusch indicated the solidarity of sin and the extension of salvation. Sin was ingrained in social institutions as well as

in individuals. While he recognized that the ultimate source of sin
is in the individual, he reminded Christians that social institutions
could uphold, inculcate, and extend sin.

At the same time, he insisted both that salvation meant primarily
the persuasion of men and women to live after God's law, and that
it also meant redeeming evil institutions from selfishness and greed.
There could be such things as saved social institutions — state, economic systems, and schools.

"The salvation of the superpersonal beings is by coming under
the law of Christ. The fundamental step of repentance and conversion for professions and organizations is to give up monopoly power
and the incomes derived from legalized extortion, and to come under the law of service, content with a fair income for honest work.
The corresponding step in the case of Governments . . . is to submit to real democracy. Therewith they step out of a kingdom of evil
into the Kingdom of God."

So the social gospel was formulated, preached, and practiced by
large numbers of American Protestant pastors. Though it was cautious concerning the time of the fulfillment of the Kingdom, it was
convinced that under the new theology they were on the right road
to the Kingdom's realization. For some men this meant a slow but
sure progress, for others it meant a more circuitous route, but for all
it meant final victory for the Kingdom of God on earth through
obedience to God's law.

At the same time that ministers were trying to relate Christianity
to the crisis of the modern economic injustice, there were others
busily engaged in attacking all who deviated from what they conceived to be the fundamentals of Christianity. This group leveled its
guns of controversy against Darwin, historical criticism, the liberal-
izing tendencies in the large Protestant Churches, and finally against
their archenemy — the social gospel.

In 1895 an impressive Bible conference was held at Niagara Falls
where a fighting creed of fundamentals was drawn up. Any who
deviated one bit from the literal acceptance of these truths was declared to be a heretic. The fundamental truths were: (1) absolute
belief in the Virgin birth; (2) literal payment for man's sins by

Christ substituting in death on the cross; (3) the physical resurrection; (4) the visible, bodily return of Jesus to the earth; (5) the absolute inerrancy of the Scriptures.

These men denied all findings of modern science and historical research as applied to the Bible. They insisted that they were protecting the faith delivered once and for all to the saints, so they seized upon these phrases as the tests of correctness. The world-shaking changes of modern life were too much for them and they clung to the "good old-fashioned religion."

Some of these men were well-trained scholars in Biblical languages, and they edited journals to support their point of view. Others were the revivalists who wished to be bothered with no intellectual problems and wanted the "old-time religion" preserved intact. Billy Sunday was a good example of that. Their favorite theme was that of the immediate return of the Lord Jesus Christ, who would burst the skies asunder in his glorious appearance and shock all the "smart aleck" professors and liberals.

Their most bitter attacks were directed against the social gospelers who were trying to make salvation meaningful for the total life. The fundamentalists recognized that the social gospel understanding of the Kingdom was based on evolution. Had not Rauschenbusch said, "Evolution has prepared us for understanding the idea of a reign of God toward which all creation is moving"?

In 1909 two extremely wealthy Californians, Lyman and Milton Stewart, firm believers in untrammeled competition and the old-time gospel, handsomely underwrote a huge campaign in publication, the *Fundamentals*. Also, they established the Los Angeles Bible Institute. The policy of the twelve volumes of the *Fundamentals* was to uphold the literal interpretation of the famous five fundamentals and to attack the rising evils of modernism and liberalism. Some saw this as "scientific evolutionism . . . [and] the rising tide of social democratic ideals." The groundwork was laid for a bitter conflict within the Churches.

So the Churches awoke to their responsibility for injustice and justice in the social order. Not all felt that the Churches had any business concerning themselves with such problems. Some felt that social concern was the consequence of forsaking the old-fashioned gospel and that it spelled ruin for the nation. Many wanted to defend the social and economic system exactly as it was, but that could not be. The social gospel movement might have been wrong in several ways, but in one respect it was absolutely correct — it pronounced a word of judgment against a society that glorified greed and lawlessness, and it bravely attempted to offer a solution on the basis of Christian insights.

Its influence was not lost. The entire nation embarked on a campaign in the first fifteen years of the twentieth century to control rapacious business, to clean up government, to democratize more fully our political institutions, to protect labor with better hours and pay, safer working conditions, and anti-child-labor laws. In addition, it undertook to extend and perfect the service of the Federal Government through such things as civil service, soil conservation, and Federal banking laws. It even attempted to put a check on the selfish accumulations of huge private fortunes by the first income tax law: what would the age of "Teddy" Roosevelt and Woodrow Wilson have been like without the moral fervor of the social gospel?

16

War and the Gay '20's

CARNEGIE HALL, in New York City, scene of many outstanding musical performances, was in 1905 the scene of a truly momentous event for American Protestantism. Representatives of the thirty leading American Protestant Churches gathered there to discuss possible plans for co-operation and unification. Though America was a country of many different Churches, each competing against the other, it had never lost the vision of the Churches working together in the spirit of unity.

During the nineteenth century there were many organizations that attempted to bridge the differences between the Churches of evangelical persuasion. Among them were the Home and Foreign Missions Societies which received support from several denominations. In 1846 the Evangelical Alliance, a world-wide movement of evangelical churchmen, was founded. At one time it counted members of over fifty Churches engaged in its activities. It embraced primarily England and America but also included other nations.

During the latter part of the century there was a growing appreciation of the union movement. Most groups were not willing to enter a true organic union; rather, they felt that some type of confederation which made possible particular co-ordinated actions was best. Each denomination was fully independent but agreed to surrender certain prerogatives with regard to general problems such as defense of the faith, spread of the gospel, and moral reform.

As America faced new tasks in religious life, two main problems appeared basic. First was the question of the Churches' relation to the rising social and economic problems. Would not greater strength be found for meeting this new challenge by pooling the wisdom, energy, and plans of the Churches? Second was the question of unrestricted competition among the Churches. Was this not both unchristian and very impractical?

At the New York meeting in 1905 a plan of federation was worked out creating the Federal Council of the Churches of Christ in America. It stated that its purpose was the prosecution of work that could better be done in union than in separation. Each member denomination was to be represented by 4 delegates for every 50,000 communicants. All problems were to be decided by a majority vote of the general delegates.

Among the stated objects of the Federal Council were:

" I. To express the fellowship and catholic unity of the Christian Church.

" II. To bring the Christian bodies of America into united service for Christ and the world.

" III. To encourage devotional fellowship and mutual counsel concerning the spiritual life and religious activities of the Churches.

" IV. To secure a larger combined influence for the Churches of Christ in all matters affecting the moral and social condition of the people, so as to promote the application of the law of Christ in every relation to human life."

Delegates enthusiastically returned to their respective Churches to plead for their participation in the Federal Council. In Philadelphia, in 1908, after a sufficient number had signified their acceptance, the Federal Council officially came into being. Co-operating in it were both social gospelers and conservatives, modernists, and the strictly orthodox. They had tacitly accepted a truce on theological discussion in order to concentrate on a task in which they were all at one — action in the spheres of public morality and social evils. It was decided that no group should surrender its integrity on theological beliefs; theology simply would not be discussed.

All groups were firmly united in the belief that the Churches lived in a great age and had a rare opportunity to further the reign of God's blessed Kingdom. Ahead was an age of peace and plenty if only the Christian forces could be marshaled to strike a deadly blow against the forces of greed, war, and selfishness. Liberal and modernist, conservative and orthodox, all believed that the real need was for " applied Christianity." Ignorance was to be overcome by knowledge, selfishness was to be conquered by service, and war was to be blotted out by fellowship.

How were the Churches to go about their contribution to the coming Kingdom? This was not an age of words but a time for action! Social activity was the mark of the hour. Vast problems had to be attacked. Public morality and general goodness were being corroded by vast waves of " pagan " immigrants, by crime, poverty, and industrial strife. This was the first line of battle.

This concern for the social problems produced by the new economic life in America was clearly expressed by the adoption, in 1908, of the Social Creed of the Churches by the Federal Council. It became the springboard for much pulpit eloquence during the early twentieth century.

" To us it seems that the Churches must stand —

" For equal rights and for complete justice for all men in all stations of life.

" For the right of all men to the opportunity for self-maintenance, a right ever to be wisely and strongly safeguarded against encroachments of every kind.

" For the right of workers to some protection against the hardships often resulting from the swift crisis of industrial change.

" For the principle of conciliation and arbitration in industrial dissensions.

" For the protection of the worker from dangerous machinery, occupational disease, injuries, and mortality.

" For the abolition of child labor.

" For the regulation of the conditions of toil for women as shall safeguard the physical and moral health of the community.

" For the suppression of the ' sweating system.'

" For the gradual and reasonable reduction of the hours of labor to the lowest practicable point, and for that degree of leisure for all which is a condition of the highest human life.

" For a release from employment one day in seven.

" For a living wage as a minimum in every industry and for the highest wage that each industry can afford.

"For the most equitable division of the products of industry that can ultimately be devised.

"For suitable provision for the old age of the workers and for those incapacitated by injury.

"For the abatement of poverty."

So the social gospel had won the day. Not all delegates in the Council were in agreement with the above statement; many felt that the real evils faced by workingmen were alcohol and working on the Sabbath, but the principles were approved by most members. This was not a basis for a political program, nor did it favor radicalism. Stress was on education and persuasion with the principles only as the ends toward which society was moving.

In the Federal Council the Churches found the stimulation and the channel through which to discuss and promote their social responsibility. It provided study groups and published findings to clarify major issues facing modern Christianity. It exhibited not only a concern for the rights of the workingmen but also for minority groups in America. Negro Churches were admitted to the Council on equal basis with whites. Again, the Council studied the causes of social conflict and deplored its presence in nation and Churches. In Christ there was neither Negro nor white. It was a sin for Christians to treat their Negro brethren as inferiors. It was the Council that sponsored conferences and literature on this problem.

Meanwhile, there were other pressing problems facing American Christians. Nearly all the major American Protestant Churches — the exceptions were the Lutherans and Episcopalians — favored either a drastic reduction of or prohibition of all alcoholic beverages. The Council became a center for the struggle against the liquor trade. While it fought against this, it also carried on a crusade against war. Just as they favored arbitration in industrial strife, so they did in international relations. The teachings of Jesus were to become the basis of settling all international disputes. One of the most important sections of the Federal Council was the Commission on Peace and Arbitration. Active until the war, it slipped for a time into inactivity.

So the Churches of America in the early twentieth century exhibited much the same concern that characterized them before the

Civil War. The center of American Protestantism was the denomination with its constant push for more members. In direct competition with all other Churches, it could not forget that it was also one with other Churches. Though the denominations maintained all their historical and theological differences, they were driven together in a spirit of fellowship for action. Reform was still the mark of American Protestantism. Just as Lyman Beecher saw the Churches acting through the tract, Bible, and missions societies of the 1820's, 1830's, and 1840's, so Lyman Abbott saw the Churches declaring a truce in theological strife in order to work through the Federal Council for reform.

In 1914 the world was stunned by the news of world war between the Central European powers of Germany and Austria-Hungary and the Allied powers of England, France, and Russia. Yet nobody should have been taken by surprise. For almost a quarter of a century Europe was teetering on the brink of war. Engaged in a mad scramble for raw materials, markets, and strategic ports, the European nations had divided between themselves the continents of Asia and Africa. It was a bitter rivalry which more than once almost resulted in open warfare.

Of all people in the Western Hemisphere, the Americans were most surprised by the advent of World War I. They too had taken some part in the scramble for colonies, yet their small commitments won from the Spanish War and their constant pressure on South America in no way deeply involved them in the intrigues and race for Asia and Africa.

The immediate reaction of the American people was to remain neutral, and under the presidency of Woodrow Wilson, son of a Presbyterian minister, they set out to do so. Their wishes turned out to be only a dream. They could not remain neutral and do business with the warring nations. Yet they insisted on doing business with both sides as Americans had always done in European wars. Profits mounted, but so did the tension.

As the British placed a strict blockade around the German ports, Germany retaliated by extensive submarine warfare. As the war dragged on, the propaganda favoring the Allied cause mounted.

Some men within the Churches favored a peace by arbitration as did President Wilson, but others painting the picture of inhuman Germans, the "Huns," demanded their total and complete defeat.

Meanwhile, American preparations went on. Wilson had been re-elected in 1916 on the slogan, "He kept us out of war." Within the nation two great forces were fighting for the future. One was the pacifist and neutrality group which wanted to remain out of the war. The other was the militant prowar group. Both groups had numerous clergymen as members.

In April, 1917, when Germany reopened unrestricted submarine warfare and when the last peace proposal had been turned down, America entered the war. Large segments of the population were still doubtful about engaging in the war. But the presses and pastors combined to stand behind the nation in order to marshal public opinion.

Suddenly the pacifist movement was all but swept from sight. Ministers stumbled all over themselves to prove their patriotism and to endorse the war. One Christian pastor said: "It is God who has summoned us to this war. It is his war we are fighting. . . . This conflict is indeed a crusade. The greatest in history and the holiest. It is . . . a Holy War."

So the Churches became recruiting centers and propaganda agencies for the nation at war. Cross and flag were united in common service. The General War Time Commission of the Churches was established to get the fullest possible co-operation from all denominations. Even the Liberty Loans were hawked through the Churches, and the temples once more became centers for the money-changers.

Also, the Churches were in the forefront in spreading the so-called atrocity stories about the German nation. Most of these were absolutely false or were doctored versions of true incidents. All these stories were used to bolster the idea that America was fighting to save democracy from Prussian militarism and Christian civilization from the Hun. The Kaiser became the personification of the devil, and the German armies became the minions of hell.

So the American troops marched off singing "Over There" and "I'm a Yankee Doodle Dandy," firm in the conviction that they were fighting to save the world for democracy and Christianity. Only one evil force was guilty of starting the war, only one foul foe committed horrible atrocities, and these men and people had to be utterly crushed and punished. There was no difficulty in recruiting sufficient chaplains to accompany the troops. Wherever men fought the Germans — in idea or by weapon — the Church was in the forefront.

In November of 1918 the big guns were silenced; peace had come. Americans shouted with exaltation. The barbarous enemy was defeated, civilization was saved, the world was safe for democracy. The Churches rejoiced that God had gotten America the victory. Through it all walked the figure of Woodrow Wilson, who wanted a just and honorable peace with no vindictive treatment of the vanquished and with a guarantee of world peace through a world organization of national powers.

In that spirit Wilson, holding high his fourteen points for a just peace, went to participate in the peace talks. At Versailles he encountered the vindictiveness of the French and the reluctance of the British. He returned home with only the promise of a League of Nations. Secret agreements and revenge buried the hopes and plans of Wilson. A rude awakening was followed by an ill temper on the part of the American people. They had been betrayed!

Isolationism was the normal reaction. After fighting a war at a high emotional pitch, they discovered that all their idealism and good intentions were scoffed at as unrealistic. Why become involved in any more European intrigues? We had gained only graves for American boys and little thanks from our allies. What many an American forgot was the three years of rich trade that none seemed willing to turn down, 1914–1917.

Wilson was repudiated; his ideals were denied. No League of Nations for America; henceforth, Europe could fight its own battles. Democracy had not triumphed — Communism conquered Russia, and a terrible economic recession gripped Europe. So the nation turned on Wilson and his peace plans and turned to the Republicans and Warren Harding, who promised a return to what he called "normalcy." That is what America wanted, the good old days of

1900–1914. But such days were gone forever.

Meanwhile, the Churches underwent a period of deep repentance. Thoroughly disillusioned by the European peace settlement, many began to question the Church's share in the war. As historians laid bare the evidence of faked atrocity stories and the smooth operations of the propaganda machines, clergymen were repentant of the extremes to which many Christians went in supporting and spreading war sentiments.

Out of this came a genuine peace movement. Many leading pastors who had supported the war turned against all war and became avowed pacifists. Such outstanding men as Dr. Harry Emerson Fosdick and Dr. Sherwood Eddy, and many others, became pacifists. Under the editorship of Charles C. Morrison, the outstanding Protestant journal, *The Christian Century,* had vigorously supported the war but now took a pacifist stand and called for the clergy never again " to put Christ in khaki or serve as recruiting officers."

During the 1920's and 1930's the peace movement grew in the Churches until it embraced most of the great preachers in the big city churches and a host of clergymen in most of the denominations. The liberal theology and social gospel emphasis combined to bring about a new devotion to the Golden Rule and the teachings of Jesus as the " basis of American foreign policy." Along with this was the constant emphasis on America participating in an international league in order to promote arbitration and international righteousness. The Federal Council had special reports published on these basic problems facing Christians.

While part of the nation was busy turning its back on Europe and concentrating on the United States, another part was trying desperately to see to it that war would never again be the policy of a Christian nation. Though they worked from opposite ends, both wanted the same goal — peace! Both thought the world was entering a new era of Christian achievement.

Little wonder that the nation was possessed with optimism. After a short business recession during 1921–1922, the country hit its economic stride. Onward and upward went prosperity. Business boomed, speculation increased, and almost every phase of economic life showed expansion. Even the population increased seventeen millions between 1920 and 1930. But in spite of tremendous increases in wealth, farmers and laborers did not share fully in the prosperity.

A revolution was taking place in America — it was but one more stage in the industrial revolution. Completely new industries developed overnight. Though the automobile was invented before the war, it was not until after the war that Henry Ford mass-produced the famous " model T." Soon automobiles were the possession of large numbers of American families. Highways spanned the nation and covered the states. Gas stations, eating stands, garages, and billboards marked the landscape. Once more America was on the move.

Also invented at the turn of the century, the airplane developed as a common and safe means of transportation after the war. Soon it was competing with the railroads and buses for passenger service. Communication had been revolutionized by the radio. Gas lights had been replaced by electricity which also performed a hundred tasks for the housewife. Even recreation was completely changed by the movies. The America of the gay '20's was a brash, new, growing, inventive, optimistic country. It was the nation of local clubs and booster organizations, and of unbounded self-confidence. It was the nation of big business.

The same spirit of hustle and drive bolstered by the latest high-pressure advertising technique invaded the Churches, conservative and liberal alike. Lighted bulletin boards, weekly parish papers, the printed Sunday bulletin, and the use of radio marked the new age. Every gadget and technique was used by the Churches. A sign on the corner announced that First Church was two blocks east, and it held two services each Sunday morning. Out in the country, just before entering town, a billboard in a strategic place announced the location of South Church and invited all to attend " the friendly church."

More and more stress was placed on the growth of the Church as an institution; hence the stress on advertising to persuade the people to come in. Because of this emphasis, much of the advertising was in bad taste and at times somewhat bizarre. Even the calling of the ministry was reconceived. The modern successful minister had to be a go-getter — a man who knew the name of every person he met, and a man who kept a complete file on every member in the congregation. At a moment's notice he could flick through the cards and brief himself on the little personal facts of a family or person, the remembering of which made a call seem so personal and thoughtful. A combination psychologist and business executive, the pastor had little time and less inclination to study or produce sermons with theological substance. Theology and doctrine were largely ignored.

But the Churches were growing. More members were brought in, larger and newer buildings were constructed, and income went up. People were urged to join a church for the sake of the community. Did it not teach children the moral rules of life? Furthermore, it was becoming ever more simple to join a church. Indeed, it was often more difficult to get into the local Rotary or Lions Club, to say nothing of the Masonic Order. In fact, the church was just one more organization in the community competing for the loyalties of people who belonged to four or five such clubs or groups. The church had changed a good deal since the early Puritans demanded a satisfactory public profession of faith before the entire congregation for admission to membership. Few Methodist pastors would think of requiring a strict personal examination of an applicant's faith by the members of a class. But was not the Church prosperous and growing? Just between 1920 and 1930 it had added 5,500,000 members.

Also, the Church was not inactive in doing works of mercy. In a magnificent way it responded to the need of the various Churches and people suffering from the war. Vast sums of money for refugees and the war destitute were raised and distributed by the Churches. In addition to the regular agencies such as Red Cross and Y.M.C.A. the Churches created new centers for giving. The Alliance for World Fellowship was one such group. The Lutherans were particularly active among the Protestants in helping their German brethren.

Another mark of the Church during the postwar years was the increasing pressure toward Church union. Though the Federal Council was only a federation of Churches, its life and work was a constant reminder of the divisions that existed between Protestant Churches and of the possible life in organic union. Many of these groups were drawn closer together by their action in behalf of better social conditions and public morality. Their most successful campaign was that which finally made the use of alcoholic beverages illegal. Prohibition was made official by the Eighteenth Amendment to the Constitution, 1919, and was to be enforced under the Volstead Act.

A number of organic unions took place between Church bodies with similar background. Norwegian Lutheran groups united into one body, but a larger union was that of the United Lutheran Church, 1918. Two Evangelical bodies of German Methodist background united into one Church in 1922. So the urge for full fellowship continued.

Several Churches negotiated with each other for organic union, but without success. The Congregationalists carried on discussions with the Episcopalians, Presbyterians, and Universalists, and finally united with the Christian Church in 1931. The Presbyterians and Episcopalians discussed union, but nothing came of it. The Methodists took steps to unite the Northern and Southern branches which had been split by the war. The Presbyterians did likewise. None of these achieved success in the 1920's.

The same spirit of mutual discussion and understanding moving toward the fuller realization of the oneness in Christ was strongly expressed by further international Church federations during the 1920's. There developed a Lutheran World Federation, a Baptist World Alliance, the Lambeth Conference of the Anglican Communion, an International Congregational Council, an Ecumenical Methodist Conference, and a Presbyterian World Alliance. Many of these started in the later nineteenth century. All these groups represented international federations of similar confessions and denominational groupings. The real thrust toward one spirit was found elsewhere.

Shortly before the beginning of the war, a great international missionary conference was held in Edinburgh, in 1910. This was one in a series of conferences in which 269 missionary societies were represented. These meetings grew out of a deep need for mutual discussion among missionary representatives in order to meet common problems on the foreign fields. How could Christians expect to gain converts in India or Africa when the natives of these lands were confronted with thirty or forty groups all claiming to be the true Church? These and other problems commanded the attention of the missionary societies.

During the war it was exceedingly difficult to continue missions. Only the Continuation Committee appointed at Edinburgh and headed by that great Christian leader from the Y.M.C.A., John R. Mott, saved the day. Under his dynamic leadership national councils embracing missionary societies and native churches alike were established. Through these groups contacts were maintained in spite of the war. All this effort for greater co-operation in missions produced the International Missionary Council as the successor to Dr. Mott's committee. At last an organ for true co-operation was present. In 1928 another great conference was held at Jerusalem and a common message of the Church for the world was accepted.

Meanwhile, the thirst for Christian unity expressed itself through other channels as well. At the Edinburgh conference in 1910, Bishop Charles H. Brent of the Protestant Episcopal Church had keenly felt the need for a full discussion of theological beliefs in order that the Churches might find the proper mutual support in the modern world. Granting certain differences in beliefs, were there not also common beliefs and practices that should be stressed? And should not even the differences be discussed in mutual forbearance so there might be a growth in understanding?

The Protestant Episcopal Church of America then raised a general call to all Churches "which accept Jesus Christ as God and Saviour to join in conference following the general method of the World's Missionary Conference, for the consideration of all questions pertaining to the Faith and Order of the Church of Christ." Unfortunately the war prevented an immediate meeting, but in 1927 at Lausanne, Switzerland, almost all the major Christian Churches throughout the world, with the exception of the Roman Catholic, were present. Discussion was a definite step toward mutual understanding, and for the first time in Christian history the Church representatives departed, after discussing differences, without excommunicating one another.

While the Churches were seeking common grounds in missionary work and doctrinal discussion, they found an area where they could exert even greater co-operation — the life of working together in facing the social tasks of the Church. In 1925, Stockholm, Sweden, witnessed the first of the great modern councils of the Church. Under the guidance of the Lutheran primate of Sweden, Archbishop Söderblom, the meeting came into being. Here were discussed the Church's relation to education, international affairs, social and moral questions, economics, and the problem of co-operation among Churches. Here again differences and similarities were brought to light. The much more active approach of the British and American Churches was quite evident. The social gospel was finding an international outlet, but it was also faced by a thorough Christian critique.

While a steady move toward fuller co-operation and a growing consciousness of the unity of all Churches pervaded the international scene, not all was peace and harmony at home. The gay '20's was not only an age of prosperity and building for the Churches, it was also an age of violent disputes, bizarre sects, and radical shifts in belief.

The optimism and pacifism of the social gospel was dealt a terrible blow by the First World War, and German scholarship had undermined its theological basis on the teachings of Jesus. These teachings were not the program of a twentieth century liberal to bring in the Kingdom of God; rather, they were the absolute demand of the Kingdom itself which Jesus believed would come at any moment. So, argued these scholars, one could not base a social program on them.

In spite of the war's terrible blow against the advance of the Kingdom and in the face of this new German scholarship, the social gospel held its grip on the gay '20's. The leading pulpits of the cities resounded with the phrases "Fatherhood of God," "the brotherhood of man," "building the Kingdom of God," and "the primacy of love." One of America's truly great preachers, Dr. Harry Emerson Fosdick, preached such a gospel with outstanding success. One of his sermons of this type was a classic formulation of these beliefs, "The Second Mile."

In addition to the great preachers, the Federal Council of

Churches, various social commissions of the denominations, and great theological schools such as Union Theological Seminary in New York, the Divinity School of the University of Chicago, and the Yale Divinity School, all presented forms of the social gospel. The very course of study in the seminaries reflected this interest. Greater time was given to sociology, social missions, social ethics, and, of course, to means of inculcating the teachings of Jesus through graded Sunday school lessons and other techniques of religious education.

But the march of liberalism and the social gospel did not go unchallenged. Some groups such as the Lutherans argued that this made a new law out of the gospel, washed out all real theological concern in favor of sheer action, and was a distortion of the full gospel of judgment and redemption. Others attacked it from another side as being largely sheer do-goodism and sentimentality. They felt that it had avoided the real problems of the day simply by running about doing things. They sought a new philosophical understanding of the Christian faith, and in doing so they seemed to be moving even farther left than the liberals.

The real attack came from organized fundamentalism. Its battle lines and creed had been mapped out before the war, but it was not until the 1920's that it struck its most telling blows. Firmly convinced that the Bible was destroyed by liberalism and that the fundamentals of the faith were not being properly taught in seminaries, the fundamentalists made an organized attempt to win the day.

One of the first groups to feel the effects of this new all-out attack was the Baptist. Several times during the early '20's the fundamentalists tried to force all members in the Northern Baptist Convention to accept a creed similar to the Niagara fundamentals. They were unsuccessful, as the Baptists insisted that no creed could be forced on any Baptist churches.

When Dr. Fosdick, a Baptist holding a Presbyterian pulpit, preached a sermon on the attempts of the fundamentalists to force subscription to a creed and to decry all liberal interpretation of Christianity, he was placed under attack. He was compelled to leave his Presbyterian church, and he became pastor of the magnificent Riverside Church in New York City. But the fundamentalists pressed for victory among the Presbyterians, Methodists, and Disciples. In no group did they win an impressive victory. They did, however, make it exceedingly difficult for sincere men honestly to relate the Christian faith to modern life. So strong was their influence that they succeeded in having laws passed in some Southern states prohibiting the teaching of evolution. America was treated to the spectacle, in 1925, of Clarence Darrow, famous agnostic Chicago attorney, defending a teacher for violating such a law in Tennessee. Against him was the silver-tongued orator of the Platte, William Jennings Bryan, Secretary of State under Wilson and great politician of the midwest.

So the battles waxed hot between fundamentalist and liberal with the conservatives generally taking a middle road and hoping to preserve both the peace and the freedom of the Church. Through it all the Church grew in numbers and prosperity. Movements toward co-operation and union were vigorous at home and abroad. With the mounting prosperity in the nation the Church shared in the material well-being.

But what of the spiritual welfare of the nation? This was the age of the speak-easy and bootlegger, the era of Al Capone and the infamous gangsters. It was the era of jazz and raccoon coats. America was disillusioned after the first war and the old appeal of the Churches no longer struck the usual responsive chord. People were still very much interested in Christianity, but somehow they equated the gospel with a general friendliness and brotherhood or with a sober, diligent life of no drinking, no smoking, no swearing, and no dancing. But this was not enough. Where was the gospel of a repentance that went beyond simply certain external moral actions? Where was the fullness of the message of redemption for all of modern life?

17

Depression, War, and Aftermath

THE SUMMER of 1929 witnessed the peak of prosperity. President Hoover talked about two chickens in every pot and a car in every garage. Wall Street was bursting with activity as trade and speculation went dizzy with speed. Business was making profits at an unheard-of rate. Everything was expanding. People talked about a new age where prosperity would wipe out destitution. There would be no poor. To be sure, not all shared alike in the booming prosperity. Farmers, never fully recovered from the 1921 depression, and laborers, though much better off, still had not won the respect of the whole community and the basic right to their unions. But these were merely little clouds lost in the endless horizon of increasing prosperity.

Suddenly the blow struck! In October of 1929 a terrible crash on the stock market resounded throughout the world. Overnight fortunes were wiped out. Within a few weeks the value of some investments was nil, and the stocks had taken an average loss of forty per cent. The sudden plunge became a steady decline in all of American economic life.

Industry and agriculture were both hard hit. Manufacturing plants began to close down. Farm products piled up, spoiling in the fields and warehouses — there was nobody with money enough to buy them. Slowly the railroads and other means of transportation ground to a halt. By 1932 industrial output was down one half. Banks were failing. Farm mortgages went unpaid, and the farms were seized. But there was nobody to buy them.

As great financial houses and local banks were forced to close their doors, people became panicky and started to rush to the banks to withdraw their money. Hoarding replaced banking. By 1931 nearly one billion dollars had been withdrawn. Wealthy men, made poor overnight, committed suicide. Long lines of discontented men were forming in the cities and towns as they murmured their distress and hatred. In 1929 there were 1,000,000 unemployed, but by 1933 this had grown to 12,000,000 or 13,000,000.

What was to be done? President Hoover insisted that this was but a temporary situation, and the nation would soon pull out of it. Many a politician said, "Prosperity is just around the corner." But 1929 passed on to 1930, then 1931, and finally 1932. Things got steadily worse. Many people felt that the Government was not taking drastic enough action to alleviate the distress of the poor or to overcome the economic collapse of the nation.

In 1932, Franklin D. Roosevelt was elected to the Presidency in the hope that he could do something. As soon as he had taken office, steps were taken to curb bank failure and hoarding; he worked out a program designed to help farmers, developed a nationwide system of relief, instituted a public works program to give the unemployed some work, attempted to develop a national recovery program for industry, and set up agencies to help home owners save their homes and businesses and their investments. Slowly but surely the nation began to recover. Much to the anger of many Church people, the Eighteenth Amendment, prohibiting the sale of alcoholic beverages, was repealed.

The depression had a devastating effect on the Churches as well as on the nation. In the optimistic flush of the '20's many congregations had built new edifices far too large and expensive. When the depression hit, they found themselves unable to pay. Most carried their huge debts; a few rejected their obligation, thus bringing shame on the Christian Church. Colleges and publishing houses, missionary enterprises, and the social work of the Churches were all hard hit by the depression. Many an institution of the Church lost its endowment in the financial crash and had to close or had to drastically cut back its activities.

But the physical effects of the depression were only part of its devastation. It left deep spiritual and mental wounds. It destroyed the utter self-confidence of the '20's, and it gave birth to a despair and lack of confidence. What an opportunity for the Churches to interpret the meaning of this event! Yet, the Churches profited little in terms of growth. There was no surge of a repentant people to the Churches. There was no appreciable increase in the numbers of churches. There was no great revival which swept the nation.

Perhaps that was good. The Churches did not lose members because of the catastrophe; neither did they make great gains. They did seem to grow in their depth of understanding the meaning of suffering and sacrifice in the Christian life. This was no time for an emotional outburst that would sweep millions into the Church. It was a time for sober reappraisal of the kind of message the Church had preached and of its relevance for modern life.

While the larger Protestant denominations were busy with their reappraisal and their ministering to the spiritual needs of the nation, there was one segment of Protestantism that profited greatly by the depression. This was the group of Churches usually called " sects." They stressed the radical, emotional conversion of the sinner and the new life lived in all holiness. They stressed the presence of the operation of God's Holy Spirit and the rebirth through him; thus, they were called Pentecostals. Some of them spoke with strange, unintelligible utterances, most practiced faith healing, and all advocated a rigorous moral life. Among these were such groups as the Nazarenes, the Assemblies of God, and the Holiness or Pentecostal Churches.

Another type of Christianity that had wide appeal at this time of dire national distress was the adventists. It believed in the immediate return of the Lord Jesus Christ, just as William Miller had in the 1840's. One of the most rapidly growing of such groups was that called Jehovah's Witnesses. Founded by Charles Taze Russell at the beginning of the century, it professed to be no Church and had no ministers. The leadership was later in the hands of " Judge " Rutherford, who, like Russell, turned out thousands of pamphlets ind tracts.

Witnesses were to be found on every street corner passing out their paper, *The Watchtower*. Nobody is certain how many members they have, for they will never release figures. However, their message of the immediate coming of God's judgment met with great appeal in an age disillusioned with the disappointments of life. It gave many faith, courage, and hope. Their slogan, "Millions now living will never die," had great appeal. Even though life was very hard, it would soon be ended, the evil would be punished, and the saints would be blessed. They refused to fight in any wars or to salute any flags. Their only loyalty was to Christ, and for him alone they were prepared to fight. Because of this, they were always under suspicion in most communities. Nevertheless, they grew.

Though the Protestant Churches did not experience a large increase in membership, except for the extreme sectarian groups, they too went through a profound and invaluable experience as a result of the depression. For too long they had preached and taught a rather shallow message which was a watering down of the full insights of the gospel. No age perfectly comprehends God's message of judgment and redemption, but some ages become so smug in their interpretation of that message that they fail to stand under it. They often pick that side of it which justifies their own well-being and earthly possessions.

Though liberal theology and the social gospel contained many valuable elements necessary for their age, they also played into the hands of the age by their emphasis. People of the '20's were convinced that Christianity meant literally following the Golden Rule — doing to others as one would wish to be treated; that it stood for the gradual building of the Kingdom on earth by men of good will if only men would exert enough good will; and that through friendliness and kindness that Kingdom was slowly being built in America.

Suddenly the Protestant Churches were confronted with the stark reality of the failure of their dreams. Under all the supposed goodness and friendliness of the prosperous '20's were to be found greed and pride. Man suddenly was shown to be no higher on the moral scale, no less selfish than his medieval brethren. In place of a new stage in the Kingdom of God men had arrived at a shattered economy. The consequence was a new look at some old Protestant doctrines that had been largely ignored — sin, faith, and justification were once more relevant.

A short time before the depression struck, a young pastor left his parish in Detroit and went to teach at Union Theological Seminary in New York City. Reinhold Niebuhr had come from the bosom of liberalism, yet he had been bred in a church of Lutheran and Reformed traditions. Furthermore, in his living through the momentous events of war, Versailles, depression, and the rise of Fascism he was forced to rethink the relevance of Christianity to these events.

He attacked the illusory faith of modern man in man as an idolatry. The twentieth century believed in man's essential goodness, in his power to subdue the forces of nature and so to overcome that which holds back progress, and it believed in the presence of God at work within man and nature, bringing through man's actions ever higher stages of progress until God's Kingdom would be established.

Niebuhr decried this naïve faith in man's ability and goodness. Man was not only good; he was also a sinner. He used his powers to make a god of himself, to pretend perfection and fulfillment in the face of his self-centeredness and disbelief. Man stood in need of repentance and faith in his Creator and Redeemer. He was not his own creator, he was a creature made in the image of God. Man could not overcome social and political problems simply by good will and by the application of the teachings of Jesus. He is not bringing in the Kingdom of God.

The social gospel was not thereby stifled. Rather, it was transformed. Professor Niebuhr had an even deeper concern for social justice and the relation of the Christian faith to economic and social problems. He insisted that two things were lacking in the old social gospel. It did not see the depth and complexity of evil in the social situation, nor did it understand that justice or the Kingdom of God could never be fully achieved by man in history.

The evils arising out of economic equality could not be solved by a simple application of the teachings of Jesus. These teachings were never intended to be used that way. The point was never reached where perfectly good men on both sides could transform a social problem into a perfect situation. Evil and selfishness could not be eradicated either from the system or the individuals, it could only be checked and made better. Thus perfection was never to be expected. Only God was perfect. Each age, each situation, had to face

God's judgment and demands. As the Christian faced this he had to seek a tolerably just solution which did not pretend to be perfect and so was always open to a new adjustment. Moving between judgment and forgiveness and not by a direct application of Jesus' teachings was the way to face social evils.

Between the '20's and the opening of the Second World War there was a general shift in both the pulpit and the theological schools of America. Reinhold Niebuhr was a symbol of, and the outstanding leader of, that change. It was directly related to the change that had taken place in Europe, particularly among German theologians. It marked the return of American Protestantism to one of its genuine roots — a deeper concern for the beliefs and theology that underlie action. Over twenty outstanding preachers and teachers wrote short articles in *The Christian Century* explaining how their minds had changed in the period 1930–1940. Truly a great change had come. Its full significance cannot be assessed yet.

Most liberal American pastors and theologians were not willing to change their liberalism and also retained their social concern. Of course, large numbers, particularly in the South and in the rural districts, had never accepted such a point of view. But some who had adopted liberalism wished to retain its good points while rejecting some of its false emphasis. This was a difficult thing to do and was made doubly difficult by those liberals who saw no need for a change. Nevertheless, progress was made.

Once more American pulpits spoke of man's sin and selfishness, not just as some temporary condition stemming from physical needs but as a basic pride and perversion in the very center of his will. No longer did one hear so much about the inevitable progress in goodness and the gradual building of God's Kingdom. God was at work in history, yet also high and mighty, lifted up, beyond history — the Creator and Redeemer. Rather than emphasis on man's good will and good deeds as the basis of man's action, stress was placed on the forgiveness of sins through God in Christ, the centrality of the cross revealing God's creative love to which man responded in trust and obedience.

So a shift occurred in American theology and preaching. This was reflected in magazine articles, in books, and in seminary curriculums.

Once more, as in the past, theology was becoming the center of the training for the pastor. This really did not get under way until during and after the Second World War, but even in the late '30's there was a move in that direction. What a man believes, that he will do. What are the basic beliefs of the Christian faith? How are they related to modern life? Are they relevant? If so, how can they be presented to modern man? These are not questions of techniques. They are questions of the wellsprings of life; they are theological questions.

Still another new development during the '30's and '40's was that of pastoral counseling. At the same time, religious education stressing movies, group discussions, and class lessons based on the latest psychological research reached its peak in the first half of the 1930's. But it worked largely on the assumption of the basic goodness of man and the need to provide an outlet through discussion and education to release that goodness. This was in direct opposition to the new theological temper critical of liberalism; so religious education continued to rely on a theological position that no longer held the field. It too faced the necessity of rethinking its basic beliefs, and it is still engaged in that task.

The new currents in pastoral counseling arose out of the new discoveries in psychology and psychiatry and the emotional breakdown of modern man. Under the stress of complex modern life, with its speed, mechanics, and disregard for personal relationships, man found it difficult to make adjustments and to find a meaningful life. Pastors were confronted by growing numbers of mentally ill. Research indicated a close correlation between spiritual and physical health. The pastor could co-operate with the physician and psychiatrist in bringing mental health to the patient. How?

It was to answer this question that the whole field of religion and personality developed. Under the direction of the Federal Council of Churches, a Committee on Religion and Health was founded. It held conferences, published reports, sponsored lectures, and encouraged research and activity in that general area. It called for better training of modern pastors so they could play their part in ministering more fully to both the physically and the mentally ill. Seminaries undertook to train men by instruction and clinical practice.

Simple conversion was not an automatic solution for all the ills of modern man.

Meanwhile, the entire world was passing through a grave economic crisis. England and France, Germany and Italy, were stricken. Russia had gone through a bloody revolution that slaughtered off the Czar and Russian nobility and placed a dictatorship of Communists in control. In the depth of their despondency Germany and Italy turned willingly to the siren ways of Fascism which extolled the glory of race and fatherland. Hitler and Mussolini took control of the destiny of Europe.

The League of Nations was powerless to stop the rise of these evil forces because it had neither the will nor the power to do so. America had turned its back on the world and said, "Let it go its own way." England and France used the League as a means of punishing Germany and of upholding their own interests. Thus, when Japan wantonly invaded China in the early 1930's, nobody in the League was willing to take real action.

In 1934, Italy, feeling proud and strong under Mussolini, invaded Ethiopia with the blessings of the pope. America was indifferent, and the best the League could do was to impose some economic sanctions. But in 1938 Europe again had a rude shock. Germany under Adolf Hitler was on the march. First came the sellout of Czechoslovakia at Munich as fearful nations attempted to appease the German wrath. Within Germany, Hitler carried on a ruthless and bloody campaign against Jewish people treating them as social inferiors. Again America remained largely indifferent.

In September of 1939, Hitler's armies struck Poland. The Second World War was on. Soon France, England, Russia, Italy, and all the lesser nations of Europe were drawn in. This time the United States was determined to stay aloof, yet in comparison with the First World War they were in far more danger morally and physically in the second war. This was the age of airplanes and flying rocket bombs. All indecision on the part of the nation was blasted by the Japanese bombs that fell on Pearl Harbor, December 7, 1941. America was again at war, this time on two fronts — east and west.

The Churches responded to this war in a fashion entirely differ-

ent from that of 1917-1918. During the '30's and right up to Pearl
Harbor the pacifist group was the most articulate group in the
Church. Through outstanding pulpits, through major religious
journals such as *The Christian Century,* and through the Federal
Council, the cry for neutrality and peace was heard. The Church
had taken part in one misguided crusade; it did not wish to err
again. Numerous denominations had passed resolutions condemning all resort to war and crying for peace. Yet some men, through
journals such as *Christianity and Crisis,* edited by Reinhold Niebuhr, condemned pacifism as a denial of moral responsibility in the
face of gross Nazi injustice and tyranny.

When war finally came, the Churches quietly took their stand
beside the Government. This time there was little hysteria and name
calling. There was a fuller recognition of the sin of war yet of its
necessity. Preachers did not compete with each other, as during the
First World War, to produce the most vile denunciations of the
enemy. There was a sober sense of the judgment of the hour and
of the role of the Church as a resource to hold back bitterness and
to tap the reservoir of a genuine concern for a just and lasting peace.

The Churches participated in the war by sending thousands of
chaplains to accompany the troops on the land, on the sea, and in
the air. They placed service flags in the sanctuaries with a blue star
for each boy in service and a gold one for each who died. They carried the grief of the nation before God in prayer. They ministered
to a determined yet saddened and often bewildered people. As our
troops liberated sections of conquered nations they sent food, clothing, and medicine to the needy. They established canteens and
recreation centers for the troops. They supported mission fields left
penniless by the war.

Thus their work was different in the second war. They were
not recruiting centers for the armed services, nor were they headquarters for selling war bonds; the pulpits were not used primarily
to fan the hatred and the emotions of the people against their enemies. The greater share of the American Christian activity during
the second great war was that of service, consolation, and interpretation. They served both troops and conquered peoples with works
of mercy. They consoled the bereaved. And above all they inter-

preted the war to their people as something necessary to put down a terrible tyranny and yet as something for which America too was responsible and for which the people must repent. Although certain that their cause was a righteous cause, the Churches, this time, had no illusion that they knew perfectly the will of God and were, through America, his chosen instrument.

In 1945 the whole world was stunned by the explosion of the first atom bomb over Hiroshima, Japan. Thousands of people were killed and an entire city was put out of operation by one great blast. A new era had dawned! Was it to be an age of atomic destruction or was it to be a new constructive era based on atomic energy? The latest scientific advance of man put him at the crossroads of destruction or co-operation. Under the threat of the atom bomb, Japan went the route of Germany and in August, 1945, surrendered.

What would be the shape of the new world? What would peace bring? The Allies had supposedly fought to gain basic freedoms for all peoples everywhere. Throughout the war the Churches had insisted on a just and lasting peace. In San Francisco, early in 1945, all of the great and most of the small nations of the world, with the exception of the defeated powers, signed the charter creating the United Nations. America was now committed not to turn its back on the question of injustice in any part of the world. Most of the Protestant Churches rejoiced to see the formation of this great organization to carry on discussion for world peace. Here was something worth fighting for.

Meanwhile, the Churches had been far ahead of the world movement for a United Nations; they progressed toward closer co-operation and mutual understanding all through the troubled years of the 1930's. In fact, not even the war could really separate some of the Churches. More than one Christian prayed for his brother Christian against whom his nation was fighting. From whence came this new spirit which was largely absent during the First World War? It came from the advance of the ecumenical movement during the '30's.

In 1937, another impressive meeting of all the major Christian Churches, except the Roman Catholic, was held in Oxford, England. The topic for study and discussion was to be the life and work of the Church, but so related was this problem to theology that a basic theological discussion was necessary. It was soon discovered that before one could discuss the relation of the Church to various social problems one had to have some conception of the nature of the Church. Much work was done on this before the conference met in 1937.

At the conference itself five commissions dealt with such major questions as Church and Community, Church and State, Church and Economic Order, Church and Education, the Universal Church, and the World of Nations. Here was evidence that the Christian Church was vitally aware of the major crisis facing Western civilization. In the face of Nazi Fascist and Russian Communist threat in the form of a totalitarian state, they dared to discuss the relation of the Church to the State and to raise the problem of the relation of the Church to all the nations of the world. This was a grand demonstration of the unity of the Church in the face of national differences.

The spirit of Oxford was expressed in the statement, " The first duty of the Church, and its greatest service to the world, is that it be in very deed the Church — confessing the true faith, committed to the fulfillment of the will of Christ, its only Lord, and united to him in the fellowship of service and love."

At Oxford, American churchmen were made fully aware of the challenge to the Christian faith by the two great forms of state absolutism. They saw the handwriting on the wall, and they were led to sympathize with and understand the plight of their fellow Christians in those lands. They were also made aware of the danger of idolizing their own state. This is one reason why American Protestantism did not become hysterical with patriotism during the Second World War.

The world conference on faith and order so ably headed by the American Episcopal bishop, Dr. Brent, also continued its activity. After the death of Brent, Archbishop William Temple, of England, became the new leader of the movement. In 1937 they too held a great world conference, at Edinburgh, Scotland. There a full, frank, and open discussion of basic Christian beliefs took place. Though full unanimity was not reached, a minimal mutual understanding was. Furthermore, it was again agreed by all that in spite of the difference and because of certain common beliefs it was possible to co-operate on many practical matters. At the conclusion, the conference recommended that they should seek to join with the life and work group of Oxford to form the World Council of Churches.

The International Missionary Conference born of the Edinburgh and Jerusalem meetings had created national missionary councils in a large number of countries. In 1938, when they held another great international council, they met in Madras, India. Though war between China and Japan had been going on for several years, both the younger Churches were well represented. Two basic questions were discussed. The first concerned the relationship of the gospel to other faiths. New faiths such as Communism, national socialism, and forms of nationalism were as potent competitors as Buddhism or Hinduism. The other problem was the relation of Christian faith to reform within the Church itself. The newer Churches wanted the external Church to reform some of the jealousies and divisions and to show a greater actuality of unity.

Out of all these meetings of world Christianity came the World Council of Churches. Archbishop Temple, of England, gathered a group of Christians to discuss bringing the three international groups into one body. At an important meeting at Utrecht, Holland, in 1938, a constitution was drawn up for the World Council providing for goals and representation. At adjournment the members looked forward to the first great World Council within three years, but within one year the world was plunged into war.

In spite of the war the provisional committee continued to function and make preparations. During the war the Council was a constant reminder to Protestant Christians that they were brothers even though caught in war. This was the only visible Protestant organization larger than the nation, the only group claiming a loyalty above and beyond the nation. In Christ there was no German, no Frenchman, no Englishman, no American, no Japanese. The Churches were all faithful to their nations but their conscience had a higher and final loyalty to God in Christ.

In 1948 after the pain and bloodshed of the war, the first World Council meeting was held in Amsterdam. Christians came from every major nation, every race, every great Church but the Russian Orthodox, which was faithful to the patriarch of Moscow who could not attend for political reasons, and the Roman Catholic, which was faithful to the pope of Rome. As a topic they chose a problem faced by the world struggling for peace — "Man's Disorder and God's Design."

The world was given the opportunity of seeing the Church tackle the most vexing problems facing modern civilization. The representatives did not equivocate. Where blame fell on the Christians, they placed such blame and called on Christians to repent of it. With a sensitive probing they uncovered the idols of modern man and showed the judgment of God against them. They decried unrestricted capitalism which led to unjust inequalities and Marxist Communism which produced tyranny. They faced up to the increasing tension between East and West, between the Western democracies and Russian Communistic nations. Once more they asserted the judgment and redemptive powers of God's Word against all forms of modern idolatry in the political, economic, and social realms.

Within the United States this same drive toward mutual understanding and unity expressed itself in a series of organic unions and finally in a great federation of co-operating Church bodies. In 1930 three independent German Lutheran synods united to form the American Lutheran Church. In 1930 this body joined with two Norwegian and Augustana Swedish Lutheran Churches to form the American Lutheran Conference. Along with the two larger Lutheran groups, the United Lutheran Church and the Missouri Synod Lutheran Church, they made large gains in membership. During the first war there developed co-operation among all groups but the Missouri Church and affiliates until under the National Lutheran Council they founded a joint organ for co-operating on world relief, missions, student work, and other activities.

While the Lutherans were learning to get along among themselves, the German Reformed and Evangelical Churches united into an organic Church in 1934. But the most important union was that which occurred in 1939. At that time the Methodist Protestant

Church and the two great Methodist Churches, North and South, which had split at the time of the Civil War, reunited. This was a great day for Methodism, making it the largest single Protestant Church in America, though there were more Baptists divided into several groups.

The effort to achieve further unification among various Protestant Churches did not cease with the successes of the 1930's. The Congregational and Christian Churches and the Evangelical and Reformed Church carried on conversations that culminated in a concrete plan of organic union. A clear majority, in both groups, favored the plan; however, some within the Congregationalists argued that the union would destroy the autonomy of local congregations and thus deny the historical Congregational view of the Church. The majority agreed that this was not the case but, rather, was in keeping with the highest Congregational traditions. The unification was stopped only by a court action obtained by its opponents in 1950. But this did not mean the end of the attempt at unification. Meanwhile, the three major Presbyterian denominations continued their discussions of organic union and in 1953 referred specific proposals for a plan of union to their ministers and churches for study.

The peace of 1945 brought no genuine peace to the world. Nazi tyranny was subdued but Communism under Russian direction arose to trouble the world. The United Nations struggled valiantly with the increasing tensions. In June, 1950, the United States, faithful to its pledge to the United Nations, went to the aid of South Korea to repel the Communist invaders from the north. Peace was an uneasy, torturous thing requiring patience as well as courage.

Under such tension a great meeting was held in Cleveland late in 1950. Four hundred and seventy-five delegates attended the formal founding of the National Council of the Churches of Christ in the United States of America. This was a great federation of co-operating agencies and Churches in America. It was not a new organic Church but a council or agency of co-operating Churches uniting on a common profession of Jesus Christ as divine Lord and Saviour, in order to carry on co-operative activities and discussions in such things as home missions problems, Christian education, foreign missions, and other activities. Thus it took up into itself the various co-operative agencies such as the Federal Council of Churches, the Foreign Missions and Home Missions Conferences of America, the International Council of Religious Education, and others. In the fall of 1952 the National Council released a new translation of the Bible, the Revised Standard Version. Millions of Protestants attended mass celebrations in honor of the new translation, and the entire stock of the first printing was quickly sold out. Already the co-ordinating role of the Council was in evidence.

The trend toward steady growth continued after the war. All the major denominations expanded their home mission work in an attempt to follow people into new areas. Concentrated programs in evangelism were carried out under able national direction. Laymen were pressed into campaigns and became evermore active within the churches. At the same time that a greater effort was concentrated on home missions, the foreign fields were not overlooked. On the contrary, many felt that a fuller foreign mission program was the best guarantee against the spread of communism and the possibility of a third world war; thus, the motivation for mission found a somewhat different basis from its earlier history among the American Churches. This was not the case with most denominational leaders nor with the majority of Christian laity; however, a considerable number of Protestant laity and some clergy felt that the political advantages of missions ought not to be overlooked. Fortunately, higher motives than these were primarily responsible for stepped-up mission efforts. The American Churches shouldered anew their responsibility of providing the major share of funds and personnel for foreign missions.

In addition to these new attempts to win people to the Christian faith, American Protestantism in the late 1940's and the 1950's witnessed a resurgence of the mass revival meetings. Once again large segments of Protestantism turned to the "old-time religion" as a means of extending the Christian faith. In the 1940's there were held a series of mass youth rallies featuring conversion preaching, gospel hymn singing, and entertainment. In 1945 an official organization was founded, Youth for Christ International. Under its direction, great mass meetings throughout the nation were held, and gospel teams invaded England and Europe. Foremost among the leaders were Torrey Johnson and Billy Graham. Within one year, rallies in

America gathered millions into their audiences. Following the Moody pattern, an attempt was made to strengthen backsliders, to convert unbelievers, and to get these people to join local churches.

Youth for Christ probably had more impact on people over thirty and forty than it did on those in their teens. In any case, it was the answer of conservative fundamentalist Christians to the challenge of the hour. It was, in fact, an attempt on the part of this segment of Protestantism to adopt the methods and approaches of modern communication in order to make their message more effective. Out of this came an outstanding new revival preacher, Billy Graham. Every modern medium of communication was used by Graham to spread his message. Radio, television, newspapers, and magazines were channels for this modern Moody. He created a superb organization that equaled anything produced by Madison Avenue's advertising industry. He systematically worked through the major American cities in his attempt to bring his understanding of the gospel to the American people. His message was essentially the same as that of Moody, Billy Sunday, and the late nineteenth- and early twentieth-century revivalists, but somehow the appeal did not appear as great. To be sure, millions had heard and attended his meetings, but there was no evidence that his impact on Protestantism was either as permanent or as deep as was that of Moody. In fact, his influence was confined largely to fundamentalist and conservative groups, especially in the South. Moody's impact was felt in all the Protestant denominations and left a permanent legacy in the American scene. Thus even a resurgence of revivalism no longer was the dominant force in large segments of those churches where it once ruled supreme — in the Presbyterian, the Methodist, the Baptist, and Disciples churches in the North. Was the world facing its doom, or was the world on the threshold of a new, rich epoch? That was the question on all lips in the mid-twentieth century. Those who always saw the bright side of things were full of confidence and hope. Others who saw all the dire consequences in life were pointing the finger at doom and destruction, and that was the road taken by the contemporary revivalists. America was filled with both kinds of men, but the majority of Christians in America still appeared hopeful.

While the Churches were busy keeping pace with or even exceeding the population growth of the nation, they also found the energy to engage in huge financial campaigns to strengthen their institutional facilities. Colleges and theological seminaries were two of the foremost contributions of Protestantism to American culture. After the war, the Churches found that many of these institutions were in need of new buildings, research equipment, and general renovation. Presbyterians, Lutherans, Methodists, Episcopalians, and other large denominations developed multimillion-dollar campaigns to provide for the needs of their various institutions. Meanwhile, the world relief program for war-ravaged Europe and Asia went on undiminished. Not only did the Churches continue to grow and to strengthen themselves through vast additions to their physical plants, they did not relent in their aid to the European and Asian homeless, needy, and orphaned. Large numbers of displaced people were brought to America, jobs were found for them, homes were furnished — all under the care of the Churches. Food and clothing continued to flow into Europe and Asia. In ten years the Lutherans alone contributed over $30,000,000 to such relief work. Thus the Churches did not forget the responsibility to their needy Christian brethren throughout the world while they were busily engaged adding to their own facilities in America.

By the end of 1952 over 53,000,000 Americans claimed affiliation with the Protestant Churches. The Baptists remained the largest denomination, with nearly 17,000,000 members, and they were followed by the Methodists, who claimed nearly 12,000,000 adherents. Lutherans were the third largest group with more than 6,500,000 members, whereas the Presbyterians had 3,500,000 and the Episcopalians more than 2,500,000 members. The Disciples of Christ embraced nearly 2,000,000 members, the Mormons had just under 1,500,000, and the Congregationalists were only slightly less than the Mormons.

The churches were full. More than fifty per cent of the American people thus claimed membership in them. If one included people who had occasional contacts through baptism, marriage, and burials, the percentage would have been much higher, probably seventy or seventy-five per cent. This was by far the largest percentage of church membership in American history. At the time of the nation's founding, only eight to ten per cent of the population were directly connected with churches. Apparently, America was going to church more and supporting the denominations more vigorously than ever before in history. Not only were more people in the churches, there was also greater financial material wealth in them than ever before. Building mortgages were paid, new structures for worship went up, and numerous beautiful new parish houses were constructed. All the Churches' many institutions were in better financial condition than they had been since the 1920's. Hospitals and houses of mercy had improved their facilities and paid off old debts, colleges had added large numbers of students and almost doubled their physical capacities. Thus from the outside, the denominations appeared to be in excellent condition.

Not all was as peaceful and serene, however, as it appeared on the surface during the early 1950's. At the very moment that the Churches seemed most successful there was an alarming outbreak of literature that attempted to speak to the conscious and subconscious insecurity of the church-going population. All religious groups in America seemed possessed by the drive to find " peace of mind." The foremost Protestant exponent of the search for techniques to produce peace of mind on the part of parishioners was a nationally syndicated minister of Marble Collegiate Church in New York City, Norman Vincent Peale. His most famous book, *The Power of Positive Thinking,* remained on the best-seller list in American bookstores for more than one year. This was followed by numerous other books and a stream of articles syndicated throughout newspapers and magazines in the United States. The titles indicate the content of concern: " The Art of Living " and " The Guide to Confident Living." Underneath the wealth, drive, ambition, and optimism of the American people there was obviously a deep sense of insecurity that Christian theology was not meeting. Dr. Peale applied the latest techniques of psychology with practical means of controlling one's fear and insecurities. This was the new gospel as preached by thousands of American ministers who followed in the footsteps of Dr. Peale. His counterpart in Roman Catholicism was Monsignor Fulton J. Sheen; but it was the Jewish rabbi, Joshua Loth Liebman, who wrote the first best seller in this category, *Peace of Mind*.

The uneasiness and insecurity that underlay the façade of optimism and wealth in the American Churches was further demonstrated by the almost hysterical outburst of anti-Communist sentiment in large segments of the American public. It was not easy for Americans and for Christians in particular to live side by side with Communists in the modern world. This was particularly difficult for Americans who in the past could simply ignore their enemies or quickly defeat them. In the new situation enemies appeared to be here to stay; in an atomic age it appeared impossible to defeat them without mutual annihilation. There were those in Protestantism who tended to identify the will of God with America and the activities of the devil with world Communism. Therefore, anybody or any group attempting to pronounce a word of judgment against any form or injustice within American life was identified as pro-Communist or anti-God. There was constant pressure from within and without the Churches to eulogize everything in American life and to decry all criticism of existing society. Agencies of social concern in the Churches were attacked as exceeding their authority in publishing statements on such problems as race relations or economic inequality. In the summer of 1952 the General Council of the Congregational Christian Churches was forced to take a vote on the propriety of the activities of its Council for Social Action. Fortunately, the right of the council was upheld. This was but symptomatic of the uneasiness in many denominations over the social concern and actions of the various boards. This attack on social concern was not sporadic and unorganized. On the contrary, it came from strongly organized centers that were well financed. Under the leadership of Senator Joseph McCarthy, of Wisconsin, and certain other members of Congress, a national Communist hunt was carried on and extended into almost every facet of American life. The Protestant Churches came in for more than their share of vilification. In spite of attempts to paint a vast plot on the part of world Communism to take over and dominate the American Protestant Churches, the best evidence that could be produced pointed to a handful of well-intentioned but sometimes naïve clergy who had at times been used by Communist-front organizations or by the party itself. It was not until Senator McCarthy was "condemned" by his colleagues in the United States Senate in 1954 that anti-Communist hysteria was brought into control.

The early 1950's appeared almost totally contradictory. On the one hand, Protestantism and religion in America appeared to be in the midst of a great revival. Religious books were avidly read, millions of people attended revivals, a popular TV program was that of Monsignor Sheen, prayer breakfasts were held by President Eisenhower and by Congressmen in Washington. University and college campuses regularly held religious emphasis week. Larger numbers of students were attending theological institutions than at any period in American history. At the same time, in spite of all the attention paid to religion, Americans seemed more insecure and less sure of themselves than they had in the days when not so many of them were present within the Churches. Many feared that Communists were about to take over the nation and that the Churches were rapidly becoming a fifth-column agency to aid and abet the enemy. Others looked to the Churches to give them a sense of personal security and some measure of peace in a world of turmoil. They did not wish the Church to prick the conscience at the same time that it sought to bring a profound sense of forgiveness and release from the burdens of the guilt of modern man.

18

The Problem of Renewal

AT THE VERY HEIGHT of external success a few prophetic voices were to be heard reminding the Christian community that all was not well in the life of Protestantism. It is common knowledge that external health in an institution is a good thing, but it does not necessarily follow that the institution is essentially sound and strong within. This is particularly true of the Christian Church; for wealth, though necessary to carry on its work, is its greatest temptation. Large numbers of people in the Church are always better than empty churches, but the real question is the intensity of spiritual devotion and of commitment of those within the Churches. Was the Christian message having a genuine impact on the totality of American life? Or were American art, literature, newspapers, television, and radio in any way influenced by Christian insights concerning life? Was there any impact of the Christian vision of life on American politics?

Viewed from this perspective, Christianity was indeed in a doubtful state. The values that determined mid-twentieth-century life in America were at their best only faintly Christian. Many Christian theologians began to speak of the " post-Christian age." They argued that Christianity had reached its maximal external influence on American life during the nineteenth century and that the most recent religious revival of the early 1950's was, in reality, only a temporary outbreak of a particular kind of vitality that did not deal with the fundamental issues of contemporary life. Christianity was now to be seen as a minority movement within a society and culture that was thoroughly secularized. That is, the Christian faith was no longer the formative influence that shaped the mores and aspirations of the American people. It was but one force among many competing forces that helped to determine and shape American life.

Nobody denied the fact that Protestant institutions were more numerous and larger than ever before in history. It was pointed out that these institutions were really irrelevant. Interestingly enough, this view was shared both by the conservative and by the so-called progressive or liberal theologians in the American scene. Dr. Carl Henry, of *Christianity Today,* a postwar conservative theological journal, and Professor Martin Marty, of The University of Chicago, found themselves in agreement as to the extent of Christianity's impact on modern culture. They disagreed, however, on the reason why the situation had come about and what ought to be done by the Christian community within the new situation. The more conservative strain of Protestants called for a return to the "old-fashioned gospel" or a movement of repristination of the basic literal Biblical insights. To be sure, they were now much more sophisticated and more theologically learned. Large numbers of churchmen, theologians, and laymen remained dissatisfied with the idea of repristination or of a more faithful literal reiteration of the Biblical message. They called for reinterpretation in order to promote renewal in the life of the Christian community.

In this situation the theological analysis of Professor Paul Tillich took on special significance for the American context. As a theology professor in Germany, he had raised the prophetic question of the possible end of the Protestant era. After his forcible removal to America in the early 1930's, it was some years before his impact was felt through the publication of his monumental *Systematic Theology* and a series of provocative sermons and essays. He exercised greater influence on the American intellectual community than any other theologian in the mid-1950's and in the 1960's, and his full impact may yet remain to be made. His call for the reinterpretation of the insights of the gospel into contemporary concepts, his insistence on a true dialectical relationship between man's basic questions and the deepest insights of the Biblical faith, and his ability to draw from and interrelate vast areas of modern man's creativity in art, literature, philosophy, psychiatry, and sociology caught the imagination of the American intellectual community. Also, he provided the Christian community with one possible way to deal responsibly and realistically with radical shifts both in the thought patterns and the institutions of the modern world.

While Paul Tillich was engaged in the task of constructing a new systematic theology for the modern situation, a group of younger theologians arose in the mid-1960's to proclaim that for many modern men and for the modern human spirit itself the possibility of God is gone forever. They declared, echoing Nietzsche, that God is dead! They argued that this did not mean the end of theology but a fresh beginning for Christian theology. This represented the most radical way of saying that the Christian community must refashion its thoughts and reconstruct its institutions if it is to carry out its role in contemporary life. Old thought patterns and concepts will not suffice for the Space Age. They argued that such concepts are not of the essence of Christianity or necessary for its survival. They were symbolic of the crisis of theological renewal within the Protestant community in America. They felt that they were calling for a reformation as necessary and yet more radical than that of the sixteenth century. At the same time, they felt they stood faithfully within the Christian tradition and, in fact, that they alone prophetically represented that tradition in the 1960's.

The struggle of the Christian community to adjust itself to the new situation in the American scene is clearly illustrated by the emergence of the Church-State issue in a radical form after World War II. The problem first emerged in special form during the war. The President had appointed a " personal representative " to the Vatican in order to expedite certain matters arising from the war. Most Protestants were very unhappy about this and worked for his recall. They argued that to appoint an official representative to the pope was to give official recognition or preference to one religion above all others. This was against the spirit of the Constitution.

For a short time excitement died down after the representative returned, but in 1951 President Truman proposed to appoint an ambassador to the Vatican. There was such an outburst of indignation and protest from both Protestants and non-Christians that he was forced to abandon the proposal. Yet the issue did not die.

Meanwhile, the real problem was emerging in the field of public education. With the large influx of immigrants from Roman Catholic sections of Europe, the Roman Catholic Church had succeeded in winning many of them into the churches in America. By the late nineteenth century it found itself to be a powerful and large Church. Roman Catholics firmly believed that their children should be instructed in their faith as well as in general educational subjects, and in the 1870's they started a program of parochial schools. Immediately after the First World War they expanded and speeded up this entire plan.

It was here that the trouble began. They felt that they should have a just share of the taxes that they paid to support public schools. Also, they argued against any prayer or Bible-reading in the public schools unless it was according to their beliefs. The fact was that many state schools had Bible-reading or school prayers at the opening of each school day. Under the constant pressure of Roman Catholics and non-Christians during the nineteenth century, most religious emphasis was gradually forced out of the public schools. Now the Protestants were worried. Does not education that ignores religion tend to influence the pupils to believe that religion is really not important? What then is to be done?

Under these conditions a whole series of problems faced American Protestants. They agreed in the separation of Church and State, but they felt that schools should not be hostile or indifferent to religion. Of one thing they were certain — public funds should not be used to support parochial schools or sectarian religious training in the public schools. Thus the problem was twofold.

Many Protestants were suspicious not only of direct aid to parochial schools but also of any indirect aid such as providing pupils with transportation or textbooks. Some states argued that it was wrong; others, that it was right. Some Protestants claimed that public schools were just as available as public beaches for all, and if any wished to use private beaches or private schools, they had to pay their own way. In fact, large numbers of Protestants agreed with strict secularists that even Horace Mann's ideal of training in basic Christian beliefs in nonsectarian fashion was wrong. What actually prevailed in public education was either indifference or hostility,

veiled or outright, against all religious beliefs. This was, in fact, a
form of faith that denied the relevance of the Judeo-Christian
tradition for modern life by denying it any place in the study
program.

But opposition to public support, direct or indirect, to any religious school did not satisfy a positive need for Protestants. How
would their children receive religious instruction along with their
regular training? Instruction in school appeared impossible and
Sunday school instruction was obviously not enough. Many states
continued to allow simple Bible-reading with no comment; others
objected.

One of the solutions tried was that of released time for religious
instruction. Students were released from classes to attend religious
instruction of their choice taught either at a church or synagogue
or by teachers who came to the school for that purpose. In 1948 the
Supreme Court of the United States ruled that such a program as
conducted in Champaign, Illinois, where school classrooms were
used for instruction, was unconstitutional. The argument was that
tax-supported property in the form of the schools was used as the
place for religious instruction. For a while this appeared to threaten
the released-time program, but in 1952 the Supreme Court ruled
that such a program was permissible if public property was not
used for the instruction.

Apparently this was an opportunity for the Churches to supply a
greatly felt need in the education of American children; but could
competent teachers, an effective program, and adequate texts be supplied? Furthermore, by removing the training from the regular
program of the student, released-time training seemed to emphasize the lack of a genuine relationship between religious beliefs and
practices and all the other educational pursuits. Certainly this would
strengthen the idea that the religious life was something apart from
and unconnected with such other areas of life as politics, economics, art, literature, or science. Here was a basic problem facing
American Protestantism in the mid-twentieth century.

Agitation on the Church-State issue continued throughout the
1950's and mounted in intensity during the 1960's. It involved the
problem of free public transportation for students attending paro-

chial schools, and it also involved the possibility of parochial students receiving various forms of Federal subsidy for such things as school lunches and textbooks. The Supreme Court ruled affirmatively on both questions. The issue that aroused the greatest public interest and a good deal of irrational zeal on both sides involved the problem of Bible-reading and the saying of prayers in public schools. In 1962 the Supreme Court ruled that specific forms of public prayer could not be required by public schools. Many Churches responded to this ruling with indignation and fury. They felt that an entire American tradition had been betrayed. It had been customary to pray or to read the Bible in public schools in many states throughout the Union from the founding days of the nation. To reject these practices appeared to many a godless attempt to subvert the Government and to kill off Christianity. Other churchmen and laymen felt that the decision was poorly timed in relation to current practice in American society, but that it was essentially a fair decision and would in no way undercut the significance or the role of Christianity within American culture.

The agitation on the Church-State issue during the late 1950's and early 1960's appeared to be but the first phase of an ongoing shift in practice in the American context. Suits were brought against the tax-exempt status of ecclesiastical organizations. Several were lost, but this does not mean that action has ceased in this area. Already some question the involvement of religious social welfare agencies in various Federal programs. Some men contend that no governmental funds, local or Federal, ought to be expended by religious organizations in such welfare activities as homes for the aged, child care, orphanages, and hospitals. The issue has only begun to be faced. The outcome is difficult to predict. One thing is clear. American society today is so diverse and pluralistic that religion can no longer play the role it once played. American culture will have to find a new basis for unity to replace that formerly provided by Protestantism. That Protestantism and other religions will and ought to play a role in the creation of this new reality in American life would be argued for by most Christians; however, both the way this is to be done and the content of what should be done would be interpreted differently by various denominations.

The dilemma of the Protestant Churches in America as they seek to serve the American people and American society is most clearly revealed in the civil rights struggle since World War II. On the one hand, the Protestant Christian Churches remained a bulwark of segregation in American life. Few if any Churches welcomed Negro members or sought to understand the problems and difficulties of the Negro people in American life. The Churches appeared more fully devoted to maintaining the *status quo* or a certain "way of life" than they did to proclaiming the brotherhood of all men in Jesus Christ. The Southern states were particularly remiss with regard to the Negro people. Negroes were completely segregated in all social activities, and they were frequently denied the basic rights of American citizenship. In many places they could not vote. By and large they received a poor education and they were not allowed to use the same public facilities as a white man. In short, they were second-class citizens. Whatever problems the Negro had in the North — and he had problems — he could exercise the franchise and by the late 1950's he could use a large number of public facilities in northern cities.

In 1954, the Supreme Court of the United States ruled, in a historical decision, that separate but equal facilities in education was not constitutional. The first positive step since the late nineteenth century had been taken to redress the injustices committed against the Negro people. The consequences were electrifying. As Negro students attempted to enroll in various high schools and universities, riots resulted, and Federal troops and marshals had to be called out. In 1957, Federal troops had to be employed by President Eisenhower to maintain peace while Central High School in Little Rock, Arkansas, was integrated. A riot resulted at Oxford, Mississippi, in 1962 when a single Negro student attempted to enroll. In both cases the governors of the respective states fought the Federal order and defied the Supreme Court of the United States. In both cases the governors lost.

Meanwhile, a very effective grass roots movement among the Negro people was started in the South. In 1956, under the leadership of a young Baptist minister, Dr. Martin Luther King, Jr., the Negroes of Montgomery, Alabama, triumphed in their struggle to break down segregation in public buses. It was a long, bitter, drawn-out struggle, but the nonviolent beliefs and tactics employed under the leadership of Dr. King finally won the day. Out of the experience of that struggle there emerged the Southern Christian Leadership Conference founded in 1957, and Martin Luther King became its first president. He demonstrated a remarkable combination of courage, patience, and political acumen as he led the movement for equality in behalf of the Negro people. Only nonviolent means were to be employed, not for the sake of strategy, but out of deep principle and belief. The civil rights movement under the leadership of Dr. King and his followers finds its center in the Christian community. Through nonviolent boycotts and sit-ins, it slowly but surely desegregated buses in many cities and desegregated restaurants and places of public accommodation. Progress was slow but steady. Next, attention was turned to the problem of voting rights.

An exceedingly small percentage of Negroes were registered to vote in the Southern states. From the time of the Fourteenth Amendment in 1868, Southern states had found one means after another to deny Negroes the possibility of voting. Dr. King and the Southern Christian Leadership Conference were not alone in their struggle to win equal rights for Negroes. The National Association for the Advancement of Colored People had long been at work in this difficult and trying field. The Urban League had done yeomanlike work in the Northern cities. Other groups developed, activistic strenuous movements, such as the Student Nonviolent Coordinating Committee (SNCC) and the Congress of Racial Equality (CORE). Both of these organizations drew their memberships heavily from Northern college students both white and Negro. Members of SNCC and CORE frequently did the initial work in behalf of voter registration in many of the Southern communities. The struggle of the Negro people for equality caught the imagination and the urge for dedication on the part of many young American collegians. Under the combined efforts of the various groups mentioned, plus the activity of the National Council of Churches, these students flocked to summer training sessions to prepare themselves to participate in teaching programs, in health programs, and in demonstration programs wherever they were needed.

The years 1964 and 1965 saw a rapid escalation of activity and of violence in the area of civil rights. In the summer of 1964, three young civil rights workers were brutally murdered in Mississippi. To this day their murderers have not been found and convicted. Violence was piled on violence as Southerners reacted to those who wished to win equality for Negroes in American life. Riots erupted in Harlem, in Rochester, New York, and in other American cities in the hot summer of 1964, and in Los Angeles in 1965. It was evident that a new page had been turned in American history, and Negroes would no longer be satisfied simply to wait another hundred years, to say nothing of fifty years or even of ten years. It is fortunate for the American people that responsible men such as Dr. King deeply believed in nonviolence as the only way to achieve their goals.

The culmination of the violence was reached on Bloody Sunday, March 7, 1965. As a peaceful group set out to march from Selma to Montgomery, Alabama, to demonstrate for redress of grievance against the state government for denying them the right to register to vote, they were brutally set upon and beaten by Alabama state troopers and local possemen. Many people were hospitalized. The entire American nation was shocked by this act of violence and savagery. Dr. King appealed to American clergymen to come to the aid of their brethren in Selma. Hundreds of clergymen — Protestant, Catholic, and Jewish — responded to his appeal. Priests, ministers, and rabbis all marched arm in arm to protest against the brutality and to demonstrate for the right of Negroes to vote. Undoubtedly the Selma incident was instrumental in speeding up the passage of a Federal right-to-vote law that was signed by President Johnson in August, 1965.

The role of the Churches in the civil rights struggle has been peculiar. On the whole, officials of the great Protestant denominations have been very much involved in behalf of Negro rights, but local ministers frequently reflect the concerns and interests of their own parishioners. However, it must be pointed out that courageous local ministers frequently suffer as they seek justice for their Negro brethren. To be sure, these men are very much in the minority in the South, but they stand firm even when their own lives and the lives of their families are in danger. It is unfortunate that the Southern

Baptist Churches have not provided greater leadership for their people in working through this exceedingly complex and difficult issue. The Christian Churches ought to have been in the forefront of the battle for civil rights, but they have only recently been drawn in. However, it cannot be denied that the movement itself, particularly under the leadership of Dr. King, has been and remains essentially a religious movement. Its songs, its dedication, its piety, even its ritual of preparation for a demonstration, all are taken from the life of the Negro Churches. The contribution of the Negro Churches to American civil rights may well be one of their major contributions to Protestantism and to American culture.

As the civil rights movement pressed with vigor for its goals, it ran afoul of the resurgence of the anti-Communist hysteria of the early 1950's. The condemnation of some of Senator McCarthy's activities in 1954 did not spell the end of the right-wing movement. To be sure, it quieted down for a short time; however, a movement called the John Birch Society, founded by an Eastern businessman, Robert Welch, picked up where McCarthyism left off and organized a national movement. In the 1960's, the American public was confronted with the revival of right-wing extremism. The extremists of the right were thoroughly convinced that there was a vast Communist conspiracy to overthrow the American form of government, a conspiracy operating primarily from within the United States of America. Some of the Birch literature called for the impeachment of Chief Justice Earl Warren and spoke of President Eisenhower as a " dupe " of the Communists. Any clergyman within the Church, and any organization of the Church concerned with civil rights or with questions of justice, was looked upon by the right-wing movement not only with suspicion but with hatred.

Singled out for special attack was the National Council of Churches because of its concern for international justice, for peace, and for civil rights. An active campaign was started by various right-wing organizations to persuade individual congregations to withdraw that proportion of their benevolence marked by their denomination for support of the National Council of Churches. Local ministers were frequently attacked by right-wing members within their congregations. The entire civil rights movement was branded as a Communist Party front fostering discord and discontent in the United States. The mid-1960's saw the right-wing movement more firmly established than it had ever been in recent American history. In fact, it appeared similar to the activity of the right-wing movements in earlier American Protestantism. It was very well financed, thoroughly organized, and determined to play a continuing role in American life. However, the Churches were prepared to cope with this irresponsible movement and would not be bullied or threatened into surrendering the responsibility of the Church for justice in all facets of life.

Nowhere was the challenge to renewal felt more fully than in the vast changes that had come to dominate American social and industrial life. By 1960, 69.9 per cent of all the people in America lived in urban centers. Automation was already making vast strides in industry with a consequent displacement of thousands of workers. Just as the computer made possible automation in industry, so it made possible the entry of the first human beings into outer space in 1961. The Protestant Churches had long been ruled by the rural mentality and institutional form. They now are confronted with the necessity of living in urban centers. They were ill prepared for this shift. Until World War II the full implications of urbanization had not yet struck the Church. Institutionally, the Church continued to live as if it were ministering to a rural culture. All that was changed after the Second World War.

Thousands of Protestant churches in America were disrupted or uprooted as their parishioners moved out of the inner city into the suburbs. They found themselves cut off from the center of decision-making and from the pulsating life of metropolitan communities. In the suburbs churches tended to become centers for privatized piety and of little or no consequence in the day-to-day lives of their people. Meanwhile, vast segments of American life were left untouched by the Churches. Churches tended to pull out of those areas which could not afford to sustain them. For a while Protestant Churches appeared more willing to support missions overseas than they were to support missions in American slums or in the declining inner-city areas. It took almost two decades for the Churches to revolutionize their methods of home missions in order to minister in creative new ways to a different situation. As early as 1948, a group of three theological students started a new type of parish in East Harlem, New York City. As they looked at the degradation and human misery of people caught in a cold, merciless, big city, they determined to bring the gospel in a fresh way. They opened a storefront church and went to live in the same area with the people. They formed a group ministry under common discipline in every phase of their lives—economic as well as religious. They worked with the everyday problems of these people — the terrible exploitation and high rent, the cruelty and inequality of law enforcement, the problem of jobs, dope addiction, and alcoholism. They attempted to find new ways of making real and meaningful God's redemptive love in Christ. They were convinced that the conventional congregational or conversion-type storefront church did not answer the needs of the dispossessed of the big cities. They developed a church in the form of a neighborhood parish administered not by a minister and his assistant or associate but by a large staff consisting entirely of specialists in a wide variety of areas all under a common discipline or in a group ministry. This type of parish spread to other cities. Industrial missions were founded in Detroit, Cleveland, Pittsburgh, and other cities in the 1950's. They were an attempt to minister to workers and to management in the industrial plant itself.

One thing was clear. The old-fashioned neighborhood church on the corner was not an adequate instrument for ministering in the inner-city situation. The storefront church was one answer, group ministry was another answer, but still new ways had to be discovered. Above all, the Church had to become involved in the power politics of the big city. This was unavoidable if the Church wished to minister to the basic needs of the dispossessed within the cities. In 1964 the Urban Training Center was founded in Chicago. Twelve denominations co-operated in its founding and development. Its special task is to do what no single denomination can do for itself. It seeks to serve as a middle institution between the denominations, the theological schools, and the local inner-city situation. It provides a training ground for experimentation and for active participation in order to learn. It is actively engaged in the central problems of the big city, not in order to be engaged in activism, but in order to train churchmen and theological students to minister in such situations. It deals with such specific issues as school dropouts, the community school issues, unemployment, and community organizations. It was symbolic of a growing concern on the part of the Churches to discover more adequate means of ministering to the inner-city situation.

The churches in the suburbs continue to flourish and to grow at an amazing rate. Whatever is to be done in the inner city cannot be done apart from what is in the suburbs and vice versa. The problem is to co-ordinate the life of the church in the suburbs with that of the church in the inner city in order that both together might minister to the total urban setting. However much division there once was between suburbs and inner city, that distinction is rapidly passing as the problems envelop and control both. As old forms of ministry and congregation continue and are modified, there must be room for the emergence of new forms and new activities. This is the primary challenge confronting Christianity today.

The challenges to renewal confronting the Church have not escaped making an impact on theological education. If the Church is deeply engaged in the civil rights movement, if it is struggling against right-wing misrepresentation of Christianity and of civil life, if it finds itself in a new phase of the Church-State relationship, if it is deeply involved in urbanization and in the passing of previous forms that once marked the so-called Christian epoch, then all these factors must have a profound impact upon theological education and the preparation of men for the ministry. The reorganization of the American Association of Theological Schools in 1956 was symbolic of the change taking place in theological education itself. There was a new concern for co-operation, for mutual planning, and for facing fundamental issues that embraced all theological institutions. The divinity schools of The University of Chicago, Harvard University, and Yale University, along with New York's Union Theological Seminary, continue to provide leadership in theological research and scholarship for the American Churches. However, certain denominational schools have taken the step of appointing men primarily on the basis of their academic competence rather than their denominational affiliation. Even the strictly denominational schools are moving in the direction of ecumenicity through appointment procedures.

The major question agitating theological institutions, along with the perennial question of systematic theology, was the question of the nature of professional education for ministry. The urbanization of the church, the changing social and institutional structures of the church, and the new demands upon the minister, all combined to pose acutely the question of the nature of the training of men for ministry. This involved nothing less than a review of the content and method of B.D. education itself. In 1956 a special study of American theological education was published by the late Professor H. Richard Niebuhr and Daniel Williams. Some of the questions posed therein, and many additional questions, continue to agitate theological institutions. The questions are not only practical as to how long the program should be or what the degree should be called; the questions are much more fundamental. What is the nature and purpose of theological education for ministry? In the light of that, what is the content and method to be?

In 1957 the Institute for Advanced Pastoral Studies was founded at Cranbrook House, Michigan, by Professor Reuel Howe. Eight years of experience with special training programs for men who have been in the ministry at least five years have provided a vast amount of evidence as to the basic problems confronting Christian ministers today. The problem is grounded in the situation in which they are called to minister, in the nature of the theological education they have received, and the failure to have adequate continuing education as they proceed in their ministry. It is evident that theological education must be rethought to the same degree and with the same precision as was true for medical education after the Flexner Report in 1910. Basic in the rethinking of theological education is the role and importance of correlation with such disciplines as psychology, sociology, modern science, and contemporary literature. These are no longer to be thought of as helpful resources for sermon hints, but as necessary disciplines to be related not only to theological construction but also to the practice of ministry itself.

Protestantism is not forced to seek renewal by the circumstances in which it finds itself. It has long been engaged in an internal effort at renewal evidenced by the ecumenical movement itself. This movement, at its best, has represented an attempt within the life of the Christian community to find the bedrock of its faith and action in order that the entire Church might be one and thus more faithfully fulfill its mission and responsibility to the world. Hence, renewal has always been one of the primary objectives of the ecumenical movement.

Within Protestantism itself, the urge for unity has continued unabated and has grown in strength and activity during the 1950's and 1960's. The earlier efforts among the Lutherans to unite were further enhanced when in 1960 The Evangelical Lutheran Church (Norwegian), the American Lutheran Church, and the United Evangelical Lutheran Church united to form The American Lutheran Church, the third largest group of Lutherans in the United States. At a constituting convention in 1962 the United Lutheran Church in America, the Augustana Evangelical Lutheran Church, the American Evangelical Lutheran Church, and the Finnish Evangelical Lutheran Church (Suomi Synod) united to form the largest Lutheran denomination in the United States. Supposedly these were not to be final unions but were to be a step on the way to uniting all Lutheran bodies in the United States. Co-operation between the Lutherans will be greatly enhanced with the formation of a new body, not a Church, but a council of co-operation involving three large Lutheran bodies in the United States, the Lutheran Church in America, The American Lutheran Church, and The Lutheran Church — Missouri Synod.

Other discussions and mergers were under way in the late 1950's and 1960's. The most important of these was that involving the Congregational Christian Churches and the Evangelical and Reformed Church. In 1957 these two Churches merged to form a new denomination, the United Church of Christ. It represented the union of Churches out of a different theological tradition as well as a different tradition of polity. It combined congregational and presbyterian polity with Reformed, Lutheran, and English Puritan theological antecedents. It represented a unique experiment in ecumenicity in the American scene.

In 1961, Eugene Carson Blake, of The United Presbyterian Church U.S.A., supported by Bishop James Pike, of the Protestant Episcopal Church, presented a proposal appealing for Christian unity among the major Protestant denominations. It included an invitation to such diverse groups as the Episcopalians, Presbyterians, Methodists, United Church of Christ, Disciples, American Baptists, and others. The appeal was to set aside temporarily theological and liturgical differences and arrive at a commonly accepted basis for union, dealing with the divisive issues at a later point. Out of the appeal has come a series of discussions between these various denominations. Not part of the original proposal, the Lutherans and Presbyterians have been carrying on theological discussions. In addition, various groups involved in the Blake-Pike proposal have engaged in conversations concerning the basic problems of Church unity. Thus, ecumenicity in the United States is proceeding at a more rapid pace than at any period in recent history.

The World Council of Churches continued and expanded its activities. In 1954, its second assembly was held in Evanston in the United States, and in 1961 its third assembly was held at New Delhi, India. At both of these, progress was made in defining the intent and purpose of the World Council and in preparing various statements on key problems involving ecumenicity and the responsibility of the Church.

The participation of Protestant Churches in America in the World Council continued undiminished. Key positions in the organization were held by American churchmen. Dr. Franklin Clark Fry remained as chairman of the Central Committee over a lengthy period of time. American theological scholars are deeply involved in the various theological commissions of the organization. The assembly at Evanston brought home firsthand to the American Churches the meaning and significance of the World Council of Churches. However, all was not peace and light within Protestantism in relation to the Council. A counterorganization of exceedingly conservative Protestants, entitled The American Council of Christian Churches, was formed to counteract the influence of the National Council of Churches and the World Council of Churches. Vitriolic attacks were leveled against both organizations and against the godless and so-called pro-Communist activities of these organizations. Fortunately, these attacks on the activities of the World Council represented a minority segment within Protestantism. The World Council had more success in bridging the gap between the Churches of a more conservative theological orientation and those of a more liberal orientation than had any previous pan-Protestant organization.

Within the United States, Roman Catholicism was beginning to play a new and creative role. It had made vast gains through immigration in the latter part of the nineteenth and early twentieth centuries and had consolidated its gains with its outstanding organizational and administrative work. Efforts had long been under way among certain Roman Catholic and Protestant leaders to understand and co-operate with each other in certain key areas. The symbol of the new relationship between Roman Catholics and Protestants, and also of the role of Roman Catholics within American culture, was provided by the election of the first Roman Catholic President, John F. Kennedy, in 1960. His running for office provided the American people a splendid opportunity for discussion of the Church-State issue and also presented them with a specific opportunity for determining the role of Roman Catholicism in American culture and life. Although he was bitterly fought by some Protestants, he was vociferously supported by many outstanding Protestant clergy and laymen. His assassination in November of 1963 saw the entire nation, religious and secular, mourn together the untimely death of an outstanding young leader. The entire nation watched and listened as Mass was said by Richard Cardinal Cushing, of Boston. Roman Catholicism had arrived at a new position in American life.

Before the full implications of the friendly exchange and growing confidence between Roman Catholics and Protestantism could be realized, a change in attitude throughout the Roman Catholic Church and in Protestantism was required. The initiative for the new level of understanding and co-operation was taken by Roman Catholicism. When Pope John XXIII called for an ecumenical council to be held in Rome in 1962, few people understood the implications and significance of that act. The Second Vatican Council was to prove itself the most significant religious event of the twentieth century and perhaps one of the most important in Christian history since the Reformation itself.

John XXIII wanted, as he stated, to "throw the windows open to the world" in order that the Church might renew itself for a more faithful ministry to the entire world. His gracious spirit, his kindliness, and his sense of humor expressed themselves in a high quality of charismatic leadership. He saw to it that Protestant and Orthodox representatives were invited from all over the world to sit as official observers at the Second Vatican Council. He was deeply concerned that Christians come to know, to love, and to understand one another at a new level in order that the Holy Spirit might lead all to unity in his own good time.

Roman Catholic bishops from the United States played an important role in the Council. In the first session they were quiescent as they attempted to feel their way through the major issues and to understand what the intent and true goal of the Council was to be. In the second session they began to exercise more leadership and the majority gradually aligned themselves with the progressive wing of the Council. The American bishops were deeply interested in two important issues, although they were interested in all the major issues under discussion. The two primary issues for them were the statement on religious liberty and the statement on the Jews. Because of their long participation in a pluralistic culture and their friendly relations with the Jewish people and with Protestants, they were perhaps better equipped than Roman Catholics from any other part of the world to understand the significance and the importance of these two issues. In the third session leadership was provided by Albert Cardinal Meyer, of Chicago, Joseph Cardinal Ritter, of St. Louis, and the outstanding Roman Catholic theologian John Courtney Murray, S.J. It was in the third session that the leadership and ability of Cardinal Meyer came to the foreground and that the full weight of the American bishops was felt for the first time.

For Protestantism, the Second Vatican Council ushered in a new

stage in American Church history to be known as the age of dialogue. It meant that for the first time serious discussion would take
place between Roman Catholics and Protestants over a wide variety
of topics. After the liturgical reforms, and the statements on ecumen-
ism and the Church, it was possible for Roman Catholics and
Protestants to worship together under limited conditions, to engage
in disciplined and continual theological discussion, and to seek co-
operation in a wide variety of areas. It also meant that the way for
dialogue was open at a new level between Christians and Jews. Thus
the importance of the Vatican Council for Protestantism in America
was incalculable. Only the future will indicate its true significance.

Meanwhile the Protestant Churches in America had moved into
a new level of discussion and understanding and respect for their
Roman Catholic brethren. Roman Catholic theological students were
to be found in Protestant theological schools and Protestant students
were beginning to attend Roman Catholic institutions. Regular discussions took place between Roman Catholic and Protestant theological students. In late 1963, Cardinal Bea, of the Secretariat for Unity,
visited the United States and participated in a special theological
conference at Harvard Divinity School. In 1964, Leon-Josef Cardinal
Suenens, primate of Belgium, one of the four Cardinal moderators
of Vatican II, delivered lectures and participated in special conferences at the University of Chicago Divinity School. Professorships
are now held by Roman Catholics in key Protestant institutions. It
is no longer possible for Protestant theologians to write their theolo-
gies as if Roman Catholicism did not exist or as if it were a straw
man to be destroyed through theological dexterity. The same fact
holds true with regard to Roman Catholic theologians. The new age
of dialogue has dawned and no one can predict its outcome or results.

Thus the Church faces the future. The two major themes that
bound together Protestantism in American life found themselves
still active, but in new form. The contemporary intellectual and
sociological scene compelled them to look once again at the profound
insights of the Biblical message. The loyalty to the Bible that marked
early Protestantism found representation both in the older literalistic
approach and in the new attempt to find creative ways to bring the
Biblical vision of life to bear in American society. Even the " God

is dead" movement of the younger theologians claims Biblical sanction for its insights. Paul Tillich's theology is but an attempt to find a new and more adequate expression to make meaningful the significance of the New Being encountered in Christ in the Biblical message. The dialogue between Roman Catholicism and Protestantism has driven both groups back to a fresh appraisal and study of Biblical themes and of Scripture itself. It is interesting that the initial contact between Protestantism and Roman Catholicism in the American scene was provided by Bible scholars and that a good deal of the leadership in the Vatican Council also came from Bible scholars.

At the same time, the experimentation that marked early Protestantism continues at a higher level and in radically new forms. Even the dialogue between Roman Catholicism, Judaism, and Protestantism represents a new experiment within Protestantism which seeks to find more relevant ways for the Church to serve the world. The experimentation that marks home missions work and theological education is but symptomatic of the continuing determination of the Protestant Churches in America to find fresh and vital ways to minister to contemporary life. New forms of ministry and experimentation in organizational structures are well under way. The Church is open to greater self-criticism than perhaps at any other time in American history. The Protestant Churches realize that they cannot go on ministering in the same old way if they wish to be responsible to their heritage and to contemporary life. Thus the Church faces the future! From the Pilgrims to the present century, it has sought a fuller, richer understanding of the gospel for each epoch. At times it has failed, at times it has been eminently successful. In the 1950's and 1960's Christianity faced one of its greatest crises in the American scene. In some lands it was under the cross enduring persecution. In America it was so prosperous that it appeared to become flabby. Could it face these multiple threats? In an atomic age, destruction might come at any moment. But on the other hand, atomic science appeared ready to usher in a new age of comfort and progress through automation. In either case, the task of the Church remained constant — to preach God's judgment against all pretension, pride, and malice and to proclaim God's creative, forgiving, and accepting love. Only in this way could modern man have a full understanding of his nature and his destiny in an age of violent extremes. The Church rests secure in the faith that God has more truth and light yet to break forth from his Holy Word and produce ever more exciting experiments and attempts to make it meaningful for modern man.

Sources

The purpose of this section is to list in consecutive order the titles from which quotations were taken. For those wishing a fully documented and detailed history of Christianity in America, the following works of Professor William Warren Sweet are indispensable: *The Story of Religion in America,* 2d rev. ed. (Harper & Brothers, 1950); *Religion in Colonial America* (Charles Scribner's Sons, 1942); *Religion in the Development of American Culture* (Charles Scribner's Sons, 1952). These three volumes have full bibliographies covering every phase of religion in America. Other indispensable tools are: H. Shelton Smith, Robert T. Handy, and Lefferts A. Loetscher, *American Christianity* (Charles Scribner's Sons, Vol. I, 1960; Vol. II, 1963); Sidney E. Mead, *The Lively Experiment* (Harper & Row, Publishers, Inc., 1963); and Edwin Scott Gaustad, *Historical Atlas of Religion in America* (Harper & Row, Publishers, Inc., 1962). The indispensable bibliographical source is Nelson R. Burr, *A Critical Bibliography of Religion in America* (Princeton University Press, 2 vols., 1961). Also, a good deal of bibliographical material is available in Professor Kenneth Scott Latourette's *A History of the Expansion of Christianity,* Vols. IV and VII (Harper & Brothers, 1941 and 1945).

CHAPTER I

Ashton, Robert, ed., *The Works of John Robinson,* Vol. I. London, John Snow, 1851. The account of Robinson's parting advice was reported by John Winslow, and there is no extant copy of the sermon; therefore, this book paraphrases the message as reported by Winslow in Ashton's edition of Robinson's works.

Miller, Perry, and Johnson, T. H., *The Puritans*. American Book Company, 1938.

CHAPTER 2

Adams, Charles F., *Antinomianism in the Colony of Massachusetts Bay, 1636–1638,* Vol. 21. Boston, Publications of the Prince Society, 1894.

CHAPTER 3

Tennent, Gilbert, *The Danger of an Unconverted Ministry.* 1740.

CHAPTER 4

Mayhew, Jonathan, Election Day Sermon, 1754.

Morill, Isaac, Sermon at Wilmington, April 3, 1755. Quoted in Baldwin, Alice, *The New England Clergy and the American Revolution*. Duke University Press, 1928.

Cleaveland, John, Letters to the *Essex Gazette,* April 18 and 25, 1775. Quoted in Baldwin, Alice, *op. cit.,* Appendix A.

Lathrop, J., *A Sermon Preached to the Ancient and Honorable Artillery-Company in Boston.* Boston, 1774.

CHAPTER 5

Penn, William, quoted in Stokes, Anson Phelps, *Church and State in America,* Vol. I. Harper & Brothers, 1950.

Van Doren, Carl, ed., *The Autobiography of Benjamin Franklin.* Pocket Books, Inc., 1940.

Stokes, Anson Phelps, *op. cit.*

Blau, Joseph L., *Cornerstones of Religious Freedom in America.* The Beacon Press, 1949.

CHAPTER 6

Peach, A. W., *Selections from the Works of Thomas Paine.* Harcourt, Brace & Company, Inc., 1928.

Crevecouer St. John, J. Hector, *Letters from an American Farmer.* New York, 1904.

CHAPTER 7

Beecher, Charles, ed., *Autobiography and Correspondence of Lyman Beecher,* two vols. New York, 1865.

Strickland, W. P., ed., *Autobiography of Peter Cartwright.* New York, 1857.

Cleveland, C. C., *The Great Revival in the West, 1797–1805.* Chicago University Press, 1916.

Finney, Charles G., *Memoirs.* A. S. Barnes & Company, 1876.

CHAPTER 8

Mode, Peter G., *Source Book and Bibliographical Guide for American Church History.* Menasha, Wis., B. Banta Publishing Co., 1921.

Finney, Charles G., *Memoirs.*

CHAPTER 9

Cartwright, Peter, *Autobiography.*

Sturtevant, J. M. Jr., ed., *An Autobiography,* J. M. Sturtevant, New York, 1896.

Lane, Daniel, Letter to A. H. M. S., July 13, 1843. Quoted in Goodykoontz, Colin B., *Home Missions on the American Frontier.* Caxton Printers, 1939.

Beecher, Lyman, *A Plea for the West.* Truman & Smith, 1836.

Finney, Charles G., *Memoirs.*

CHAPTER 10

Emerson, Ralph W., *An Address Delivered Before the Senior Class in Divinity College, Cambridge, 1838.* Boston, American Unitarian Association, 1941.

Sears, Clara Endicott, *Days of Delusion.* Houghton Mifflin Company, 1924.

CHAPTER 11

Quoted in Jenkins, William Sumner, *Pro-Slavery Thought in the Old South.* University of North Carolina Press, 1935.

CHAPTER 12

Stern, Philip Van Doren, *The Life and Writings of Abraham Lincoln.* The Modern Library, 1940.

Bushnell, Horace, *Christian Nurture.* New York, Baker & Scribner, 1861.

CHAPTER 13

Quoted in Day, R. E., *Bush Aglow*. The Judson Press, 1936.

Mott, John R., *The Evangelization of the World in This Generation*. New York, Student Volunteer Movement, 1901.

CHAPTER 14

Quoted in Roberts, Windsor H., "The Reaction of the American Protestant Churches to the Darwinian Philosophy, 1860–1900." Unpublished Ph.D. Dissertation at the University of Chicago, March, 1936.

Abbott, Lyman, *Reminiscences*. Houghton Mifflin Company, 1915.

Briggs, Charles A., *The Authority of Holy Scripture: an Inaugural Address*. Scribner's, 1891.

Eddy, Mary Baker, *Science and Health with Key to the Scriptures*. Boston, Joseph Armstrong, 1907.

CHAPTER 15

Adams, Charles Francis, quoted in Gabriel, Ralph H., *The Course of American Democratic Thought*. New York, The Ronald Press, 1940.

Bushnell, Horace, *Women's Suffrage; the Reform Against Nature*. New York, 1869.

Quoted in May, Henry F., *Protestant Churches and Industrial America*. Harper & Brothers, 1949.

Baer, quoted in Garrison, W. E., *The March of Faith*. Harper & Brothers, 1933.

Gladden, Washington, *Working People and Their Employers*. New York, 1894.

Quoted from Cole, Stewart G., *The History of Fundamentalism*. New York, Richard R. Smith, Inc., 1931.

CHAPTER 16

Sanford, E., ed., *Church Federation*. Fleming H. Revell Company, 1906.

Sanford, E., ed., *The Federal Council of Churches of Christ in America*. Fleming H. Revell Company, 1909.

Quoted in Abrams, Ray H., *Preachers Present Arms*. Philadelphia, Round Table Press, 1933.

Suggestions for Further Reading

Barnes, Gilbert Hobbs, *The Anti-Slavery Impulse 1830–1844.* D. Appleton-Century Company, Inc., 1933.

Billington, Ray Allen, *The Protestant Crusade 1800–1860.* Rinehart & Company, Inc., 1938.

Braden, Charles Samuel, *These Also Believe.* The Macmillan Company, 1950.

Carter, Paul A., *The Decline and Revival of the Social Gospel.* Cornell University Press, 1956.

Clark, Elmer T., *The Small Sects in America.* Cokesbury Press, 1937.

Cross, Whitney R., *The Burned-Over District.* Cornell University Press, 1950.

Ellis, John Tracy, *American Catholicism.* The University of Chicago Press, 1956.

———, *Documents of American Catholic History.* Bruce Publishing Company, 2d. ed., 1962.

Furniss, Norman F., *The Fundamentalist Controversy 1918–1931.* Yale University Press, 1954.

Gaustad, Edwin Scott, *The Great Awakening in New England.* Harper & Brothers, 1957.

Glazer, Nathan, *American Judaism.* The University of Chicago Press, 1957.

Goodykoontz, Colin Brummitt, *Home Missions on the American Frontier.* Caldwell, Idaho: Caxton Printers, Ltd., 1939.

Koch, Adrienne, *The American Enlightenment.* George Braziller, Inc., 1965.

Koch, G. Adolf, *Republican Religion.* Henry Holt and Company, Inc., 1933.

Latourette, Kenneth Scott, *The Great Century* (*A History of the Expansion of Christianity,* Vol. IV). Harper & Brothers, 1941.

McLoughlin, William G., Jr., *Modern Revivalism.* The Ronald Press Co., 1959.

Marty, Martin E., *The New Shape of American Religion.* Harper & Row, Publishers, Inc., 1959.

Maxson, Charles Hartshorn, *The Great Awakening in the Middle Colonies.* The University of Chicago Press, 1920.

May, Henry F., *Protestant Churches and Industrial America.* Harper & Brothers, 1949.

Mead, Sidney E., *The Lively Experiment.* Harper & Row, Publishers, Inc., 1963.

Miller, Perry, *The New England Mind: From Colony to Province.* Harvard University Press, 1953.

Niebuhr, H. Richard, *The Kingdom of God in America.* Willett, Clark & Company, 1937.

————, *The Social Sources of Denominationalism.* Henry Holt & Company, Inc., 1929.

Simpson, Alan, *Puritanism in Old and New England.* The University of Chicago Press, 1955.

Smith, H. Shelton, Handy, Robert T., Loetscher, Lefferts A., *American Christianity.* 2 vols. Charles Scribner's Sons, 1960, 1963.

Smith, Timothy L., *Revivalism and Social Reform.* Abingdon Press, 1957.

Stokes, Anson Phelps, and Pfeffer, Leo, *Church and State in the United States.* Harper & Row, Publishers, Inc., 1964.

Sweet, William Warren, *Revivalism in America.* Charles Scribner's Sons, 1945.

Tillich, Paul, *The Protestant Era.* The University of Chicago Press, 1951.

Tyler, Alice Felt, *Freedom's Ferment.* University of Minnesota Press, 1944.

Weatherford, W. D., *American Churches and the Negro.* Christopher Publishing House, 1957.

Weisberger, Bernard A., *They Gathered at the River.* Little, Brown and Company, 1958.

Chapter 1

H. Shelton Smith, Robert T. Handy, and Lefferts A. Loetscher, *American Christianity*, Vol. I, pp. 20–35, 41–65, 82–114, 123–126.

John Tracy Ellis, *American Catholicism*, pp. 1–39.

John Tracy Ellis, *Documents of American Catholic History*, 2d. ed., pp. 1–93.

H. Richard Niebuhr, *The Kingdom of God in America*, pp. 17–44.

Alan Simpson, *Puritanism in Old and New England*, pp. 1–60.

Chapter 2

Smith, Handy, Loetscher, Vol. I, pp. 35–40, 114–123, 126–140, 143–183, 197–229, 231–271.

Ellis, *American Catholicism*, pp. 1–39.

Ellis, *Documents*, pp. 95–124.

Nathan Glazer, *American Judaism*, pp. 1–21.

Sidney E. Mead, *The Lively Experiment*, pp. 16–27.

Perry Miller, *The New England Mind: From Colony to Province*, pp. 19–26, 82–104, 173–190, 367–384, 481–485.

Niebuhr, *Kingdom of God in America*, pp. 45–126, 164–198.

Chapter 3

Smith, Handy, Loetscher, Vol. I, pp. 276–292, 295–297, 310–371, 398–407.

Edwin Scott Gaustad, *The Great Awakening in New England*, pp. 102–140.

Charles Hartshorn Maxson, *The Great Awakening in the Middle Colonies*, pp. 139–151.

Mead, pp. 27–37.

Miller, pp. 105–118.

Niebuhr, *Kingdom of God in America*, pp. 88–163.

Chapter 4

Smith, Handy, Loetscher, Vol. I, pp. 374–414, 419–442, 448–450.

Ellis, *American Catholicism*, pp. 40–81.

Ellis, *Documents*, pp. 124–141.

Mead, pp. 38–54.

CHAPTER 5

Smith, Handy, Loetscher, Vol. I, pp. 442–448, 450–459, 465–475.
Ellis, *Documents,* pp. 142–197.
Mead, pp. 55–71.
Glazer, pp. 43–59.
H. Richard Niebuhr, *Social Sources of Denominationalism,* pp. 54–76.
Anson Phelps Stokes and Leo Pfeffer, *Church and State in the United States,* pp. 3–82.

CHAPTER 6

Smith, Handy, Loetscher, Vol. I, pp. 481–516, 545–547, 559–576.
Ellis, *Documents,* pp. 197–325, 329–342, 405–408.
Mead, pp. 90–133.
Niebuhr, *Social Sources of Denominationalism,* pp. 3–25.

CHAPTER 7

Smith, Handy, Loetscher, Vol. I, pp. 519–545; Vol. II, pp. 10–28, 42–48.
Whitney R. Cross, *The Burned-Over District,* pp. 1–51, 353–357.
Ellis, *Documents,* pp. 269–272.
William G. McLoughlin, Jr., *Modern Revivalism,* pp. 3–11.
Timothy L. Smith, *Revivalism and Social Reform,* pp. 45–62, 225–237.

CHAPTER 8

Smith, Handy, Loetscher, Vol. I, pp. 576–586; Vol. II, pp. 28–36, 66–79, 92–105, 108–112.
Ray Allen Billington, *The Protestant Crusade 1800–1860,* pp. 1–25.
Adrienne Koch, *The American Enlightenment,* pp. 19–48.
G. Adolf Koch, *Republican Religion,* pp. 3–27, 285–298.

CHAPTER 9

Smith, Handy, Loetscher, Vol. I, pp. 547–577; Vol. II, pp. 48–58, 88–92.
Colin Brummitt Goodykoontz, *Home Missions on the American Frontier,* pp. 15–39, 406–427.

Kenneth Scott Latourette, *The Great Century* (A History of the Expansion of Christianity, Vol. IV), pp. 175–462.

CHAPTER 10

Smith, Handy, Loetscher, Vol. I, pp. 273–276, 586–596; Vol. II, pp. 80–84, 119–164.
Niebuhr, *Kingdom of God in America*, pp. 164–198.
Alice Felt Tyler, *Freedom's Ferment*, pp. 47–224.

CHAPTER 11

Smith, Handy, Loetscher, Vol. I, pp. 292–295; Vol. II, pp. 167–210.
Gilbert Hobbs Barnes, *The Anti-Slavery Impulse 1830–1844*.
Ellis, *Documents*, pp. 322–329.
Niebuhr, *Social Sources of Denominationalism*, pp. 187–199.
Smith, *Revivalism and Social Reform*, pp. 178–224.

CHAPTER 12

Smith, Handy, Loetscher, Vol. II, pp. 215–221, 270–275.
Ellis, *American Catholicism*, pp. 82–121.
Ellis, *Documents*, pp. 342–383.
Glazer, pp. 60–78, 151–152.
Mead, pp. 72–89.
W. D. Weatherford, *American Churches and the Negro*.

CHAPTER 13

Smith, Handy, Loetscher, Vol. II, pp. 36–41, 320–324.
McLoughlin, pp. 523–530.
William Warren Sweet, *Revivalism in America*, pp. 162–182.
Bernard A. Weisberger, *They Gathered at the River*, pp. 175–265.

CHAPTER 14

Smith, Handy, Loetscher, Vol. II, pp. 215–253, 255–270, 276–282, 290–306, 309–317, 324–332.
Charles Samuel Braden, *These Also Believe*.
Elmer T. Clark, *The Small Sects in America*, pp. 7–29.
Ellis, *Documents*, pp. 385–391, 490–507, 533–545.

Norman F. Furniss, *The Fundamentalist Controversy 1918–1931*, pp. 14–45.
Mead, pp. 134–156, 168–175, 183–187.

Chapter 15

Smith, Handy, Loetscher, Vol. II, pp. 282–290, 359–394, 401–414.
Paul A. Carter, *The Decline and Revival of the Social Gospel*, pp. 3–28.
Ellis, *Documents*, pp. 391–393, 428–437, 440–459, 485–490, 507–509, 561–564, 585–617, 621–625, 642–654.
Henry F. May, *Protestant Churches and Industrial America*, pp. 263–265.
Mead, pp. 156–168, 175–183.
Smith, *Revivalism and Social Reform*, pp. 148–162.

Chapter 16

Smith, Handy, Loetscher, Vol. II, pp. 345–356, 394–401.
Ellis, *American Catholicism*, pp. 124–159.
Glazer, pp. 79–105.
Carter, pp. 31–45.

Chapter 17

Smith, Handy, Loetscher, Vol. II, pp. 332–336, 419–443, 505–536, 563–585.
Ellis, *American Catholicism*, pp. 122–159.
Ellis, *Documents*, pp. 620–621.
Carter, pp. 220–231.
Glazer, pp. 106–149.
Weisberger, pp. 266–274.
Paul Tillich, *The Protestant Era*, pp. 261–269.

Chapter 18

Smith, Handy, Loetscher, Vol. II, pp. 443–502, 536–562, 585–611.
Ellis, *Documents*, pp. 617–620, 642–654.
Martin E. Marty, *The New Shape of American Religion*, pp. 1–89.
Stokes and Pfeffer, pp. 351–446.

Index